GREEN PICKLED *peaches*

GREEN PICKLED *peaches*

- - - - - -

A COLLECTION OF
RECIPES AND MEMORIES

CHUI LEE LUK

Contents

Introduction 6

Chapter 1: *Scent* 10

BLACHAN FRYING IN THE REMPAH 12
HAWKER STALLS AT NIGHT 26
BLACK TEA BREWING AND OTHER INFUSIONS 38
HIDDEN IN OLD TIN BOXES 50
THE CURVING ROAD TO MY GRANDMOTHER'S LITTLE FARM 60

Chapter 2: *Sight* 74

FESTIVAL DAYS 76
MAGICAL TROPICAL FRUITS 88
MEALS AT OUTDOOR CASUAL RESTAURANTS 102
THE TEMPTATION OF PICKLED PEACHES 114
MY MUSHROOM AVERSION 128

Chapter 3: *Sound* 140

A BIRTHDAY TREAT OF CLAWS AND SHELLS 142
A LIVE GOAT IN THE GARDEN 154
EAVESDROPPING ON ADULT CONVERSATIONS 168
PAINSTAKING PREPARATIONS 182
DOWN THE LONG PEBBLY PATHWAY 196

Chapter 4: *Touch* 206

MORTAR AND PESTLE CUISINE 208

THE TEMPERATURE OF THINGS 220

IS THIS A CUISINE OF ENTRAILS AND INTESTINES? 232

FISH HEADS AND WHOLE FISH 246

UNUSUALLY FORAGED FOODSTUFFS 258

Chapter 5: *Taste* 270

AN OUTRAGE OF TASTES 272

FAMILY BANQUETS 282

CHICKENS AND PIGS 296

SWEET MEMORIES 310

WHAT ARE COLOURS MEANT TO TASTE LIKE? 324

Glossary 338

Index 340

A SENSE OF MEMORY and INSPIRATION: an invitation

If you were to ask me, as a chef, to explore the place from which I derive inspiration, I'd immediately choose memories of my early childhood in Malaysia. This was the time when I discovered my deep-seated interest in cooking and eating. (If you're familiar with Malaysia, you'll know that I'd be considered rather odd if I hadn't actually followed this national preoccupation.) This background has shaped me to think and cook in a particular way.

In the present day, I'm a chef and restaurateur, firstly running Claude's Restaurant and more recently Chow Bar & Eating House. I have been involved with Claude's in Sydney for over a decade. I learned and fine-tuned technical aspects of cooking here, graduating to creating dishes and then orchestrating menus. Claude's is also where I learned the craft of running a restaurant. It's a dual role that bridges creativity with practicality. Duality is what interests me: the point at which tension is created; even if it's tension only of my own making, it keeps me amused.

In recent years, it's become clearer to me that individual expression comes from a deeper understanding of the evolving concept of self. One of my methods for reaching this understanding is to mine memories for emotional resonance. My dishes, menus and the personality of the restaurant are an authentic reflection of self and also a reflection of the journey I've taken to arrive at this juncture.

I spent the first seven years of my life in Sabah, Malaysia. It's a place that has had difficulty feeling that it belonged anywhere. Located at the north-eastern part of Borneo Island, Sabah is physically removed from the main part of Malaysia. It was part of the colonial British empire until 1963, when it chose to join the Malaysian Federation. Whenever I look at the land mass on a map I feel it resembles an amphibious lion, with Sabah the head of this creature.

The household in which I grew up comprised my two parents and younger sister and sometimes,

MY FAMILY, SANDAKAN — 1972

perhaps, a member of our extended family. Grandparents, uncles, aunts and cousins were never far away and formed part of our daily community. The various tables around which we shared meals have become some of my most formative memories of first-time food sensations, creating my likes and dislikes of certain dishes and ingredients.

We lived mainly in Sandakan and for a short period in Tawau. There was an abundance of stimuli for a curious child in these environments. The main industries of the towns were aggressive, environmentally unfriendly agriculture: rubber plantations; harvest of timber from first-growth tropical rainforests; palm oil plantations. (I now wonder if my vivid memory of the resinous smell of the rubber being extracted from the deliberately carved spiral trail on the trunk of the tree is indeed memory or imagination.) As a family living in Sandakan, we heard and spoke a mixture of Malay, English, and Chinese dialects. Here again, the mix of stimuli, in this case of cultures, filled my head with further questions as I struggled to understand what was being said. The Chinese population in my part of Sabah spoke mainly Hakka or Cantonese with local inflections, coloured by words adopted in an organic way from the cultures with which they mixed. Walking through the wet market in the early morning, the adult I was with (mother, grandmother, aunt or cousin) would switch languages and dialects with ease. I heard words from different languages which initially were unintelligible babble. With the passage of growing up and learning, these became languages that I understood. And, with further passing of time, have now forgotten.

Every day was an adventure, although there was a discernible routine dictated by the harshness of the weather. The daily climate, I remember, seemed to range from sometimes intolerable tropical heat to heavy rain. The routine in the morning would be to go about errands as early as possible to avoid the onslaught of heat and then hunker down within the cool walls of our darkened house, perhaps napping, when the sun was at its most fierce. Sometimes this daily routine was punctuated by thunder or lightning storms, the rumblings and flashes of which scared but fascinated me. It was a thrill to listen to the distant rumbles that gradually came closer, passing overhead with the threat of danger and then, little by little, drawing away.

My memories have influenced me to cook in a certain way. I believe that the child comprehends most of the factual points of any remembered situation, but doesn't necessarily comprehend the context. As an adult, I'm now able to read the background, undertone, implications and inter-linked relationships of the remembered situation. This is like a forensic examination of memory. The common touchstone that links the child in me with the adult is memory processed through the senses. When I try to understand and then explain how I've developed in the way I have, I inevitably file these memories by my five senses: it is the senses that form the anchors for my memories.

In the chapters that follow, you'll find dishes that have been created with the knowledge and experience I have now, inspired or influenced by the original memory or meal from my childhood. I'd like to reveal what goes through my head when I'm planning a dish, and I also want to encourage you to think independently and use my thoughts as the beginnings of your own explorations.

OUTSIDE CLAUDE'S, SYDNEY — 2012

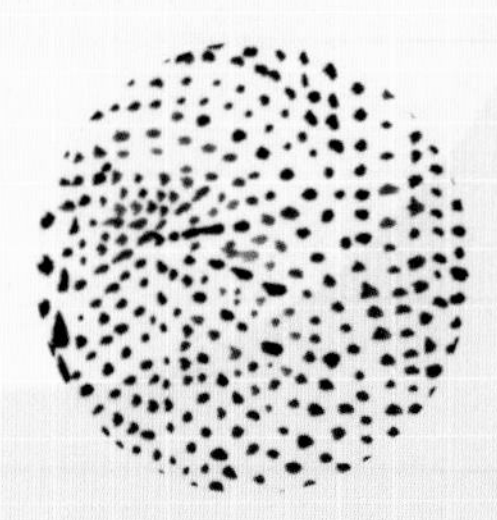

S C

NT

BLACHAN FRYING *in the* REMPAH

Curiosity drove me back to the kitchen time and time again. Food, and an appreciation of the mechanics of cooking, played a large part in my immediate childhood environment and took up a lot of my attention. Perhaps it was a lull in playing in the garden, an increase in the humid heat, or pangs of expectant hunger that would lure me back to peek at what might be happening in the kitchen? Certainly another inviting drawcard was that the tiled walls of our kitchen made it seem constantly cooler than other rooms in the house.

My aunt, who lived in the apartment building near the harbour in town, had a kitchen through which I was curious to wander and rummage. It opened onto the balcony and was stacked with ingredients in bags, bottles and boxes, all hermetically sealed so the competing smells weren't so apparent.

My paternal grandmother had an old-fashioned kitchen. It was dark and, because of this, seemed to have a slightly threatening air: smells pervaded the atmosphere but I wasn't sure what they were. And I was a little bit too frightened to poke around and search them out.

No matter which kitchen it was, there was a different smell every time I wandered in. New ingredients had been brought home and laid out on the bench in readiness for the next meal. As I skipped in and out during preparations for cooking, I sensed a different nuance to the smells every time I returned. I could discern the smell of a fish cut up for steaming — perhaps a mullet, hinting at iron and fish leather. The mullet might be set on a steaming dish and covered by sharply scented salted cumquat, pungent garlic and metallic-smelling slices of chilli. These smells would be augmented by the more appetising savoury aroma of soy sauce.

Everything smelt raw and inedible at this stage; it was a wonderful transformation as these ingredients amalgamated and the new smell of the dish was delicately brought out.

I was a child who demanded to stand on a chair so that I could look at what was happening at heights invisible from my rather low vantage point. I was a keen stirrer of pots and pans, curious to see the chemistry that transformed these raw ingredients into something completely different.

The question that always came from my mouth at a much younger age (and still does, even now) was: 'How do you know whether a dish is done or not?' I was usually met with vague, and thus disturbingly dissatisfying, answers: 'A couple of minutes'; 'Oh, you know when ...'; 'Just leave it for a little bit longer'. These answers were given by the adults as they poked their heads further over the stove to smell what they were cooking, having warned me away for the very reason that it was hot and dangerous. Isn't it exasperating when adults find it so hard to articulate what's going on?

When I was banished from my high outpost for being naughty (insisting on stirring when my help wasn't welcome), it was the smells that signalled change was happening. The wet spice paste or rempah of shallots, ginger, garlic and chilli hitting the hot wok smelt intense and raw. The peanut smell of the swirling oil was instantly acrid and sharp and that hint of toasty seafood was in the air: that would be the roasted blachan. The sharpness would gradually recede and become more mellow and increasingly more appetising. A piece of fish added to the sauce makes the smell strange again; the scents of iron and fish scale momentarily stop the aroma being so delicious. And what's that fruity sour smell that has crept in: tamarind or lime? With time, all becomes harmonious again, the ingredients still discernible yet blended. At table, the dish reveals itself to be assam of fish.

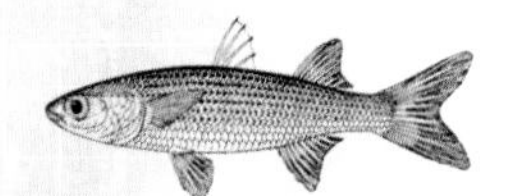

Mullet steamed with Salted Cumquat

The key ingredient of this dish is the salted cumquats, which need to be prepared about a month in advance. Wash and thoroughly dry a couple of tea cups full of cumquats. In a sterilised glass preserving jar, sprinkle a layer of fine sea salt, lay down a layer of cumquats and keep repeating until all the cumquats have been salted. Leave to mature in the pantry.

The mullet should be scaled and eviscerated but otherwise left whole. Rub 1 teaspoon of salt over the cavity and the outside of the fish and then brush with some vegetable oil. Put on a tin plate in readiness for placing in the steamer. The paste can now be prepared: grind a couple of salted cumquats with 1 tablespoon of salted soy beans, 1 teaspoon of chopped ginger and 1 teaspoon of sugar until you have a fine paste. Spoon the paste over the exposed surface of the fish and add a couple of halved hot red chillies. Steam over high heat for about 15 minutes until the fish is cooked, then serve immediately.

Betel leaves, spiced lentils and grilled okra

I was wondering what would happen if the cooking of the rempah was interrupted at a preliminary stage, or if anything was shifted into a different context? Here, I'm using a lentil fritter called masala wadai as the basis for the dish, introducing an additional ingredient (the okra) and playing with the fritter so that it becomes the coating for a betel leaf. This is intended to be eaten as a snack or small plate.

Betel leaves, spiced lentils and grilled okra

SERVES 4

Ingredients

FOR THE CARAWAY SEASONING

1 TEASPOON CARAWAY SEEDS
½ TEASPOON WHITE PEPPERCORNS
1 TABLESPOON SALT

FOR THE OKRA

300 G (10½ OZ) SUGAR
300 G (10½ OZ) SALT
12 MEDIUM GREEN OKRA

FOR THE BETEL LEAVES

50 G (1¾ OZ) URAD DHAL (BLACK GRAM DHAL), SOAKED IN COLD WATER OVERNIGHT
50 G (1¾ OZ) RED SPLIT LENTILS, SOAKED IN COLD WATER OVERNIGHT
50 G (1¾ OZ) YELLOW SPLIT LENTILS, SOAKED IN COLD WATER OVERNIGHT
3 LARGE RED CHILLIES, DESEEDED AND CHOPPED
1 RED ASIAN SHALLOT, FINELY DICED
1 TEASPOON FINELY CHOPPED CURRY LEAVES
1 TABLESPOON FINELY CHOPPED CORIANDER (CILANTRO)
1 TEASPOON FINELY CHOPPED GINGER
200 G (7 OZ) SKINLESS COLD-SMOKED SALMON OR OCEAN TROUT
16 BETEL LEAVES
1 EGG WHITE, LIGHTLY BEATEN
PEANUT OIL FOR DEEP-FRYING

Method

MAKE THE CARAWAY SEASONING

Preheat the oven to 160°C (320°F). Roast the caraway seeds for 10 minutes or so, adding the peppercorns for the last 5 minutes. Cool for 5 minutes, then grind to a fine powder with the salt.

PREPARE THE OKRA

Make a brine by bringing the sugar, salt and 500 ml (17 fl oz) water to the boil. Cool. Drop the okra in the brine and leave for 2–3 hours, removing from the brine when you're ready to grill. Preheat the grill to medium–hot. Add the okra and grill until they colour and are cooked through. They should be bright green and will have lost their raw flavour, but have a slight charred flavour from the grill. Sprinkle with the caraway seasoning as soon as you take them off the grill.

PREPARE THE BETEL LEAVES

Drain the dhal and lentils, drying them as much as possible. Put in a blender or food processor and add the chillies and shallot. Blend to a fine paste. Add the curry leaves, coriander and ginger, blend, then add the salmon and blend to a paste.

Brush the back of each betel leaf with egg white. Use a small palette knife to spread ½ teaspoon of paste over each leaf. Set aside on a tray in the refrigerator for 1 hour to allow time for the egg white to dry and stick the mixture to the leaf.

Heat oil in a deep-fryer to 170°C (340°F). Gently lower a few leaves at a time into the oil and fry until the paste is golden, but the leaf unburnt. Drain on paper towels and serve as quickly as possible.

ASSEMBLE THE DISH

The okra and betel leaves have similar importance in the dish as a whole, so, instead of piling everything onto a central serving plate for all to share, think of arranging them separately on plates so that the delicate betel leaf fritters aren't damaged.

Fish fragrant watermelon

For me, watermelon has the fragrance of the freshest fish. The raw ingredients here are those which the Sichuanese conceive as complementary to fish, but which are generally used in chicken, eggplant or pork dishes. I'm imagining what the chemistry of those flavourings might be like if they were used with raw fish.

Fish fragrant watermelon

SERVES 4

Ingredients

FOR THE AVOCADO DRESSING

1 TEASPOON UNSALTED BUTTER
80 ML (2½ FL OZ) GRAPESEED OIL
50 G (1¾ OZ) YOUNG GINGER, MINCED
65 G (2¼ OZ) GARLIC, MINCED
1 TABLESPOON CHILLI BEAN PASTE (DOU BAN JIANG)
50 ML (1¾ FL OZ) DRY SHERRY
½ BUNCH (ABOUT 5) SPRING ONIONS (SCALLIONS), THINLY SLICED
SUGAR TO TASTE
½ AVOCADO, PUREED JUST BEFORE USING
1 TEASPOON LEMON JUICE

1 TABLESPOON SEA SALT
300 G (10½ OZ) STRIPED TRUMPETER OR FLAME-TAIL SNAPPER FISH FILLETS, SKIN REMOVED
150 G (5½ OZ) RIPE WATERMELON, SEEDS REMOVED
ICING (CONFECTIONERS') SUGAR IN A SUGAR SHAKER
A LITTLE LIGHT SOY SAUCE TO SEASON
CHILLI OIL TO SERVE

Method

MAKE THE AVOCADO DRESSING

Soften the butter in a saucepan over medium–high heat. Add the oil and, when hot, stir in the ginger and garlic. Cook gently until soft and with mellow flavours. Season with salt and white pepper. Add the chilli bean paste and fry until fragrant. Add the sherry and cook until the mixture becomes syrupy. Stir in the spring onions but don't overcook them as this will draw out moisture into the mixture. Season generously with salt, white pepper, and sugar to taste. Leave at room temperature for about 30 minutes to allow to mature. Pass the mixture through a fine sieve (reserving the solids) and fold the oil into the freshly puréed avocado. Add the lemon juice to the avocado dressing. Taste to check that the dressing is well flavoured with ginger and chilli paste and that the richness is cut by the lemon juice.

PREPARE THE FISH

Gently rub the salt onto the fish fillets. Leave for 30 minutes and then wipe off the excess with a damp paper towel. Don't rub hard or you will damage the flesh. When ready to assemble the dish, cut the fillets into paper-thin slices across the grain of the fish.

PREPARE THE WATERMELON

Cut the watermelon into thick steaks. Sprinkle with salt, pepper and icing sugar. Cook in a hot frying pan for 30 seconds on each side until lightly browned. Dice very finely.

ASSEMBLE THE DISH

Arrange the slices of fish on individual serving plates. Add the watermelon dice, intermingling them with the fish. Add a little avocado dressing around the plate. Season the reserved solids from the avocado dressing with a little light soy sauce to taste and add to the plate. Drizzle the plate with a little chilli oil.

Veal sweetbreads, soured and grilled

The flavourings in this dish are derived from the traditional Malaysian assam of fish. I now wonder what would result if the spicy and strong-flavoured sauce was used as a seasoning paste and grilled?

Ingredients

MAKES ABOUT 10

FOR THE ASSAM PASTE

- 4 CANDLENUTS
- 10 RED ASIAN SHALLOTS
- 2 RED CHILLIES, DESEEDED
- 8 GARLIC CLOVES, PEELED
- 1.5 CM (½ IN) PIECE OF YOUNG GINGER
- ½ TEASPOON BLACHAN (SEE GLOSSARY), ROASTED
- 1 CM (½ IN) PIECE OF CASSIA, GROUND TO POWDER
- 2 CLOVES, GROUND TO POWDER
- 1½ TABLESPOONS PEANUT OIL
- ½ TEASPOON SUGAR
- 1½ TEASPOONS TAMARIND PULP MIXED WITH 250 ML (8½ FL OZ) WATER

FOR THE VEAL SWEETBREADS

- 500 G (1 LB 2 OZ) VEAL SWEETBREADS, SOAKED OVERNIGHT IN WATER
- 2 BANANA LEAVES (EXCESSIVE, BUT ALLOWS FOR MISTAKES)

Method

MAKE THE ASSAM PASTE

Grind the candlenuts, shallots, chillies, garlic, ginger and roasted blachan to a fine paste. Mix in the ground cassia and cloves. Heat the oil in a frying pan over medium–high. Fry the paste until it separates and there's no longer any taste of raw shallot or garlic. Season with the sugar and add salt to taste, letting it colour slightly in the residual heat. Strain the tamarind water, add to the paste and cook until it is rather thick. Season with additional salt so that it tastes slightly saltier than a normal sauce (it's to be used as a seasoning). Leave to cool completely.

PREPARE THE SWEETBREADS

Drain the sweetbreads. Put in a pot of cold water, bring to the boil and simmer for 5 minutes. Remove from the pot and, when cool enough to handle, clean away the membrane and other unpleasant things. Put on a plate, cover with another plate and load this with weights (tins of tomatoes are good). This is to prevent a spongy unpleasant texture. Leave for at least 3 hours in the fridge. When ready to grill, cut the sweetbreads into 3 cm (1¼ in) squares. Mix the assam paste through the pieces of sweetbread to ensure they are thoroughly coated.

Cut the banana leaves into 15 x 8 cm (6 x 3¼ in) rectangles and an equal number of 5 cm (2 in) squares. Put a piece of sweetbread on a banana rectangle. Fold each of the long sides towards the centre, place a square over the sweetbread and then turn each of the shorter sides of the rectangle over towards the centre. Using kitchen string, tie up neatly, as you would a parcel. Continue in this way until you have used up all the sweetbreads and cut banana leaves. Preheat the grill to medium–low. Grill the parcels for 20–25 minutes, turning them frequently. Serve hot straight from the grill as a snack or canapé.

HAWKER STALLS *at* NIGHT

Certain smells evoked irrepressible food cravings in me as a child. From the moment when something triggered a reminder of what might be missing in my day, it felt like an itch that wouldn't go away, a gnawing need that bothered me through play or school, even when I wasn't hungry. It wasn't beyond me to beg and cajole until I got what I wanted. The intensity of that craving remains a very immediate sensation for me to this day.

One of the strongest cravings I experienced as a child was for the Malaysian version of banana fritters, and these had to be the fritters from the Indian hawker stalls. I can remember when it was all a new experience for me. After dinner one day my father or one of my uncles must have thought it a good idea to take my cousins and me to the stalls that sold banana fritters. (These outings always seemed to happen only at twilight or night and so, of course, made me feel as if I were doing something forbidden or cheating my parents of the opportunity to put me to bed at the designated time.) Perhaps the adults were prey to the same cravings I would later suffer?

I can remember being driven in someone's car, stopping in a so-called car park that was sticky with ochre mud, a mud which had an acrid stink about it, and wandering through a slippery, precipitous, circuitous path to a surprisingly crowded area. There were roughly set up stalls and all sorts of people hovering about. I admit to having no recollection of what the other stalls might have sold — it seemed our sole mission was to hone in on the banana fritter stall. All I can remember of the stall is a dirty blue and white awning in a ragged state, which had a persistent but rather pleasant smell of old cooking oil. I think it was because I was such a shy child at times that I shirked having any contact with strangers or even satisfying my curiosity about what went on in the stall, hence the vagueness of my visual memory of the place.

The greatest pleasure and most intense memory is the smell of the freshly fried fritters through the white paper in which they were wrapped. Believe me when I say that the smell of the paper formed just as important a part of this indelible scent memory as the very particular banana smell and the sweetness of the batter. We'd purchase a number of large packages to take home to the assorted family members. When the packages were unwrapped, the satisfaction of biting into the still hot and crispy fritters was immense, to say the least. I believe I always consumed more than was probably right for a child of my size.

Banana Fritters

Mix a cupful of non-glutinous rice flour with half a cupful of water and leave for 30 minutes. The mixture will be quite hard to stir, so use a wooden spoon or a pastry card rather than a whisk. Mix a cupful of water with ¼ teaspoon of lye water or concentrated alkaline water. (Don't drink this or touch it with bare hands. It's optional, if you're worried about using it, but it will keep the fritters crispy.) Beat into the batter with 1 teaspoon of salt and 1 lightly beaten egg.

Choose floury but sweet bananas for fritters, perhaps just-ripe sugar bananas (in Malaysia, the pisang rajah is the preferred variety). I like to deep-fry the whole banana split in half lengthways. Dredge the bananas in egg yolk then rice flour before dipping in the batter. Deep-fry in oil at 180°C (350°F) until dark golden. Wrap in butcher's paper and leave to sit for 15 minutes before serving. Let the companions at your table unwrap and fight over the fritters amongst themselves.

Green tomato, hazelnut and shiitake

I feel a super sensitivity to the deliciousness of the deep-fried banana because of the context in which I came across it during a particular time of my life. I find the mixture of hazelnut and shiitake meets a certain concept in my head about what constitutes super-charged umami-ness. So this composition is about harnessing ingredients which play up to the primary focus on hazelnut and shiitake.

Green tomato, hazelnut and shiitake

SERVES 4

Ingredients

FOR THE RED CAPSICUM SALT	1 RED CAPSICUM (BELL PEPPER) 1 TEASPOON CORIANDER SEEDS ½ TEASPOON BLACK PEPPERCORNS SUGAR TO TASTE
FOR THE HAZELNUT AND SHIITAKE MUSHROOM PASTE	400 ML (13½ FL OZ) LIGHT CHICKEN STOCK 5 DRIED SHIITAKE MUSHROOMS, STEMS REMOVED, SOAKED IN WATER FOR 1 HOUR 75 G (2¾ OZ) SKINNED HAZELNUTS 2 GARLIC CLOVES, SMASHED 3 CM (1¼ IN) PIECE OF GINGER, SMASHED 2 CORIANDER (CILANTRO) ROOTS, SCRAPED OF DIRT 50–100 ML (1¾–3½ FL OZ) EXTRA VIRGIN OLIVE OIL LIGHT SOY SAUCE TO TASTE
FOR THE CHICKEN THREADS AND GREEN TOMATO	12 CONFIT CHICKEN WINGS (SEE PAGE 306) OLIVE OIL FOR FRYING PEANUT OIL FOR DEEP-FRYING 2 GREEN TOMATOES 1 QUANTITY RICE BATTER FROM BANANA FRITTERS (SEE PAGE 27) 2 EGG YOLKS, LIGHTLY BEATEN RICE FLOUR FOR COATING FEW SMALL LEAVES OR GARLIC FLOWERS TO SERVE (OPTIONAL)

Method

MAKE THE RED CAPSICUM SALT

Remove the seeds and membrane from the capsicum. Cut it into smaller pieces and dry overnight in a convection oven on the lowest heat until crisped but not coloured. Grind to a powder. Grind the coriander and black peppercorns to a fine powder and combine with the capsicum. Season with salt and sugar so that it tastes appetising and savoury.

MAKE THE HAZELNUT AND SHIITAKE PASTE

Put the stock, mushrooms, hazelnuts, garlic, ginger and coriander roots in a pot and bring to the boil. Simmer gently for about 2 hours until the mushrooms and hazelnuts are soft. The flavours and fragrances are very delicate so the mixture can't be allowed to boil too strongly. (An alternative is to cook the pot in the oven at 170°C (340°F) for about 2 hours with a lid three-quarters on.) Strain. Pick out the mushrooms and hazelnuts from the solids and put them in a blender or food processor along with the strained liquid. Blend to a fine paste, adding some of the olive oil if necessary to help it pass through a fine sieve. To accentuate the umami taste (savouriness), add light soy sauce, salt and white pepper to taste. Keep warm.

MAKE THE CHICKEN THREADS AND FRY THE GREEN TOMATO

Prepare this just before serving. Remove the skin from the chicken and separate the meat. Using the part closest to the body which has longer strands, shred the meat into fine strands. Brush a non-stick frying pan with olive oil, put over low heat and slowly dry the strands to a crisp. Season generously with finely ground salt.

Heat oil in a deep-fryer to 180°C (350°F). Cut the tomatoes into quarters and cut each quarter in half across the mid section. Dip each piece in the batter, then shake off any excess. Deep-fry until golden. Drain on paper towels and season with the red capsicum salt.

ASSEMBLE THE DISH

You may like to use small leaves or flowers such as garlic flowers or torn-up nasturtiums to soften the bristly look of this dish. I picture this as a canapé, so serve the fried tomato with some of the hazelnut and shiitake paste. Pile the chicken threads on top and dress with additional capsicum salt and the flowers.

Oysters, eggplant custard and rose petals

Foods like banana fritters never seem to be defined as pre- or post-meal treats, simply snacks to be indulged in on a whim. This is my version of an appetiser or snack that treads the fine line between sweet and savoury.

Oysters, eggplant custard and rose petals

SERVES 4

Ingredients

FOR THE PICKLED ROSE PETALS	40 G (1½ OZ) SUGAR 175 ML (6 FL OZ) WHITE WINE VINEGAR PETALS FROM 4 ROSES
FOR THE ROSE PETAL AND CHILLI PASTE	30 G (1 OZ) DRIED CHILLI, COARSELY CHOPPED, RECONSTITUTED IN WATER THEN DRAINED 50 ML (1¾ FL OZ) ROSE PETAL SYRUP (SEE BOX OPPOSITE) 30 G (1 OZ) FRESH CHILLI 1 GARLIC CLOVE ½ TEASPOON CORIANDER SEEDS ½ TEASPOON CARAWAY SEEDS ½ TEASPOON DRIED MINT LEAVES 1 TABLESPOON CORIANDER (CILANTRO) LEAVES 1 TEASPOON SALT A LITTLE OLIVE OIL TO LOOSEN THE PASTE
FOR THE EGGPLANT CUSTARD	1 LARGE EGGPLANT (AUBERGINE) 2 EGGS 1½ TABLESPOONS SAKE 50 ML (1¾ FL OZ) EXTRA VIRGIN OLIVE OIL 1 TEASPOON MIRIN
FOR THE DEEP-FRIED OYSTERS	PEANUT OIL FOR DEEP-FRYING 12 PACIFIC OYSTERS, SHUCKED 1 QUANTITY RICE BATTER FROM BANANA FRITTERS (SEE PAGE 27)

Method

PICKLE THE ROSE PETALS

Put the sugar, vinegar and 125ml (4 fl oz) water in a pot and bring to the boil, stirring to dissolve the sugar. Put the petals in a sterilised preserving jar. When the temperature of the pickling solution reaches 80°C (175°F), pour it over the roses. Seal the jar and leave for a couple of days before use.

MAKE THE ROSE PETAL AND CHILLI PASTE

Put all the ingredients except the olive oil in a blender or food processor and blend to a fine paste. Add a little olive oil to loosen the mixture if it is not puréeing smoothly.

MAKE THE EGGPLANT CUSTARD

Preheat the oven to 200°C (400°F). Sear the whole eggplant in a hot frying pan until brown all over. To ensure the eggplant is thoroughly cooked, transfer it to the oven and bake until it feels soft all the way through when pressed. Leaving the oven on, transfer the eggplant to a tray to cool, pressing out the juices and draining them off as it cools. Peel off the skin. Purée the flesh, then pass it through a sieve into a bowl. Measure out 180 g (6½ oz) of purée for the next stage of the recipe. Beat the eggs and pass through a sieve into the bowl to ensure there's no foam or albumen. Mix in the sake, oil and mirin. Season with salt and white pepper. Lightly oil an ovenproof dish large enough to take the custard. Add the custard and cover the dish with foil. Place in a roasting tin and pour hot water into the tin to come halfway up the side of the dish of custard. Reduce the oven to 180°C (350°F) and bake for 25–30 minutes until set. Cool completely.

PREPARE THE OYSTERS

Heat oil in a deep-fryer to 180°C (350°F). Dip the oysters in batter, then drain off the excess. Deep-fry until golden. Drain on paper towels and serve straightaway.

ASSEMBLE THE DISH

Arrange 3 oysters on each plate with some of the custard, rose petal and chilli paste and pickled petals.

TO MAKE ROSE PETAL SYRUP

Take 20 g (¾ oz) petals from unsprayed dark-coloured roses (not tea roses). Heat 175 g (6 oz) sugar in a cupful of water until dissolved. When the syrup reaches 80°C (175°F), add the petals. Keep the petals in the syrup to continue infusing; store in the fridge or in sterilised jars for a couple of days before use.

Plums, curry leaf syrup and baked coffee cream

I'm using the smell of deep-fried bananas as an anchor for whatever ideas might reveal themselves. For some reason, when I think further about that particular banana aroma, I've arrived at contrasting the zing of the curry leaf with the comfort of milky coffee.

Ingredients

SERVES 4

FOR THE CURRY LEAF AND BLOOD PLUMS IN SYRUP

- 4 BLOOD PLUMS
- 220 G (8 OZ) CASTER (SUPERFINE) SUGAR
- 1 TABLESPOON CURRY LEAVES

FOR THE BAKED COFFEE CREAM

- 140 ML (4½ FL OZ) MILK
- 60 G (2 OZ) WHOLE COFFEE BEANS
- 125 G (4½ OZ) CASTER (SUPERFINE) SUGAR
- 2 EGGS
- 4 EGG YOLKS
- 500 ML (17 FL OZ) THICKENED CREAM

FOR THE SOUR CREAM PASTRY

- 310 G (11 OZ) PLAIN (ALL-PURPOSE) FLOUR
- 100 G (3½ OZ) SOUR CREAM
- 4 EGG YOLKS
- 1¼ TABLESPOONS RUM
- PEANUT OIL FOR DEEP-FRYING
- ICING (CONFECTIONERS') SUGAR FOR DUSTING

- FROSTED CURRY LEAVES (SEE BOX BELOW) TO SERVE

TO MAKE FROSTED CURRY LEAVES

For frosted curry leaves, take the most tender leaves and brush them lightly all over with beaten egg white. Pat them lightly in caster (superfine) sugar to coat and spread on a baking tray lined with baking paper to dry.

Method

MAKE THE CURRY LEAF AND BLOOD PLUMS IN SYRUP

Halve the plums, remove the stones and then cut the halves into quarters. Combine the sugar and 250 ml (8½ fl oz) water in a saucepan and bring to the boil. Add the curry leaves and plums and simmer for 5 minutes or so. Remove from the heat and leave the plums to cool in the syrup. Taste the syrup as it cools and if it is starting to taste too strongly of curry leaf, remove the leaves.

MAKE THE BAKED COFFEE CREAM

Bring the milk to scalding point in a saucepan. Add the coffee beans, remove the pan from the heat and cover. Leave to infuse until cool. Strain. Preheat the oven to 150°C (300°F). Whisk the sugar and eggs and when smooth, whisk in the milk. Cook over medium heat, stirring all the time, until thickened like crème anglaise or other custard mixtures. Off the heat, stir in the thickened cream. Pour into an ovenproof dish and cover the dish with foil. Place in a roasting tin and pour hot water into the tin to come one-third of the way up the side of the dish of custard. Bake for 1 hour or until set. Cool.

MAKE THE SOUR CREAM PASTRY

Sift the flour and a large pinch of salt into a bowl. Mix the sour cream, egg yolks and rum together until smooth. Gradually add to the flour, mixing until you have a loose moist dough. Knead until smooth. Alternatively, process to a tight shiny dough in a food processor. Cover in plastic wrap and rest for 1–2 hours.

Heat the oil in a deep-fryer to 160°C (320°F). Roll the dough through a pasta machine to one of the finest settings, about 2 mm (⅛ in) thick. Cut into 3 cm (1¼ in) squares. Deep-fry the squares in batches until lightly golden. Drain on paper towels and dust with icing sugar before using.

ASSEMBLE THE DISH

Spoon small 'chunks' of baked coffee cream into bowls and scatter with pieces of blood plum and sour cream pastry. Top with frosted curry leaves and serve.

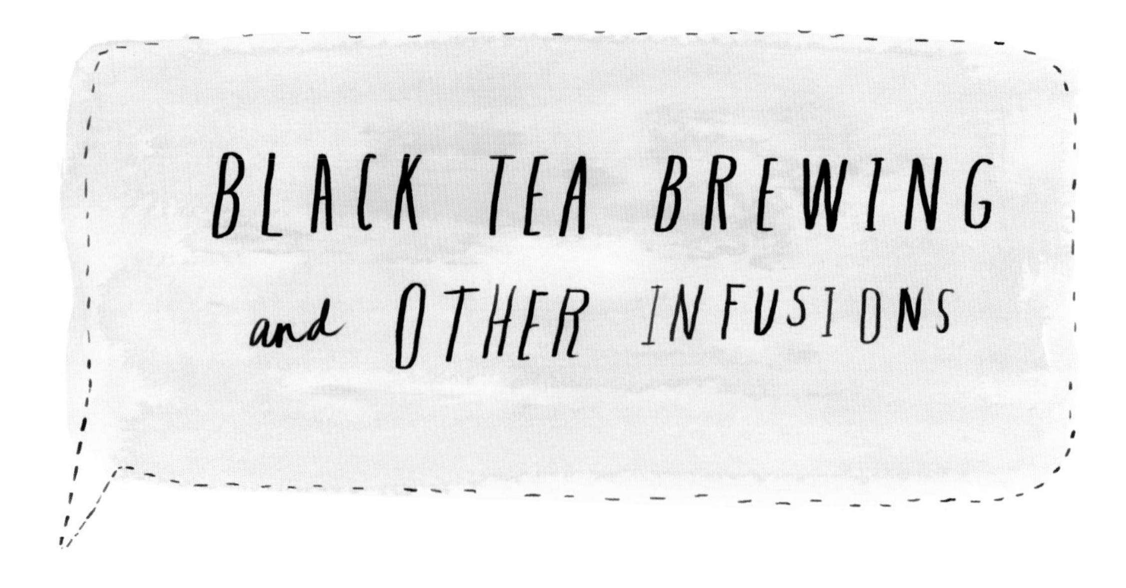

I remember many afternoons sitting in the shaded verandah of a hotel in Kota Kinabalu that my parents liked to take us to (there were many such verandahs in that part of the world, such is the legacy of colonial architecture and the practicality of tropical living). For me, those outings always felt like very grand experiences because we would drink tea. Not only were we away from home and the normal routines of the domestic afternoon, but we were partaking in what I considered to be a very civilised adult custom.

Can the smell of something be thirst-quenching? I remember trying to work this out a long time ago, but without adequate powers of language and logic to draw any feasible conclusion. When I think about it now, perhaps smells can hint at fulfilling promises with such certainty that I wanted to believe them.

Was the scent of that tea brewing in the pot before us thirst-quenching? Imagine the heat of the late afternoon, the hot stillness barely relieved by any breeze. The pink and yellow flowers of the frangipani trees close to the verandah were sharp and intense but emphasised the heat rather than providing any relief. That particular black tea may have been in a bag, just a simple commercial blend, but it held all the potential in the world to make me feel less thirsty and so was the most tantalising smell. My recollection of that scent and the physical sensation it elicits, sets the benchmark for how I consider tea now.

And can a smell shake us from the torpor of ill health? For an age, while we were living in Sandakan, I nursed a bad cough. It came on suddenly and chose not to leave me. My parents tried everything, from the supposed restorative properties of snake soup, to more conventional herbal remedies from the Chinese doctors, boiled up into strong-tasting broths. (For some reason, I have no recall of the Western medicines used.) The strong odours that I associate with these inflicted remedies created an apprehension of illness rather than appetite. So, now, when I'm offered bak kut teh, or other soup that contains any measure of Chinese herbs, part of me is slightly repelled by the aromatic reminder of a time when I was ill.

One day in our garden a friend of my mother's pointed out that one of the decorative plants we'd always ignored had some medicinal properties, including improving coughs. (She had obviously noticed my persistent, and most likely quite annoying, cough.) By now my mother was no longer conservative in choosing her treatments for me; an extra herbal concoction was probably just another way of covering the myriad bases. I protested greatly when I was offered the infusion that stank of crushed ants and citrus peel. While I can't tell you now how bitter or how unpleasant the drink might have been, I know that my cough disappeared shortly afterwards.

My mother and I have long wondered over the identity of this possibly cough-dispelling plant. We think now it was eau de cologne mint, but can't be sure, so its mystery lives on in our minds. That scent lingers with me, reminding me of the past experience of suddenly getting better.

Roasted fish: Chinese herbal concoction

This dish comes from my revisiting of my childhood demons of the pungent and bitter Chinese herbal soups drunk to relieve symptoms of illness and build up the constitution. The combination of the sweetness and bitterness of various herbs creates a great foil for fish. All the ingredients are available from Chinese herbalists.

Roasted fish: Chinese herbal concoction

SERVES 4

Ingredients

FOR THE BAK KUT TEH (CHINESE HERBAL CONCOCTION)

5 PIECES RHIZOMA LIGUSTICI
3 PIECES RHIZOMA POLYGONATI ODORATI
2 PIECES RADIX ANGELICA SINENSIS
4 PIECES RADIX REHMANNIA GLUTINOSA
2 TABLESPOONS HAWTHORN BERRIES
5 DRIED RED CHINESE DATES
5 WHOLE DRIED SHIITAKE MUSHROOMS
500 G (1 LB 2 OZ) PORK SPARE RIBS
1 CASSIA STICK
½ STAR ANISE
2 CLOVES
1 TABLESPOON WHITE PEPPERCORNS
1 TABLESPOON BLACK PEPPERCORNS
1 HEAD OF GARLIC, PEELED
4 RED ASIAN SHALLOTS, PEELED
1 PIECE OF YOUNG GINGER, PEELED
COGNAC TO SEASON
DARK SOY SAUCE TO SEASON
LIGHT SOY SAUCE TO SEASON
SUGAR TO SEASON

4 WHITE FISH FILLETS (EG MULLOWAY, HAPUKA, SNAPPER) ABOUT 90 G (3 OZ) EACH, WITH SKIN ON
1–2 TABLESPOONS GRAPESEED OIL
6 BRUSSELS SPROUTS, LEAVES SEPARATED OUT
6 CHESTNUTS, SHELLED (SEE PAGE 132), LIGHTLY COOKED IN CHICKEN STOCK UNTIL SOFT

Method

MAKE THE BAK KUT TEH

Soak the first 6 ingredients together in cold water for at least 30 minutes. Soak the shiitake in a separate bowl of cold water for 30 minutes. Blanch the ribs in boiling salted water, then rinse and pat dry with paper towels. Wrap the cassia, star anise, cloves and both peppercorns in a muslin bag. Put in a pot with the drained soaked herbs and mushrooms and the ribs. Add the garlic, shallots and ginger and 3.5 litres (118 fl oz) water. Bring to the boil and simmer for 2 hours to develop the herbal and pork flavours. Strain this into another pot, discarding the solids. Bring the broth to the boil and simmer until it becomes quite concentrated. Season to taste with cognac, dark and light soy sauce for colour and saltiness, and sugar if desired. Keep hot.

COOK THE FISH

Do this as close to serving as possible with the aim of serving the fish directly from the oven. Preheat the oven to 160°C (320°F). Score the fish skin with a handful of slashes. Heat the oil over medium–low heat in a large skillet with an ovenproof handle. Fry the fish fillets, skin side down, for 4–5 minutes until the skin is crisp. Turn them over and transfer the skillet to the oven. Bake for 5 minutes so that the fish will cook through but remain succulent.

ASSEMBLE THE DISH

Lightly steam or fry the brussels sprouts leaves until they turn an even brighter green and are slightly softened. Break the chestnuts into slightly smaller pieces and scatter into bowls. Spoon over a little of the hot herbal concoction for the chestnuts to warm through. Add the brussels sprouts leaves and fish to the bowls and a generous amount of the herbal concoction to serve.

Borage and other cucumber-like flavours

Writing of evocative scents and smells puts me in mind of borage. The flowers of the borage plant are lovely blue star-shaped things. Both the flowers and the hairy leaves have a taste of cucumber about them. This dish is based on the premise that we can indulge in an abundance of the flowers: I want them to hold more than the position of garnish on the dish and be enjoyed for their flavour also. (This highlights my perpetual conundrum with garnishes, that they shouldn't be simply visual enhancements, but should have a meaningful place in the make-up of the dish.)

Borage and other cucumber-like flavours

SERVES 4

Ingredients

FOR THE MARINATED RADICCHIO

1 HEAD TREVISO (LONG) RADICCHIO, WASHED, OUTER LEAVES REMOVED
200 ML (7 FL OZ) APPLE CIDER VINEGAR
1 TEASPOON BLACK PEPPERCORNS
EXTRA VIRGIN OLIVE OIL

FOR THE MARINATED CUCUMBER

1 TELEGRAPH CUCUMBER (NOT OLD AND GONE TO SEED)
50 ML (1¾ FL OZ) VERJUICE

FOR THE SMOKED RAINBOW TROUT

ONE 500–700 G (1 LB 2 OZ–1 LB 9 OZ) RAINBOW TROUT, CLEANED
2 LITRES (68 FL OZ) POACHING BRINE (SEE BOX BELOW)
1 CUPFUL OF SMOKING CHIPS (EG HICKORY, APPLEWOOD OR EVEN WOODY HERBS LIKE THYME OR BAY)

FOR THE CHOPPED SALAD

50 G (1¾ OZ) FRESHLY SHELLED WALNUTS, BLANCHED AND SKINS REMOVED
6 BORAGE LEAVES, BLANCHED, REFRESHED AND THOROUGHLY DRIED
1 TABLESPOON FINELY CHOPPED FLAT-LEAF (ITALIAN) PARSLEY
2 TABLESPOONS EXTRA VIRGIN OLIVE OIL

OLIVE OIL FOR DRIZZLING
A FEW BORAGE FLOWERS TO SERVE

TO MAKE BRINE

Put 2 litres (68 fl oz) water, 35 g (1¼ oz) sea salt, 25 g (1 oz) sugar, 1 teaspoon of coriander seeds, 1 teaspoon of white peppercorns, 2 peeled and crushed garlic cloves and 1 teaspoon of peeled and crushed ginger in a pan. Bring to the boil. Remove from the heat and let the mixture cool completely before using.

Method

MARINATE THE RADICCHIO

Keeping the radicchio whole, cut it into quarters from top to bottom, leaving the core in place so the wedges are kept intact. Combine the vinegar, peppercorns and 500 ml (17 fl oz) water in a stainless steel saucepan and bring to the boil. Add the radicchio wedges, either one by one or together, depending on the level of liquid and the saucepan size. Keep the wedges submerged in the boiling liquid for 2 minutes. Remove and drain well, gently squeezing out the excess liquid. Place in a sterilised preserving jar and cover with extra virgin olive oil. Seal with the lid and leave to marinate for a couple of days before use.

MARINATE THE CUCUMBER

Peel the cucumber and halve lengthways. Scrape out the seed structure from the middle. Cut into 5 cm (2 in) lengths and then slice these into thick matchsticks. Spread on a metal tray and put in the freezer for 2–3 hours until thoroughly frozen. Bring a pot of salted water to the boil. Thaw the cucumber by blanching in the boiling water then refreshing under cold water a couple of times. Drain and gently squeeze dry without distorting the shape too much. Cut into small cubes, place in a bowl and mix thoroughly with the verjuice and salt to taste.

PREPARE THE RAINBOW TROUT

Using paper towels, dry the fish inside and outside. Put in the brine, cover and store overnight in the refrigerator. The next day dry the fish. Preheat the oven to 100°C (210°F). Light the smoking chips in a foil-lined hot pan until they give off smoke, then transfer the pan to the bottom of the oven. Put the fish on a rack in the oven and smoke for about 20 minutes until the fish is smoked through but still moist.

MAKE THE CHOPPED SALAD

Finely chop the walnuts and borage leaves separately. Combine with the parsley in a bowl and season generously with salt and freshly ground white pepper. Mix with the olive oil.

ASSEMBLE THE DISH

Take a couple of drained leaves of radicchio for each person and trim them down. Toss with salt and freshly ground white pepper to taste and drizzle with a little fresh olive oil. Put a large piece of skinless trout on each plate. Arrange some cucumber and radicchio alongside. Scatter with some of the chopped salad and, of course, the borage flowers.

White peach in pastry, drenched with jasmine syrup

I associate the heady scent of jasmine flowers with walking through gardens during the languid heat of summer. A hot, fragrant and sweet confection that is both intense and delicate came to mind. Serve this with cream if you like.

TO MAKE STRUDEL PASTRY

Mix 400 g (14 oz) strong flour, 1 teaspoon salt and 100 ml (3½ fl oz) olive oil in a mixer with a dough hook. When combined, gradually add 200 ml (7 fl oz) water and keep mixing until it comes together. Leave for 10 minutes and then knead again for 15 minutes, either in the machine or by hand. The dough should be very shiny and elastic. Cover with plastic wrap and leave for 2 hours. Cover a wide bench with a cloth and dust it liberally with flour. Stretch the dough out with the palms of your hands until it is even and very thin. Cut into 12 squares with 15 cm (6 in) sides and store on a tray, separated by sheets of baking paper. To prevent drying out, cover with plastic wrap.

Ingredients

SERVES 4

FOR THE JASMINE SYRUP

- 350 G (12½ OZ) SUGAR
- 50 G (1¾ OZ) UNSPRAYED OPENED JASMINE FLOWERS (SEE GLOSSARY)

FOR POACHING THE WHITE PEACHES

- 100 G (3½ OZ) CASTER (SUPERFINE) SUGAR
- ½ VANILLA BEAN, SPLIT LENGTHWAYS, SEEDS SCRAPED
- JUICE OF ½ LEMON
- 400 G (14 OZ) WHITE PEACHES (OR PEARS)

FOR THE GLAZE

- 12 G (½ OZ) PECTIN

FOR THE CAKE BATTER

- 60 G (2 OZ) UNSALTED BUTTER, AT ROOM TEMPERATURE
- 40 G (1½ OZ) SELF-RAISING FLOUR
- 20 G (¾ OZ) PLAIN (ALL-PURPOSE) FLOUR
- 60 G (2 OZ) CASTER (SUPERFINE) SUGAR
- 3 TEASPOONS MILK
- 1 EGG
- 1 TEASPOON NATURAL VANILLA EXTRACT

FOR THE CROUSTADES

- 12 PIECES OF 15 CM (6 IN) SQUARE STRUDEL PASTRY (SEE BOX OPPOSITE) OR FILO PASTRY
- MELTED CLARIFIED BUTTER FOR BRUSHING
- ICING (CONFECTIONERS') SUGAR FOR DUSTING

Method

MAKE THE JASMINE SYRUP

Stir the sugar and 500 ml (17 fl oz) water in a saucepan until dissolved. Add the flowers when the temperature reaches 80°C (175°F). Pour into sterilised preserving jars while still hot. Seal and refrigerate for at least a week before straining and using.

POACH THE WHITE PEACHES

Combine the sugar, vanilla pod and seeds, lemon juice and 300 ml (10 fl oz) water in a saucepan and bring to the boil. Add the peaches and 200 ml (7 fl oz) of jasmine syrup and bring to just simmering point. Remove from the heat and cover with baking paper so the peaches are submerged. Leave until completely cold. Remove the peaches and peel. Slice into quarters and then halve again.

MAKE THE GLAZE

Gradually mix the pectin with 100 ml (3½ fl oz) of jasmine syrup. Place in a small saucepan and bring to the boil. Cook for 2–3 minutes. Take off the heat and stir in 120 ml (4 fl oz) of jasmine syrup. Cool.

MAKE THE CAKE BATTER

Using electric beaters, beat the butter until very light and soft. Sift the flours into a bowl. Mix the sugar, milk, egg, vanilla and 1 teaspoon of jasmine syrup together. Fold the flour into the butter, alternating with the liquid mixture. Mix well.

MAKE THE CROUSTADES

Preheat the oven to 200°C (400°F). Butter four 10 cm (4 in) ring moulds with clarified butter. Brush 3 pieces of pastry on both sides with the butter. With one corner of each sheet pointing upwards, line one mould in an overlapping layer. The 3 corners should form an overhang. Repeat with the remaining moulds. Spoon the cake batter into the moulds. Arrange the peach slices over the batter. Dust the overhanging pastry with icing sugar and fold into the middle of the moulds to look like wrinkled sheets in a pile. Dust generously with icing sugar. Bake for 15 minutes. Remove the rings and brush the croustades with glaze. Put on a tray and return to the oven for 5–7 minutes until well coloured. Brush with more glaze before serving. Serve warm, dusted with icing sugar. If you're using cream, mix it with 50 ml (1¾ fl oz) of jasmine syrup and spoon around each croustade.

HIDDEN in OLD TIN BOXES

The sight of old biscuit tins fills me with nostalgia. I suspect they conjure up similar emotions in anyone brought up in a place or age when tin boxes were the most efficient way to store and carry fragile items. At Claude's the various pastry chefs I've worked with have also mused about the sentimental, and perhaps not totally practical, way we've stored tuiles and pastries in biscuit tins, passed on from chef to chef.

When I was a child in Malaysia, biscuits were transported from Britain, continental Europe and the United States by cargo ship. They travelled in tin boxes, themselves packed into larger boxes and stowed in containers. We saw quite an array of biscuit tins of varying sizes and designs (and still do in the grocery stores in town). Wafer biscuits, water crackers, butter cookies, those oh-so-rare chocolate or chocolate-filled biscuits, all stacked neatly and deliberately in boxes. There could be quite misleading designs on the tins, with the contents revealed only when we'd peeled away the transparent sticky tape (much too much of it) that sealed the gap where the lid joined the base. We'd pull off the lid and be hit by a strong waft of the scent of these objects contained so long in their airtight home: a buttery, sweet smell. Then, the sight of them: butter cookies in a multitude of shapes, in multiple layers of fluted papers.

The most intriguingly shaped tins were tall and square with round lids. The memory associated with the opening of these tins comes from my very early years: some adult, probably my father, cleaved open the tin with a butter knife. The smell that I remember is of something dry, one-dimensional, biscuity but not holding much promise. What was inside wasn't so interesting when I was looking for a sweet fix (they were water crackers and, for me, the association was that they were eaten when I was sick and seen to require 'a plain diet').

My memories of old tin boxes are fuelled by how they were used after the commercially manufactured biscuits were consumed. Imagine turning up to visit a beloved aunt or grandmother and being presented with a well-worn biscuit tin that you're invited to open. The labelling on the tin no longer bears any relation to what the contents might be. That moment always brought me such open delight, for the only thing one could expect was to be happily surprised. And then, the rush of displaced air as the lid is quickly removed and the release of the delicious scent: salty and sweet fermented bean curd cookies, pineapple tarts, coconut cookies, walnut cookies or the pastries I used to find the most intriguing, the delicate scrolls known as 'love letters'.

Love Letters

(kuih kapit)

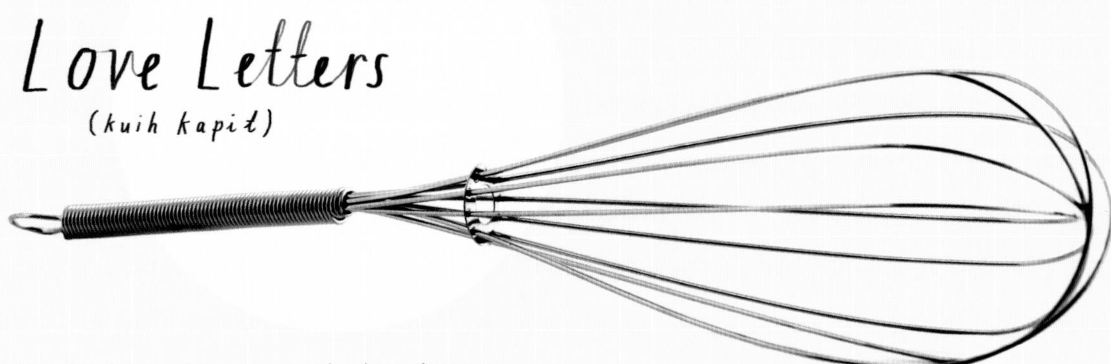

The traditional way to make love letters is in patterned metal moulds over a charcoal fire. This recipe has been adapted for use within the confines of a modern kitchen. Whisk together 5 eggs with 150 g (5½ oz) caster (superfine) sugar. Combine with 125 g (4½ oz) of rice flour which has previously been sifted with a couple of tablespoons of tapioca flour and a pinch of salt. Then, whisk in 200 ml (7 fl oz) of fresh coconut milk. Pour the batter through a fine sieve to isolate any lumps. Brush a non-stick frying pan with some oil and heat over medium heat. Pour in enough batter to thinly cover the surface. When the batter is set but not coloured, flip it onto a tray covered with baking paper and place in an oven preheated to 150°C (300°F) for 10 minutes until the biscuit is dark golden brown. Roll into a scroll while it's hot and soft. The love letters are best stored in old airtight biscuit tins, of course.

Fermented shiso and pickled mussels

There's no way of knowing what lies hidden within boxes without opening them. Similarly with foodstuffs wrapped in leaves. My thoughts then moved on to featuring the leaves themselves: here, the fragrant and striking shiso leaves. The starting point of hidden things was then overturned.

Fermented shiso and pickled mussels

SERVES 4

Ingredients

FOR THE FERMENTED SHISO LEAVES

3 TABLESPOONS FISH SAUCE
40 G (1½ OZ) FINELY CHOPPED BROWN ONION
4 GARLIC CLOVES, CHOPPED
2 SPRING ONIONS (SCALLIONS), CHOPPED
1 TEASPOON HONEY
1 TABLESPOON CHILLI FLAKES
2 TABLESPOONS FINELY CHOPPED CARROT
130 G (4½ OZ) SHISO LEAVES (SEE GLOSSARY) WASHED AND DRIED

FOR THE PICKLED MUSSELS

3 TABLESPOONS OLIVE OIL
1 CELERY STALK, FINELY SLICED
½ CARROT, FINELY SLICED
1 RED ASIAN SHALLOT, FINELY SLICED
JUICE OF 2 LEMONS
20 BLACK MUSSELS

LOVAGE OR MITSUBA LEAVES TO GARNISH

Method

PREPARE THE FERMENTED SHISO LEAVES

Combine all the ingredients except the shiso leaves in a blender and purée to a fine paste. Brush the paste over each shiso leaf and arrange in a stack on a plate. Cover with plastic wrap and refrigerate for 3 days before using.

PICKLE THE MUSSELS

Heat 2 tablespoons of the oil in a saucepan over medium–high heat. Add the celery, carrot and shallot and season with salt and freshly ground black pepper. Cook for about 5 minutes until softened. Add the lemon juice, then remove from the heat and keep warm. Heat the remaining oil in a frying pan on very high heat. Add the mussels, put a lid on and steam them open. Take the mussels out as the shells open, debearding them at the same time. Drop them into the warm pickling mixture. Cool, then refrigerate for 2–3 hours before using.

ASSEMBLE THE DISH

I picture serving this as a shared appetiser, so lay the shiso leaves out individually on a platter. Take the mussels from their pickling mixture and scatter them over the leaves. Garnish with small leaves of lovage or mitsuba.

Shards, things hidden, shattered and revealed

Wafers in my memory have an amazing ability to crunch and shatter, and it was always deemed a tragedy if they were found broken or imperfect in some way. Assembly of this dish should follow the principle that everything lies as it falls on the plate.

Shards, things hidden, shattered and revealed

SERVES 5

Ingredients

FOR THE CHOCOLATE AND COFFEE CREAM	50 G (1¾ OZ) DARK CHOCOLATE, FINELY CHOPPED 250 ML (8½ FL OZ) THICK (DOUBLE/HEAVY) CREAM 2 TABLESPOONS CASTER (SUPERFINE) SUGAR 2 TEASPOONS WARM ESPRESSO COFFEE
FOR THE BLACK SESAME DUST	50 G (1¾ OZ) BLACK SESAME SEEDS 30 G (1 OZ) CASTER (SUPERFINE) SUGAR
FOR THE WAFERS	2 EXTRA LARGE EGGS 225 G (8 OZ) CASTER (SUPERFINE) SUGAR 250 G (9 OZ) PLAIN (ALL-PURPOSE) FLOUR 100 G (3½ OZ) UNSALTED BUTTER, MELTED 3 TEASPOONS VANILLA SUGAR
FOR THE LEMON CURD	85 G (3 OZ) UNSALTED BUTTER 85 G (3 OZ) CASTER (SUPERFINE) SUGAR 3 EGGS, LIGHTLY BEATEN FINELY GRATED ZEST AND JUICE OF 3 LEMONS
FOR THE BLACK SESAME PUDDINGS	125 G (4½ OZ) RICOTTA 45 G (1½ OZ) QUARK (SEE GLOSSARY) 30 G (1 OZ) CASTER (SUPERFINE) SUGAR 1 EGG 65 G (2¼ OZ) CONDENSED MILK 65 G (2¼ OZ) LEMON CURD (SEE ABOVE) 35 G (1¼ OZ) TOASTED BLACK SESAME SEEDS, ROUGHLY CHOPPED
	BLUEBERRIES AND RASPBERRIES TO GARNISH

Method

MAKE THE CHOCOLATE AND COFFEE CREAM

Put the chocolate in a large bowl. Bring the cream and sugar to the boil, stirring to dissolve the sugar. Pour over the chocolate and whisk until smooth. Add the coffee. Cool in the refrigerator for a couple of hours before use.

MAKE THE BLACK SESAME DUST

Preheat the oven to 160°C (320°F). Spread the sesame seeds on a tray and bake for about 15 minutes until fragrant. Cool. Tip onto a board and chop until all the seeds are shattered. Mix with the sugar.

MAKE THE WAFERS

Increase the oven to 165°C (330°F). Bring a small saucepan of water to the boil. Using an electric mixer, beat the eggs and sugar together in a bowl. Set the bowl over the pan of simmering water and continue beating until the mixture is thick, frothy and light in colour. Remove from the heat. Sift the flour and fold it into the bowl along with the melted butter. The batter should be thick but slightly runny, so add some lukewarm water if required to thin it out. Cover with plastic wrap and rest in the refrigerator for an hour or so before use. Spread as thinly as possible with a palette knife on silicone mats. Bake for 6 minutes until light brown. Cool.

MAKE THE LEMON CURD

Heat the butter gently until just melted (but not clarified). Add the sugar and stir until dissolved. Over low heat gradually stir in the eggs, and then the lemon zest and juice. Continue to cook, stirring, until thick and smooth. Strain, cover the surface with plastic wrap to avoid a film forming and set aside.

MAKE THE BLACK SESAME PUDDINGS

Have the oven at 160°C (320°F). Butter and lightly flour five 125 ml (4 fl oz) dariole moulds or ceramic soufflé moulds. Beat the ricotta and quark in a food processor until smooth. Add the sugar and blend in, then the egg, and process well until combined. Add the condensed milk and lemon curd and blend to combine. Turn the mixture out into a bowl and fold in the sesame seeds. Spoon into the moulds and bake for 40–50 minutes until set but slightly wobbly in the middle. Turn out to serve.

ASSEMBLE THE DISH

Using a spoon, break up the black sesame puddings into irregular pieces and arrange on serving plates. Scatter a few berries around the plates. Spoon a tablespoon or so of the chocolate and coffee cream about and sprinkle the black sesame dust in between. Sprinkle the wafers with vanilla sugar, shatter them into shards and let them fall on the plates as they will.

THE CURVING ROAD to my GRANDMOTHER'S LITTLE FARM

Seeing our maternal grandparents wasn't an everyday occurrence. They lived out of town in the hills and, though the distance to their little estate probably wasn't that great, it seemed a major excursion. The keen excitement that I felt was in anticipation of both the journey and what I expected to find at the end.

The road to my grandmother's house was very quiet in those days. There were not many other homes on it, so the trip felt like an expedition through territory that very few knew and this fuelled my excitement. The road was narrow and arced uphill at a steep gradient with many sharp turns. I had a tendency to car sickness, so learned to prevent dizziness by focusing on the interesting things I could spot through the window. I loved to imagine the jungle was slowly covering all traces of human encroachment (creepers seemed to start growing as soon as anyone even thought of abandoning their house). As we sped by in the car, I imagined the smell of the green-ness I could see, an overpowering odour of energy and power suggested by the hidden, but very apparent, strength of the vegetation. The trees I remember seemed to have oversized leaves, which made no sense to me. Sometimes these peculiarly unbalanced trees bore familiar fruits, as pointed out by the adults sitting in the front.

On our arrival, we were always warmly greeted by my grandparents. Their little house was in the middle of the estate. I have the impression (perhaps my present-day imagination is intruding here?) that highly active vegetation had taken over much of their land. It always seemed dimly lit with trees and creepers blocking out light, giving the atmosphere a damp and fertile air. My grandparents were, in my eyes, expert growers of all types of fruits and vegetables. Small plots of land were deliberately allocated to different fruits and vegetables, all being things they enjoyed eating. Here were banana trees bearing heavy loads of ripening bananas; I would run up to them and scrunch up the leaves, the smell reminding me of green banana skin. Over there was a stand of papaya trees, tall lean trunks with leafy

limbs sprouting at the top and the oddly surprising sight of embryonic green papaya-shaped fruit hidden among the foliage. I wondered if these had the same peculiar combination of smells I found in the ripe fruit: rotting flesh with an arresting floral fragrance coming through. On the perimeter, trellises supported climbing plants: snake beans, my grandfather indicated to me. Leaf vegetables were arrayed in their individual plots.

We would gradually proceed into the little house for refreshments. It was one of the old-style dwellings and parts of it still had an earthen floor. The smell was inviting (strange as it was for me to see earth as a floor cover) and it was a much-loved home. One of the things I was most excited to find out was what treats (kuih) my grandmother might have made for our visit. She was an expert at many of the Nyonya and Chinese sweets. She knew how much I loved the deep-fried pastries filled with coconut and gula melaka and never failed to make sure there were some ready whenever I visited. At that time, these seemed the most intricately shaped pastries I could ever hope to encounter: tiny semi-circular pouches with finely pleated edges. The thin pastry was extremely crisp and the shredded coconut filling delicately moistened with palm sugar. I recall very clearly the scent of those pastries: the richness of coconut oil combined with lard for deep-frying. This was a smell that held promise for stimulating the sense of taste also, offering a salty-sweet pastry and satisfyingly sweet filling. My recall of the smell of those coconut pastries holds the memory of my history with my grandmother — a very precious intangible. To this day I never fail to think of her when I come across anything delicately wrought, and the evocation of emotion through scent is an important consideration for me.

Deep-Fried COCONUT Crescent Puffs

Fry 100 g (3½ oz) grated fresh coconut in a wok until fragrant, season with 60 g (2 oz) sugar and a little salt and then set aside to cool. To make the pastry for the puffs, sift 120 g (4½ oz) plain (all-purpose) flour onto the work bench, add a pinch of salt and 1 tablespoon of sugar to the flour. Combine 2 tablespoons of water and 2 tablespoons of peanut oil with 1 egg yolk and work into the flour to make a soft dough. Cover the dough with plastic wrap and rest for 30 minutes. Roll the dough out to a thickness of 2 mm and cut shapes with a 6 cm (2½ in) round cutter. Fill with a teaspoon of the coconut mixture. Bring the edges together and pleat as finely as your fingers allow to create finely wrought edges. The approximate yield for this recipe is 20 puffs. Deep-fry in a wok filled with hot oil over medium heat until golden. Drain and cool a little before eating.

Coconut, gula melaka and sweet potato

Ingredients and recipes are like pieces of a jigsaw puzzle. It's possible to reconfigure everything to make something that's both unfamiliar yet familiar. The pieces of this puzzle are the shreds of coconut dressed in gula melaka, moved from their original place as filling in the coconut crescents. The sweet potato hints at a rich sweet soup called bubur cha-cha.

Coconut, gula melaka and sweet potato

SERVES 6

Ingredients

FOR THE SWEET POTATO JELLY

200 G (7 OZ) ORANGE SWEET POTATO (OR PERHAPS YELLOW OR PURPLE, ON A WHIM)
500 ML (17 FL OZ) COCONUT MILK
50 G (1¾ OZ) SUGAR
2 PANDAN LEAVES, BRUISED AND TIED INTO A KNOT
150 ML (5 FL OZ) ALMOND MILK (SEE BOX BELOW)
60 G (2 OZ) CASTER (SUPERFINE) SUGAR
6 G (¼ OZ) GELATINE SHEETS
55 ML (1¾ FL OZ) THICKENED CREAM

FOR THE PEANUT PASTRY

180 G (6½ OZ) PLAIN (ALL-PURPOSE) FLOUR
50 G (1¾ OZ) ICING (CONFECTIONERS') SUGAR
60 G (2 OZ) PEANUTS, ROASTED
1 TEASPOON SALT
60 ML (2 FL OZ) GRAPESEED OIL

FOR THE STEEPED COCONUT

100 G (3½ OZ) GULA MELAKA (MALAYSIAN-STYLE PALM SUGAR)
1 PANDAN LEAF, BRUISED AND TIED INTO A KNOT
½ TEASPOON TAPIOCA FLOUR
FLESH OF ½ MATURE COCONUT, GRATED

FOR THE BURNT ORANGE SAUCE

FINELY GRATED ZEST AND JUICE OF 3 NAVEL ORANGES
40 G (1½ OZ) CASTER (SUPERFINE) SUGAR
25 G (1 OZ) UNSALTED BUTTER, SOFTENED
75 ML (2½ FL OZ) POURING (SINGLE/LIGHT) CREAM

TO MAKE ALMOND MILK

Coarsely grind 250 g (9 oz) of almonds in a food processor. Add 500 ml (17 fl oz) of filtered water and blend as finely as possible. Leave covered in the fridge overnight to infuse. Strain through fine muslin.

Method

MAKE THE SWEET POTATO JELLY

Peel the sweet potato and cut into 3 cm (1¼ in) cubes. Combine the coconut milk, sugar and pandan leaves in a saucepan and add the sweet potato. Bring to a very gentle simmer (or the coconut milk will split) and cook with the lid slightly covering the pan for about 15 minutes until the sweet potato is soft. Cool, then discard the pandan leaves. Purée to a fine paste with a blender, then pass through a fine sieve. You will need 300 g (10½ oz) of purée. Combine the almond milk and caster sugar in a saucepan and heat until just warmer than body temperature (test by dipping in your finger). Meanwhile, soak the gelatine in cold water until soft. Drain, squeeze out the excess water and stir into the almond milk. Set aside. Beat the cream to soft peaks, then fold the sweet potato purée through. When the almond mixture is cool but not set, fold the sweet potato cream into it. Spread in a shallow tray and refrigerate for about 2 hours until set.

MAKE THE PEANUT PASTRY

Preheat the oven to 170°C (340°F). Spread the flour on a baking tray and toast in the oven for 20 minutes or until a sandy gold colour, stirring halfway through. Cool. Grind the icing sugar, peanuts and salt together in a food processor. Add the cooled flour and grind to a rather fine powder. Pour the oil in quickly and combine for a second or so at high speed to give a loose dough. Turn out onto a work bench and knead until smooth. Roll out to a thickness of 1 cm (½ in). Cover with plastic wrap and refrigerate for 1–2 hours. Preheat the oven to 170°C (340°F) and line a baking tray with baking paper. Break the dough into 16 small shards and place on the tray. Bake for 10 minutes until set and lightly coloured.

STEEP THE COCONUT

Chop up the palm sugar and put in a saucepan with 50 ml (1¾ fl oz) water and the pandan leaf. Stir over medium heat until the palm sugar dissolves and the syrup is brownish and fragrant with pandan. Strain, then pour back into the pan. Set aside to cool. Dissolve the tapioca flour in 1 tablespoon of syrup and stir back into the pan. Add the coconut and a pinch of salt. Bring to the boil and cook for 2–3 minutes. Take off the heat and cool to room temperature before serving.

MAKE THE BURNT ORANGE SAUCE

Put the orange zest and juice into a non-reactive saucepan. Bring to boiling point and simmer until reduced by half. Meanwhile, make a caramel. Heat the sugar in a heavy-based pan over lowish heat until melted. Continue cooking without stirring until golden. Remove from the heat and gradually add the reduced orange juice, returning the pan to the heat if necessary to facilitate this. Avoid stirring, but tilt the pan so that the caramel and juice swirl together. Cool slightly. Mix in the butter and then the cream. Serve at room temperature.

ASSEMBLE THE DISH

Place a fragment of pastry on each person's plate. Add a spoonful of the sweet potato jelly. Garnish with 2 teaspoons of the coconut and drizzle a little of the burnt orange sauce on the plate.

Painted and smoked kingfish

I'm inspired by the memory of the finely wrought forms of my grandmother's carefully made coconut crescent pastries. Their memory is also associated with the greenery surrounding the place where she lived. The remembered smell of scrunched leaves on her farm pushes me to experiment with ways to preserve the green colour and floral scent of sorrel, which disappear when the leaf comes into contact with heat.

Painted and smoked kingfish

SERVES 4

Ingredients

FOR THE PAINTED KINGFISH

3 TABLESPOONS EXTRA VIRGIN OLIVE OIL
1 BROWN ONION, FINELY DICED
4 GARLIC CLOVES, CHOPPED
1 TEASPOON THYME LEAVES
100 G (3½ OZ) SORREL LEAVES, CENTRAL STEMS REMOVED
1 TABLESPOON WHITE SOY SAUCE
400 G (14 OZ) KINGFISH FILLETS, WITHOUT SKIN
1 CUPFUL OF SMOKING CHIPS (EG HICKORY OR APPLEWOOD)
1 SMALL HANDFUL OF GREEN TEA LEAVES, RECONSTITUTED IN COLD WATER

FOR THE PISTACHIO PASTE

1 TABLESPOON NOILLY PRAT (DRY VERMOUTH)
60 ML (2 FL OZ) WHITE WINE
2 TEASPOONS WHITE WINE VINEGAR
500 ML (17 FL OZ) LIGHT CHICKEN STOCK
100 G (3½ OZ) SHELLED PISTACHIOS

20 SHELLED PISTACHIOS TO GARNISH
SMALL SORREL LEAVES TO GARNISH

Method

PAINT AND SMOKE THE KINGFISH

Heat the oil in a frying pan over medium heat. Add the onion and cook until golden, soft and sweet. Add the garlic and thyme and continue cooking until the smell of raw garlic has gone. Remove from the heat and cool completely. Use a hand-held blender to purée the onion mixture with the sorrel and white soy sauce. Add salt to taste and season quite generously with freshly ground white pepper. Put through a fine sieve. Cut the fish into long pieces along the natural separation of the fillet (so there will be larger and smaller pieces). Brush all over with the onion mixture.

Preheat the oven to 100°C (210°F). Light smoking chips in a hot foil-lined pan until they give off smoke, place thoroughly drained green tea leaves over the chips, then transfer the pan to the bottom of the oven. Put the fish on a rack in the oven and smoke for 15 minutes. The intention is to flavour the fish, not cook it through, so keep an eye on it. If in doubt, remove the fish from the oven and check whether it has enough smoked scent. Return to the oven if necessary.

MAKE THE PISTACHIO PASTE

Put the noilly prat, white wine and vinegar in a saucepan and simmer until reduced to one-third of its original volume. Pour into a clean pan with the chicken stock and bring to the boil. Add the pistachios and simmer gently for about 1 hour until the pistachios are soft. Place the pistachios in a food processor or blender. Mix together equal amounts of strained braising liquid and water and gradually blend into the pistachios until the mixture has the consistency of a smooth nut paste. Pass through a fine sieve and season with salt if desired.

ASSEMBLE THE DISH

Cut the fish into small slices. Arrange a few pieces on each plate and add a little pistachio paste. Scatter with pistachios and garnish with sorrel leaves.

Hollow bread chicken

This is based on a daydream about how plants in the tropics seem to run amok when you turn your back on them. The idea of hollow bread, kong xin bing in Chinese, suggests forgotten items to me: things hidden away in the pockets of memory (but what excitement when they're found again). Salted and pickled foods have the suggestion of having been forgotten or left to their own devices, the result being that they are transformed at the end of the process.

Ingredients

SERVES 4

FOR THE HOLLOW BREAD

- 60 ML (2 FL OZ) PEANUT OIL
- 85 G (3 OZ) STRONG FLOUR
- 1 TEASPOON SALT
- 260 G (9 OZ) PLAIN (ALL-PURPOSE) FLOUR
- 180 ML (6 FL OZ) BOILING WATER, COOLED WITH 2 TABLESPOONS COLD WATER

FOR THE GREEN CHILLI, CORIANDER AND CHILLI RELISH

- 50 ML (1¾ FL OZ) EXTRA VIRGIN OLIVE OIL
- 10 GARLIC CLOVES, PEELED
- 4 LONG MILDLY HOT GREEN CHILLIES, DESEEDED AND CHOPPED
- 100 G (3½ OZ) CORIANDER (CILANTRO) LEAVES
- 2 CM (¾ IN) PIECE OF YOUNG GINGER, PEELED AND FINELY GRATED

FOR THE CHICKEN FILLING

- 2 CHICKEN BREASTS, SALTED AND STEAMED (SEE PAGE 302)
- 85 G (3 OZ) PICKLED MUSTARD GREENS, STEMS CUT INTO 1 CM (½ IN) DICE, LEAVES FINELY CHOPPED
- 2 SALTED DUCK EGGS, PLACED IN A PAN OF COLD WATER, BROUGHT UP TO BOIL, BOILED FOR 5 MINUTES, PEELED AND FINELY CHOPPED
- 2 SMALL CUCUMBERS, PEELED AND CUT INTO 1 CM (½ IN) DICE

Method

MAKE THE HOLLOW BREAD

Make a laminating paste first. Heat the oil in a saucepan to 80°C (175°F). Add the strong flour and half the salt and stir to form a paste. If it appears to be too dry, add more oil, cautiously. Cook the paste for about 5 minutes. It should have a dried-out appearance, a nutty smell and be of a consistency that drops off the spoon in splodges. Take off the heat and set aside.

Make up the dough next. Mix the plain flour and remaining salt in a bowl. Gradually mix the water into the flour. Knead to a smooth dough. Cover with plastic wrap and set aside for 1 hour or so. Lightly grease the work bench with oil (to stop the dough sticking) and roll out the dough to 42 x 10 cm (17 x 4 in). Spread 5 tablespoons of the laminating paste along the length of the dough, leaving a margin of 5 cm (2 in) on all sides. Store any leftover paste in the freezer for another time.

Bring the edges together along the length of the dough and pinch together. Pinch the edges on the shorter ends as well. Cut the roll into 12 pieces. With a cut side facing you with the piece flat on the bench facing upwards, roll into a 15 x 12 cm (6 x 5 in) rectangle. The width will be slightly expanded from the original size. Turn the dough through 90 degrees. Fold into thirds by folding the left third into the centre then the right third over the left. Roll out again to a 20 cm (8 in) square with the open seam facing you. Roll up the dough into a cylinder and rest with the seam side down to prevent unfurling while you roll the remaining pieces. Cover with plastic wrap, then a tea towel and leave for 2–3 hours. Roll each cylinder into a 15 x 8 cm (6 x 3 in) rectangle. Leave, covered, for at least 1 hour prior to cooking.

Preheat the oven to 220°C (430°F) and grease two or three baking trays. Bake the breads for about 15 minutes until golden and puffed. Cool on cake racks.

MAKE THE RELISH

Heat the oil in a saucepan to 60°C (140°F). Add the garlic and cook slowly for 30 minutes. Transfer the garlic to a blender or food processor and add the chillies, coriander leaves and ginger. Grind to a paste, gradually adding the flavoured oil. Season with salt and white pepper.

FILL THE BREADS

Shred the chicken breasts roughly. Combine with the mustard greens, salted duck egg and cucumber and fold in 3 tablespoons of the relish. Cut the top off each bread or split it through the centre. Fill with the chicken mixture. Have extra relish available on the side.

SIG

HT

Late one afternoon our cousins brought over a large flat package wrapped in the sort of brown paper that I knew came from one of the dusty stores in town. They had excited looks on their faces and seemed complicit in a secret knowledge they weren't yet ready to share. They were older and wiser, in my eyes, but not unkind, and quickly told us we should wait until after dark to open the parcel. Obedient as I was (on occasion), it was a long wait until they deemed the night inky black enough to satisfy their rule.

We were instructed to open the wrapping carefully. This did slow down progress but they were watchful that we should follow their instruction. Inside were beautifully coloured animals drawn on rice paper and mounted on wire frames. Our much more worldly cousins showed us how these could be folded out into three-dimensional forms. To our further surprise, they had candles inside which, when lit, gave illumination to a bright red goldfish, grey and black striped cat, caramel brown monkey, gold and black tiger, white and grey goat, and chestnut dog (what now, in my memory, seems a large menagerie shepherded by our four cousins, my sister and me).

Children are universally told not to run around with fire, but on this evening an exemption was granted to the rule. We cautiously proceeded around the border of our garden, unused to traversing territory that was familiar during the day but alien and frightening at night. There were uneven patches in the grass, areas without any lighting, where insects sounded their loudest and closest with their slightly threatening noises, and looming shadows way above normal human height. Once the territory grew more familiar and we became accustomed to carrying our lanterns, we ran with abandon, scaring each other with the shadows we made. It was an occasion for boisterous, unrestrained joy, running ragged late into the night. Only later did I find out that we had been celebrating the Autumn Moon Festival that evening.

Celebrating the Lunar New Year is a confusion of frenetic memories for me. It meant dressing up early in the day to visit relatives and friends, sitting quietly and nibbling on sunflower seeds while the adults chatted together, then receiving the red packets. The convention, if you're not aware, is that married adults present to children, or unmarried adults they meet on that day, vivid red packets embossed with lurid gold characters denoting wishes for prosperity and auspiciousness. These packets potentially contained generous (or token) amounts of money.

We would make our way into the town and see men, in a long line, covered with a costume representing the Chinese conventional image of a lion. The lion danced to a drum beating amidst the light flashes and exploding bits of paper from the fire crackers. We feasted among a large group of relatives, with dishes laid out on the table all vying for our attention. Food ranged from the extremes of extravagance to the apparently humble, yet symbolic: whole steamed fish; dried oysters braised with black moss and dried shiitake mushroom; prawns; drunken chicken; and sweet niangao slices, dipped in egg and then fried.

Festival days could also be quietly contemplative events. The fifth day of the fifth month of the lunar calendar was an occasion to gather to eat sticky rice parcels wrapped in bamboo leaf. My mother had become quite expert at forming these four-cornered parcels, which I would describe as asymmetrical pyramids. The filling was fiddly to make, with layers radiating from the centre: pork, then dried shrimp, chestnut, shiitake mushroom, mung beans and rice. The first sign of her intention to make rice parcels was finding her in the kitchen rubbing the green skins off the soaked mung beans. I would try my best to wrap the rice in the complicated arrangement she demonstrated, but much greater dexterity than mine was demanded, so my attempts were either abandoned or stood out as rather irregularly shaped objects among my mother's perfect parcels.

The parcels were taken into the garden to be boiled in a large pot over the fire pit. It seemed to take an age, with my mother periodically going outside to stir them around and make sure the parcels were unbroken. Once they were cooked, the already plump parcels appeared even fatter, straining against the hemp string that held them together. I was sure my mother made these more than once in my childhood conception of a year, that it was on more than one occasion we gathered around to unwrap the leaves, which tended to stick a little to the rice, and savour the bamboo-infused flavour and marvel at the distinct layers of the parcel. It was only years later, talking to my mother about why she chose to teach herself this complicated process, that she admitted she made sticky rice parcels whenever she felt like it, rather than observing the particular festival traditions.

Going back to that firelit night of the Autumn Moon Festival, you might ask: what did we eat? It seemed that the joy of running around with lanterns overshadowed any thought of food. However, the snacks and celebratory dishes are ever present and have symbolic meaning and on this occasion it was moon cakes: lotus seed paste encased in a soft pastry, sometimes with a centre of salted duck egg yolk. My mother added her individual celebratory touch to the evening: she had split the top off a watermelon and scooped the red flesh into balls, which she then piled back into the hollowed-out shell.

When we had tired of running and scoffing down cake and fruit, the end of the evening saw us lying in a lighted patch of garden until the rain suddenly poured in a torrent to cool down the evening. My last memory is of the abandoned watermelon in the garden, slowly filling to the brim with rainwater.

Luminous things

The memory of running wild with lanterns is constructed around feelings of unconstrained happiness. For me, favourite tastes and colours can go a long way towards recapturing that elation. (For practical reasons of measuring, the amount of marshmallow buttons you will make here is far greater than required for the recipe. The excess can be stored for later use in an airtight container and enjoyed as bonbons or snacks.)

Luminous things

SERVES 8

Ingredients

FOR THE MARSHMALLOW BUTTONS

1½ GELATINE LEAVES
100 ML (3½ FL OZ) ELDERFLOWER LIQUEUR
1 TEASPOON LIQUID GLUCOSE
150 G (5½ OZ) CASTER (SUPERFINE) SUGAR
85 G (3 OZ) EGG WHITES (ABOUT 2 EGGS)
80 G (2¾ OZ) ICING (CONFECTIONERS') SUGAR AND 20 G (¾ OZ) CORNFLOUR (CORNSTARCH), SIFTED TOGETHER

FOR THE HAZELNUT MERINGUE

75 G (2¾ OZ) SKINLESS HAZELNUTS
200 G (7 OZ) EGG WHITES (ABOUT 5 LARGE EGGS)
200 G (7 OZ) CASTER (SUPERFINE) SUGAR
40 G (1½ OZ) PLAIN (ALL-PURPOSE) FLOUR

FOR THE VANILLA CREAM

2 EGG YOLKS
75 G (2¾ OZ) CASTER (SUPERFINE) SUGAR
20 G (¾ OZ) CORNFLOUR (CORNSTARCH)
250 ML (8½ FL OZ) MILK
1 VANILLA BEAN, SPLIT, SEEDS SCRAPED OUT
1 TEASPOON LIQUID GLUCOSE
80 G (2¾ OZ) EGG WHITES (ABOUT 2 EGGS)

1 SOFT PERSIMMON, CUT INTO LOGS WITH AN APPLE CORER
12 MULTI-COLOURED ROSE PETALS IN SYRUP TO GARNISH (SEE BOX BELOW)

TO MAKE ROSE PETALS IN SYRUP

Dissolve 50 g (1¾ oz) of caster (superfine) sugar in 50 ml (1¾ fl oz) of water over medium heat. When the syrup temperature reaches 70°C (160°F), pour it over a handful of perfect unsprayed rose petals. Leave to cool before use.

Method

MAKE THE MARSHMALLOW BUTTONS

These can be made 2–3 hours in advance. Soak the gelatine in cold water until softened. Drain and squeeze out the excess water. Heat the liqueur, add the gelatine and glucose and stir until dissolved. In a saucepan bring 50 ml (1¾ fl oz) water and 120 g (4½ oz) of the caster sugar to the boil. Simmer until the syrup reaches 127°C (260°F) on a thermometer. Meanwhile, have the egg whites ready in the bowl of an electric mixer with the whisk attachment and start whisking to soft peaks when the syrup is at 114°C (237°F). Add the remaining 30 g (1 oz) of caster sugar gradually to stabilise the egg whites. Add the gelatine liqueur to the sugar syrup as it reaches 127°C (255°F). Start slowly pouring the syrup into the egg white, whisking constantly. Continue whisking until all the syrup is in and the meringue is thick and cooled. Line trays with baking paper and dust generously with the icing sugar mixture. Use a piping bag with a large piping nozzle to pipe 12 discs of 2 cm (¾ in) diameter and 12 discs of 4 cm (1½ in) diameter, all to a height of 1 cm (½ in). Flatten any irregular peaks with a dampened finger. Dust with the icing sugar mixture and refrigerate to set. You will have enough mixture to make more marshmallows, so pipe, bake, store and eat them as you wish.

MAKE THE HAZELNUT MERINGUE

Preheat the oven to 110°C (220°F) and line two baking trays with baking paper. Grind the hazelnuts to a moderately fine powder. Whisk the egg whites to soft peaks, then gradually add the sugar until stiff peaks are formed. Fold in the flour and hazelnuts. Spread over the baking trays to a thickness of 5 mm (¼ in). Bake for 20 minutes until thoroughly browned. Turn out onto wire racks, place a damp tea towel over the top for a few minutes and then remove the baking paper. Cool thoroughly before using.

MAKE THE VANILLA CREAM

Whisk the egg yolks and 1 tablespoon of the sugar until thickened and white. Whisk in the cornflour. Pour the milk into a saucepan and add the vanilla pod and seeds and 2 teaspoons of the sugar. Bring to scalding point. Mix some of the hot milk into the yolk mixture, then whisk this mixture back into the saucepan. Bring to the boil and cook for 2–4 minutes until you can't taste any gritty uncooked starch in the mixture. Transfer to a bowl and immediately cover with plastic wrap directly on the cream to prevent a skin forming. Leave to cool.

Heat the remaining caster sugar with the glucose and 50 ml (1¾ fl oz) water. Heat until the syrup reaches 110°C (230°F) on a thermometer. Start whisking the egg whites in a mixer with whisk attachment until soft peak stage. When the syrup reaches 120°C (248°F) slowly pour it into the egg whites in a slow stream, whisking all the time. Continue whisking until the meringue is thick and cooled. Fold into the pastry cream.

ASSEMBLE THE DISH

Place spoonfuls of the vanilla cream onto each plate and spread one side of it flat. Shatter the hazelnut meringue into large and smaller pieces, retaining the integrity of it being crunchy pastry. Scatter a large spoonful around the cream. Add the marshmallow buttons and persimmon and garnish with rose petals.

Green tea dressing, shoots and fungi

In recalling the customs and activities surrounding festivals, I am trying to understand what might signify 'celebration'. I feel it's a celebration to share a specially created dish with others, and this doesn't necessarily require a festival that designates the food as culturally and symbolically important. For some reason, I keep coming back to a very humble dish of selected mixed vegetables.

Green tea dressing, shoots and fungi

SERVES 4

Ingredients

FOR THE GREEN TEA DRESSING

250 ML (8½ FL OZ) LIGHT CHICKEN STOCK
20 G (¾ OZ) IKAN BILIS (DRIED ANCHOVIES), ROASTED
10 G (¼ OZ) JADE TIE GUANYIN (TIE KUAN YIN) TEA LEAVES, PULVERISED TO POWDER
20 G (¾ OZ) WATERCRESS LEAVES
20 G (¾ OZ) CHRYSANTHEMUM LEAVES
30 G (1 OZ) ROASTED PEANUTS
30 G (1 OZ) WHITE SESAME SEEDS, TOASTED
1 TABLESPOON MIRIN

FOR THE GLAZED BAMBOO SHOOT

1 WHOLE BAMBOO SHOOT
50 G (1¾ OZ) SUGAR
100 ML (3½ FL OZ) LIGHT SOY SAUCE
50 ML (1¾ FL OZ) DRY SHERRY

FOR THE MUNG BEAN NOODLES

30 G (1 OZ) MUNG BEAN STARCH
½ TEASPOON SALT
1 TEASPOON SESAME OIL
1 TEASPOON RICE VINEGAR

FOR THE FUNGI

8 OYSTER MUSHROOMS
2 TABLESPOONS CLARIFIED BUTTER
4 GREEN ASPARAGUS SPEARS
OLIVE OIL FOR BRUSHING

2 TABLESPOONS DRIED MULLET ROE (BOTARGA), FINELY SHAVED

Method

MAKE THE GREEN TEA DRESSING

Bring the chicken stock to the boil in a saucepan. Remove from the heat and add the ikan bilis. Leave to infuse for 30 minutes or so. Add the green tea and infuse for a further 30 minutes. Transfer to a blender and purée with the watercress and chrysanthemum leaves. Grind the peanuts and sesame seeds together and then combine with the leaf purée. Pass through a fine sieve and season with the mirin and salt to taste.

GLAZE THE BAMBOO SHOOT

Cut off the tough outer leaves of the bamboo shoot and trim away the tough end of the root. Place in a pot, cover with cold water and bring to the boil. Simmer for 1 hour or until soft when tested with a skewer. Leave in the poaching liquid until cool enough to handle. Trim off any remaining tough leaves. Cut into quarters. Preheat the oven to 200°C (400°F). Combine the sugar and 25 ml (¾ fl oz) water in a saucepan and bring to the boil. Add the soy sauce and sherry. Place the bamboo on a baking tray and pour the glazing liquid over it. Bake for 40 minutes until browned, basting with the liquid and turning the pieces once or twice for a more even glazing.

MAKE THE MUNG BEAN NOODLES

Mix the starch, salt and 270 ml (9 fl oz) water together in a stainless steel bowl. Place over a pan of simmering water and stir slowly with a wooden spoon. The mixture will slowly thicken and become translucent as it cooks. Once cooked, pass through a spaetzle plane set over iced water and let droplets fall into the water and set. Drain and dress the noodles with sesame oil and rice vinegar.

PREPARE THE FUNGI

For the oyster mushrooms, heat a frying pan over very high heat, melt the butter and fry the mushrooms until they turn an appetising golden colour. Season with salt and white pepper and drain on paper towels. Trim the hard ends of the asparagus. Brush with some olive oil and fry on a plancha (metal griddle plate) until just cooked but still with a slightly charred appearance.

ASSEMBLE THE DISH

Cut the bamboo into attractive cross-sections, allowing a few slices per person. Arrange on individual plates. Create a jumble of the vegetables and noodles on each plate and finish with shavings of the mullet roe and droplets of green tea dressing around and over everything.

The concept of celebration

Another aspect of celebration is, of course, to indulge in luxury. However, sometimes the most simply presented of extravagant delicacies holds the most meaning for me.

Peel some good waxy potatoes, such as russet burbank or kipfler. Wipe them dry, but don't wash them, as this rinses off the starch. Cut the potatoes into 2 mm (⅛ in) slices, then cut the slices into uniform rounds with a cookie cutter. Work quickly to prevent discolouration, if browning bothers you. Gently toss with melted clarified butter and some salt, coating them well. Spread on a paper-lined baking tray and bake in a preheated oven at 190°C (375°F) for about 15 minutes or until golden and crisp. If they are colouring unevenly turn them over and move them around.

The luxury is indulging in hand-cut potato crisps. It can further be heightened by eating them with thin slices of lardo and black sturgeon caviar (ethically farmed, of course).

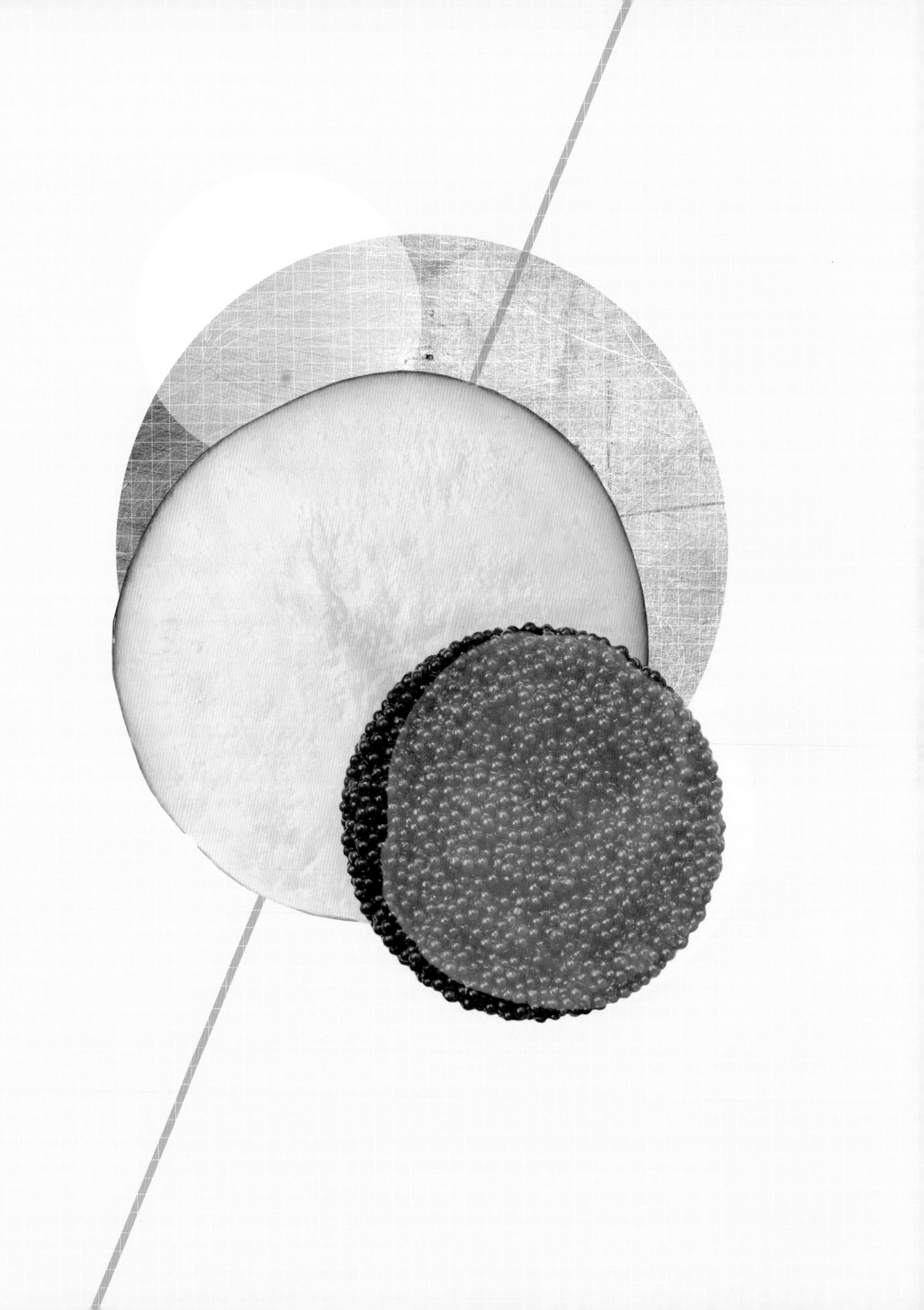

MAGICAL TROPICAL FRUITS

This is a tale of expectations based on appearances. I wonder where you might be reading what I've written? Wherever it is, I hope you've encountered the fruits of the tropics, which I've always viewed as magical forms.

In my early attempts to rationalise, tropical fruits fell into several groups. There were the visually stunning, such as the rambutans: vivid red globes, possessing spikes that looked threatening but proved to be an illusory self-defence mechanism (more like hairs, welcoming and nice to the touch). And the terribly plain, such as the langsat with its dull, dun-coloured skin. And those fruits that appeared armour-plated: the durian, jackfruit or tarap. Spiky or dimpled, these were misshapen, like balloons that had been wrongly blown up because of a manufacturer's mistake.

We would come across these fruits in great abundance when they were in season, piled high at the specialist market stalls. The leader of our expedition to seek them out (perhaps my mother or father, or a grandparent, aunt or uncle — an aficionado or self-designated expert of that particular fruit) would negotiate to obtain what, in their opinion, was the best available product and exchange advice on eating and storing. Abundance and overindulgence are also abiding memories of these favourite fruits. How, otherwise, would I have come to know the intimate details of each one?

Then there were the fruits whose symmetry elevated them to objects of elegance, such as the yellow and green star fruit, or pink or green rose apples. I was less excited by the sight of these. We were presented star fruits sliced in cross-section to reveal a five-pronged star shape with seeded innards. The rose apple had a similarly objective beauty. Their perfection rather bored me. It was echoed in the rather unexciting taste; there was no adventure involved to provoke the imagination of my curious self. So, it seems, appearance does count for something: it potentially holds my imagination in thrall.

It was probably one of my parents who patiently taught my sister and me how to extract a tasty reward from various small fruits; how to peel away the delicate skin of the langsat to reveal the segments of translucent white flesh that sometimes encased a large seed; that sap from the skin, and not just juice, was likely to make our fingers sticky. We were taught to pinch the rambutan shell hard so that it

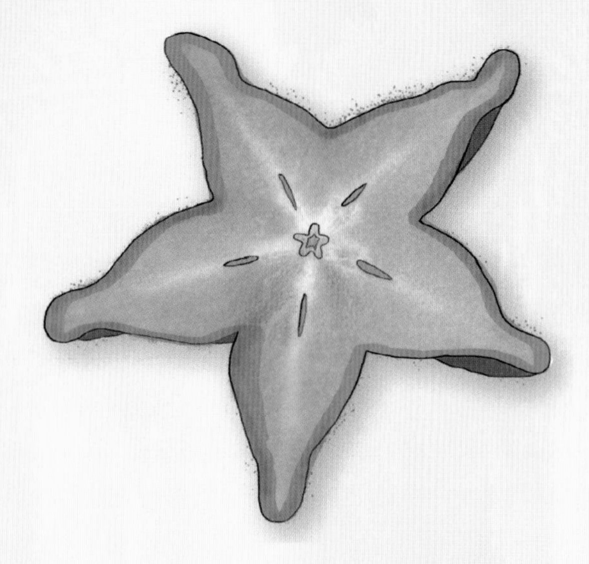

would puncture, and crack away the red casing before feasting on the, again, translucently delicate white flesh. The mangosteen, by far my favourite of the small fruits, was, I realised, structurally an amalgam of the rambutan and langsat. Its purple-black shell was eased open in the same way as the rambutan's and the creamy white flesh was already divided into segments.

The most exciting way to eat would be in a session devoted entirely to indulging in one prized large fruit. There was a certain ceremony associated with this process, if we were lucky enough to source the thing in the first place. Newspapers were laid out over the small, flecked blue tiles in the kitchen and one of those large round wooden chopping boards was set down upon the newspaper. Then, father or uncle would cleaver open a durian, jackfruit or tarap (these exaggerated actions seemed to reflect the larger than life nature of the fruit and paralleled the oversized proportions of the trees on which they grew). Revealed inside were pods of seeds encased by succulent sweet flesh: creamy in texture with a unique stink in the case of the durian, crunchy and thinly sweet for the jackfruit and creamy tasting with a resinous perfume in the case of the tarap. Perhaps you can guess from this which was my favourite?

Now, I wonder how I have completely overlooked one of the most important fruits of my early years, the mango. Perhaps because I'm not sure how it would be categorised according to my early classification system? Or maybe, subconsciously, I don't want to trespass on another's territory, for mangoes are my father's favourite. Numerous trees grew in the garden where his parents lived. They stood in an untidy fashion in a long avenue, their trunks often stained with sap and their branches hung with aerial orchids. The mystery surrounding mangoes was increased by the fact that they were wrapped in brown paper as soon as they were noticed, the paper-bag fruit attached to the main tree by exaggeratedly long stems.

Someone, most likely my father or grandfather, would sniff and prod the bags every day for signs of growth until it was determined that the mangoes were mature enough to be eaten, or until they fell from the tree of their own will. The mangoes of those days were green skinned, elliptical and eaten relatively unripe — resinous sweetness balanced with a sour tang was favoured as a taste. And if, for some unfortunate reason, a mango fell before it was sufficiently matured, there was a solution for that: incorporation in a snack.

a Traditional recipe for Fallen Mangoes

Windfall mangoes can be a boon and not a disappointment, even if they haven't reached maturity on the tree. The sappiness and sourness of green mangoes can be offset by a dressing of 1 tablespoon of dark soy sauce, a pinch of salt and 1 teaspoon of sugar. Dip wedges of peeled green mango into the dressing and adjust the proportions to your taste.

NATURALLY BREWED
SOY SAUCE
5 FL OZ (148 mL)

A savoury tropical fruit salad

The distinctiveness of most fruits compels me to enjoy them without too many embellishments. I was inspired to decide which tropical fruit might best be described as 'versatile' and for me it is the pineapple. The pineapple can be savoured as a sweet or savoury ingredient, as in this recipe, inspired by a hawker-style salad called Rojak.

A savoury tropical fruit salad

SERVES 4

Ingredients

FOR THE DUCK SALAD

2–2.5 KG (4½–5½ LB) DUCK
1 BANANA FLOWER
2 TABLESPOONS SUGAR
¼ PINEAPPLE, PEELED AND CORED, CUT INTO 1.5 CM (½ IN) PIECES
2 TABLESPOONS OLIVE OIL
1 TEASPOON WHITE PEPPER

FOR THE MARINATED ONIONS

100 ML (3½ FL OZ) RICE VINEGAR
4 PICKLING ONIONS

FOR THE DRESSING

2 RED CHILLIES
1 TABLESPOON BLACHAN (SEE GLOSSARY), ROASTED
4 TABLESPOONS GULA MELAKA (MALAYSIAN PALM SUGAR) (SEE GLOSSARY)
1 TABLESPOON HEIKO (CREAMY SHRIMP PASTE)
1 TABLESPOON LIME JUICE
½ TEASPOON SALT
1 TABLESPOON TAMARIND PULP, MIXED WITH 170 ML (5½ FL OZ) WATER AND PASSED THROUGH A SIEVE
110 G (4 OZ) PEANUTS, ROASTED AND COARSELY GROUND

Method

PREPARE THE DUCK

This initial preparation should be done about 12 hours in advance. Cut the legs off the duck and trim off the wings, reserving these for another use. Cut away the tail part of the duck so the cage is exposed. Dip the duck in a pot of boiling water for a few seconds and hang to dry in a cold spot with circulating air (ideally, a coolroom).

PREPARE THE MARINATED ONIONS

Prepare these at least 1 hour in advance. Have the vinegar in a bowl. Peel the onions, halve them and separate out into leaves. Blanch in boiling salted water, then drop into the vinegar, adding salt to taste. Toss to coat well.

MAKE THE DRESSING

Pound the ingredients with a mortar and pestle as you would see done in the open air markets. Pound the chillies to a fine paste. Gradually add the blachan and then the gula melaka, pounding constantly. Mix in the heiko, lime juice, salt and tamarind water. Gently incorporate the peanuts (you want to keep their texture). Taste that the flavour is hot, sweet, sour and salty and add more salt if desired.

PREPARE THE BANANA FLOWER AND PINEAPPLE

Remove the tough or discoloured outer petals of the banana flower, separate out the remaining individual petals and thinly slice lengthways. Place in acidulated water if slicing ahead of serving. Place a non-stick frying pan over high heat. Sprinkle with half the sugar and melt to a light caramel brown. Spread the pineapple pieces over the surface and let the caramel colour the pineapple. Remove the pineapple and add the remaining sugar. Melt as before, and this time colour the other side of the pineapple. Finish by seasoning the pineapple with salt.

ROAST THE DUCK

Preheat the oven to 200°C (400°F). Score the skin of the duck breasts. Remove the breasts from the carcass and fry, skin side down, in the oil until the skin is golden and crisp. Place on a tray, skin side up, and roast for 15–18 minutes. My preferred cuisson (degree cooked) is medium-rare. Leave to rest for about 10 minutes in a warm spot before carving.

ASSEMBLE THE DISH

Carve the duck across the breast and arrange slices on each plate. Place a teaspoon of the dressing around the duck. Scatter the pineapple, banana flower and marinated onion about the plate.

The ritual of preparing globe artichokes

I recall, as near ritualisation, the care my family members took in preparing tropical fruits. The ritual signalled how highly valued were these fruits and also how important it was to do things for the family. This leads me to think about how, as a chef, I sometimes have to follow rigid rules in ingredient preparation. Traditionally, the great fear about globe artichokes lies in their potential to discolour (something which may or may not affect the flavour in its cooked state). My basic method for preparing the artichoke is simply not to hesitate but to forge ahead with relentless determination.

The ritual of preparing globe artichokes

SERVES 4

Ingredients

FOR THE GLOBE ARTICHOKES	1 LEMON 2 GLOBE ARTICHOKES
FOR THE CUSTARD	3 LARGE EGGS 400 ML (13½ FL OZ) LIGHT CHICKEN STOCK 2 TEASPOONS DRY SHERRY 1 TEASPOON LIGHT SOY SAUCE
FOR THE PIQUANT SHRIMP DRESSING	3 CM (1¼ IN) PIECE OF CINNAMON 1 STAR ANISE 1 TEASPOON BLACK PEPPERCORNS 1 BROWN ONION, FINELY DICED 4 GARLIC CLOVES, CHOPPED 2 BIRD'S EYE CHILLIES, DESEEDED AND CHOPPED 3 TABLESPOONS DRIED SHRIMP, SOAKED IN WATER FOR 1 HOUR 6 PRAWN (SHRIMP) HEADS, GILLS AND TOP HARD SHELLS REMOVED 1 CUBE OF FERMENTED RED BEAN CURD 150 ML (5 FL OZ) VEGETABLE OIL 3 TABLESPOONS SUGAR 50 ML (1¾ FL OZ) RICE VINEGAR 2 TABLESPOONS LIGHT SOY SAUCE A FEW DROPS OF SESAME OIL

Method

PREPARE THE GLOBE ARTICHOKES

Have about 1 litre (34 fl oz) of cold water ready in a bowl. Halve the lemon and squeeze the juice into the bowl, then throw in the halves, too. Also have a pot of simmering water ready. Cut off an artichoke's stem, and peel it if it is fleshy (that is, with a lot of translucent white under the tough outer skin) and so worth cooking. Put in the bowl of acidulated water. Peel the artichoke base with a small knife until you reach the yellow-green flesh. Peel off the leaves one by one until the really small tender leaves are revealed. Reserve some of these leaves in the acidulated water. Continue until the fleshy heart is revealed. Using a spoon, scrape out and discard the hairy choke in the centre. Rinse quickly in cold water and drop into the acidulated water. Repeat with the other artichoke. When ready to cook, place a couple of teaspoons of salt into a saucepan of boiling water, add the artichoke hearts and stems and cook for 15 minutes until the flesh can easily be pierced without much resistance. Drain, cool and cut into chunks.

MAKE THE CUSTARD

Preheat the oven to 180°C (350°F). Break the eggs into a bowl and whisk lightly. Whisk in the chicken stock, sherry and soy sauce. Leave for 10 minutes, then skim off any foam. Divide the artichokes among four ovenproof bowls or ramekins. Pour the custard over the artichokes to cover. Place the bowls in a roasting tin and pour hot water into the tin to come two-thirds of the way up the sides of the bowls. Cover the whole roasting tin with foil. Put in the oven and bake for 30 minutes. The custards should turn a lighter colour and be set but wobbly.

MAKE THE PIQUANT SHRIMP DRESSING

Lightly roast the cinnamon, star anise and black pepper in a preheated 160°C (320°F) oven for 10 minutes. Grind the spices to a fine powder. Blend the onion, garlic, chilli, dried shrimp, prawn heads and bean curd with 50 ml (1¾ fl oz) of the vegetable oil to a fine paste. Fry in a pan with the rest of the oil over medium heat until the raw prawn flavour has disappeared and the paste has separated. Meanwhile, melt the sugar in a heavy-based pan over medium heat until a dark caramel colour. Take off the heat and cool with 2 tablespoons of water, then add the rice vinegar and soy sauce. Allow the caramel to dissolve into the rice vinegar and soy sauce over low heat. When dissolved, stir into the cooked paste. Season with a few drops of sesame oil.

ASSEMBLE THE DISH

Blanch the reserved young artichoke leaves and refresh under cold water. Dry thoroughly. Take 3 tablespoons of the shrimp dressing, being mindful to scoop some of the oil from the top also, and dress the young artichoke leaves. Place a few leaves on top of each cooked custard. Spoon some more of the shrimp dressing over the leaves so it floods the custard's surface. Serve warm.

A surprising fruit flavour appears in the rabbit pie

When I hear people describe tropical fruits it's often with reference to something familiar in their flavour, rather than taking their complexity as a given. This has made me consider how it might be possible to surprise with a flavour combination. I wanted to capture flavour in a sealed environment and a pastry casing is one of my favourite methods to do so. This pie is deliberately designed to fall apart; technically minded perfectionists will hate its messiness (no apologies forthcoming).

Ingredients

SERVES 4

FOR THE PASTRY

- 150 G (5½ OZ) SOUR CREAM
- 1 EGG, BEATEN
- 20 G (¾ OZ) FRESH YEAST, CRUMBLED, OR 10 G (¼ OZ) DRIED YEAST
- 250 G (9 OZ) COLD UNSALTED BUTTER, DICED
- 50 G (1¾ OZ) CASTER (SUPERFINE) SUGAR
- ½ TEASPOON SALT
- 500 G (1 LB 2 OZ) PLAIN (ALL-PURPOSE) FLOUR

FOR THE PIE FILLING

- 350 G (12½ OZ) RABBIT MEAT, CUT INTO STRIPS
- 50 ML (1¾ FL OZ) DRY SHERRY
- 3 TABLESPOONS GRAPESEED OIL
- 2 CM (¾ IN) PIECE OF GINGER, JULIENNED
- 6 SPRING ONIONS (SCALLIONS), THINLY SLICED
- 90 ML (3 FL OZ) RED SEDIMENT (HONGZAO) (SEE GLOSSARY)
- 100 G (3½ OZ) PINE NUTS, TOASTED UNTIL GOLDEN AND FRAGRANT
- 1 TEASPOON TAPIOCA OR POTATO FLOUR DISSOLVED IN 2 TEASPOONS WATER
- LIGHT SOY SAUCE TO SEASON

FOR THE RABBIT SAUCE

- 500 G (1 LB 2 OZ) RABBIT BONES (AND RABBIT LEGS IF POSSIBLE), ROUGHLY CHOPPED
- 4 CM (1½ IN) PIECE OF GINGER, BRUISED
- 2 RED ASIAN SHALLOTS, ROUGHLY CHOPPED
- 6 GARLIC CLOVES, ROUGHLY CHOPPED
- 2 LITRES (68 FL OZ) BROWN CHICKEN STOCK
- 100 ML (3½ FL OZ) RED RICE WINE (OBTAINED BY STRAINING THE RED SEDIMENT)

- BEATEN EGG WHITE FOR BRUSHING
- BEATEN EGG YOLK FOR GLAZING

Method

MAKE THE PASTRY

Prepare this the day before you need it. Warm the sour cream to blood temperature (test with your finger) and mix with the egg and yeast in a bowl. In a larger bowl work the butter into the caster sugar, salt and flour until evenly incorporated. Add the wet ingredients and bring the mixture together into a soft and pliant dough. Cover with plastic wrap and leave overnight in the refrigerator.

MAKE THE PIE FILLING

Marinate the rabbit meat in half the sherry for 1 hour. Heat a large frying pan or wok over high heat and add 2 tablespoons of the oil. Quickly brown the rabbit in batches so that there's no stewing of the meat, only quick frying. Set the rabbit meat aside. If the pan is clean (otherwise use a fresh one), add another tablespoon of oil and lightly fry the ginger. Add the spring onions and let them wilt. Add the red sediment and cook for 1–2 minutes for the ingredients to meld. Stir in the rabbit meat, pine nuts and remaining sherry and reduce the heat. Add the flour to thicken the mixture. Season with salt, white pepper and light soy sauce (it should be a little more salty than usual as it's a pie filling). Take off the heat and cool completely in the fridge before using.

MAKE THE RABBIT SAUCE

Preheat the oven to 220°C (430°F). Put the rabbit bones on a baking tray and roast to a dark golden colour. Transfer them to a pot and add the vegetables and chicken stock. Bring to the boil and simmer for 1 hour. Strain into a saucepan and bring to the boil. Simmer until reduced by two-thirds. It should smell intense but not gluey. Finish by adding the red rice wine. Reheat the sauce for serving.

BAKE THE PIE

I suggest using a rectangular flan form (metal tart bracket) 25 x 10 cm (10 x 4 in), or a 20 cm (8 in) tart tin with a removable base. Butter and flour the tin. Roll out the pastry to a thickness of 4 mm (⅙ in). Cut a larger piece for the base of the pie and a slightly smaller piece for the top, taking into account overhang. Ease the pastry base into the tin, then spoon in the filling. Brush the pastry rim with egg white and cover with the pastry top. Press the pastry edges together to seal. Trim off the excess and crimp the rim. Refrigerate for 30 minutes. Preheat the oven to 200°C (400°F). Bake the pie for 20 minutes then glaze with egg yolk. Bake for another 10–20 minutes until the pastry is crisp and a dark burnished copper colour. I picture this served casually: have the pie in the centre of the table, cut a piece for each person and let them pour the sauce for themselves.

MEALS at outdoor CASUAL RESTAURANTS

As a child I considered going out to eat to be an exciting adventure, an unmissable treat and even, occasionally, something that I'd manipulate into occurring. However, this isn't the place to discuss the machinations I employed in the past to get my own way, but an exploration of my love for all types of eating environments.

In the small town where I grew up there wasn't a culture of haute cuisine. We had simple places in which to eat and, from my child's view, these were generally divided into air-conditioned spaces and those without. The memories I have of the various restaurants we frequented form a visual montage: there were restaurants located at the bottom of apartment blocks that were open on all sides and served a small number of specialities from morning to night; there were air-conditioned restaurants in the middle of what seemed like industrial estates, offering a more formal experience with tables laid, albeit carelessly, with cloths and chipped porcelain plates and bowls and chopsticks balanced on stands; and there were the eateries that we called 'cafés' in the middle of town, serving coffee, snacks and also noodles, porridge or rice and a simple array of other set dishes. These cafés had a traditional spot in Malaysian culture and, although there was no sense of nostalgia about them at the time because of their proliferation, there certainly is now. And, of course, there were the food stalls set up in groups in the markets or congregated together near a popular park, scenic spot on the beach or residential estate.

There wasn't any sign generally given by my parents as to whether we would be going to a formal or less formal eating establishment. If we were going out to dinner, my sister and I would still have to scrub up and dress up; that was simply the ceremony of getting ready to go out, regardless of the formality (or lack thereof) of the establishment to which we were heading. I enjoyed enacting this ceremony.

Although I did adjust my expectations in response to each of these different types of eating places, there were different joys to be discovered in each one. I liked the common ritual involved in being greeted on our arrival, being seated, the pouring of the tea, negotiating the menu with the waiter — and all this as a precursor to the dishes even arriving.

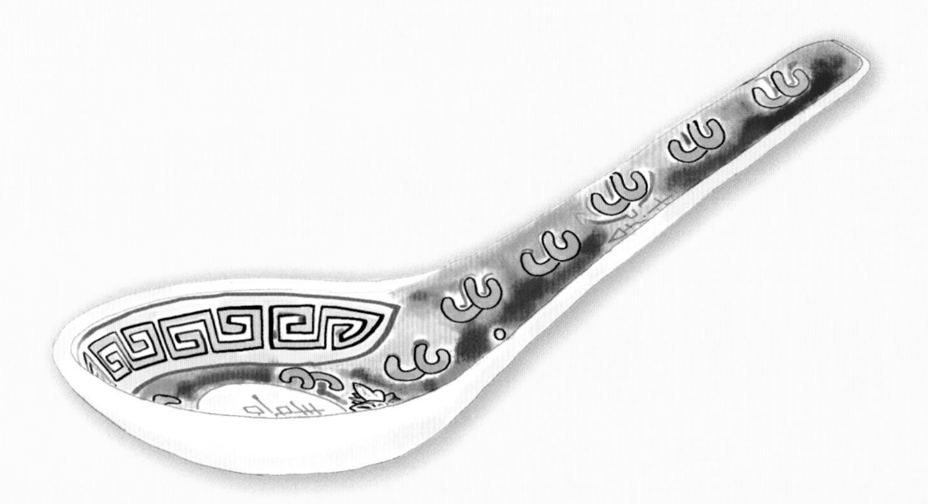

'Array' is the word I'd use to describe the sight of the dishes on the table when we ate out. That was the way of the culture. It was array in excess in the formal restaurants if we were attending a banquet: crab and shark's fin soup served by a waiter from a tureen, to which we then added droplets of black rice vinegar; a communal platter of crisp-skinned chicken skilfully divided into chopstick-friendly pieces; braised abalone with bok choy, served like Western-style steaks with knives and forks, and so it went on ... In the casual cafés the array was perhaps less impressive: a platter of rice noodles with beef in black bean sauce and maybe some roast pork and a stir-fry of vegetables.

My favourite curiosities were the Malaysian equivalent of greasy spoon cafés. These places usually had some speciality that turned them into local attractions. After shopping at the early morning markets, there might be a detour to a favourite noodle stall for a breakfast of tea and what I liked to call 'black noodles' — boiled noodles dressed with dark soy sauce and redolent with sesame oil and spring onion.

There was a seafood restaurant on the road out of the main town in Sandakan. It seemed to be situated in a hangar-like space, open on all sides to the tropical heat, with fans slowly turning above to help a little with air circulation. Concrete was the other predominant feature of its décor, its main use being to fabricate the ground level tanks of live fish, prawns and crabs (guests could wander among them to choose what they favoured for their meal). The plastic-topped tables weren't set in any fashion; plastic containers or baskets held chopsticks and spoons. Then, as now, we'd polish plates and cutlery with paper napkins, usually brought from home. I was a little repulsed by the dirt floor, and the thin and mangy cats ranging around looking for titbits, but grew to realise that the greatest attraction was the quality of the seafood and the skill with which the dishes were cooked.

This has built up an expectation I still possess, that the most obscure, humble-looking, dirty place anywhere in the world should surely harbour some hidden treasure of an eating place.

FRAGRANT Black Noodles FROM Outdoor Stalls

Blanch a handful of fresh egg noodles for each person and make the dressing. For each person, combine 2 tablespoons of dark soy sauce with 1 tablespoon of light soy sauce, a pinch of sugar, a few drops of sesame oil and 2 teaspoons of garlic and scallion oil (made by deep-frying a couple of garlic cloves and a couple of thinly sliced spring onions/scallions until golden, then straining the oil). Toss the hot noodles in the black dressing. The simpler the accompaniments, the better in my opinion, as the noodles and dressing are the primary components; so a few slices of barbecued pork, some blanched choy sum, coriander (cilantro) and sliced spring onion should be ample.

Grilled squid and candied ikan bilis

This and the following recipe share a common ingredient and are reflections on what makes a dish 'casual' or 'formal'. This is what I'd call the casual dish: simple ingredients, simply put together without too much fuss.

Grilled squid and candied ikan bilis

SERVES 4

Ingredients

FOR THE CANDIED IKAN BILIS	100 G (3½ OZ) IKAN BILIS (DRIED ANCHOVIES, SEE GLOSSARY) 1½ TABLESPOONS CASTER (SUPERFINE) SUGAR 3 TEASPOONS DARK SOY SAUCE OR THE TREACLY TAIWANESE SOY SAUCE
FOR PICKLING THE GREEN PAPAYA	PEANUT OIL FOR FRYING 2 LONG GREEN CHILLIES (HUNGARIAN PEPPERS) ¼ GREEN PAPAYA 375 ML (12½ FL OZ) RICE VINEGAR 2 TABLESPOONS SALT 1 TABLESPOON CASTER (SUPERFINE) SUGAR
FOR GRILLING THE SQUID	4 WHOLE SQUID, ABOUT 100 G (3½ OZ) EACH ½ TEASPOON SALT 1 LIME, CUT IN WEDGES TO SERVE EXTRA VIRGIN OLIVE OIL FOR DRIZZLING

Method

CANDY THE IKAN BILIS

Toast the ikan bilis in a medium–hot pan with a little oil until crispy. Drain on paper towels. In another pan heat the sugar until it turns light caramel. Add the ikan bilis and toss to coat well. Add the soy sauce and toss again to coat with that. Tip the ikan bilis onto a foil-lined baking tray brushed with a little oil and separate them out so they don't clump while they're cooling.

PICKLE THE GREEN PAPAYA

Heat a pan and drizzle with oil. Add the chillies and reduce the heat to medium. Char the chillies by pressing one side against the bottom of the pan, then turning them and charring the other side. Refresh in iced water. Peel, chop roughly and put in a bowl. Peel the green papaya, scrape out the seeds and membrane and slice the flesh thinly. Add to the bowl. Bring the vinegar, salt and sugar and 500 ml (17 fl oz) water to the boil in a saucepan, cool to room temperature and then pour over the papaya and chillies. Leave to sit for a couple of hours before serving.

GRILL THE SQUID

Clean the squid by cutting off the heads and removing the wings (but keep the skin on). Pull out the innards then rinse out and dry the inside of the tubes. I'd suggest using a plancha (metal griddle plate) or a stainless steel frying pan for grilling the squid. Heat the pan on the highest flame until it's smoking hot. Scatter the salt on the pan then add the squid and cook for about 10 seconds. Use a fish slice to keep the underneath of the squid flat against the pan so that it's golden and crusted. Turn the squid and repeat the process. Take out of the pan and season with white pepper.

ASSEMBLE THE DISH

The squid should be served immediately. Cut the squid into rings and arrange on a platter with a pile of the pickled green papaya and chillies. Scatter about some of the ikan bilis. Serve with lime wedges and drizzle the plate with extra virgin olive oil.

Grilled squid and white beans

The difference in this more formal presentation of the dish lies in the greater complexity in the composition of the accompaniments, and greater attention to creating a balance in the dish. The choice of grilled squid emphasises the importance I place on capturing spontaneity in taste and heightening flavour through the cooking method chosen.

Grilled squid and white beans

SERVES 4

Ingredients

FOR THE CUCUMBER JUICE

1 LEBANESE CUCUMBER OR CUCUMBER WITH THE GREENEST FLESH
2 GELATINE LEAVES, SOFTENED IN COLD WATER
125 ML (4 FL OZ) MILK
2 SICHUAN PEPPERCORNS, LIGHTLY CRUSHED
80 ML (2½ FL OZ) EXTRA VIRGIN OLIVE OIL

FOR THE WHITE BEANS

200 G (7 OZ) SHELLED BORLOTTI BEANS
2 TABLESPOONS OLIVE OIL
1 LEEK, FINELY DICED
4 GARLIC CLOVES, FINELY CHOPPED
1 TABLESPOON COGNAC
1 BAY LEAF
2 LONG SPRIGS OF THYME
JUICE FROM 2 FRESH TOMATOES
ABOUT 250 ML (8½ FL OZ) EXTRA VIRGIN OLIVE OIL

FOR THE SQUID

4 WHOLE SQUID, ABOUT 100 G (3½ OZ) EACH
1 TABLESPOON COGNAC
½ TEASPOON SALT
2 TABLESPOONS PEANUT OIL
1 TEASPOON FINELY CHOPPED GARLIC
1 TEASPOON FINELY SLICED SPRING ONION (SCALLION)

Method

PREPARE THE CUCUMBER JUICE

Peel the cucumber and cut into chunks about 2 cm (¾ in) thick. Put in a bowl and sprinkle with a little salt. Leave for 30 minutes to draw out some of the liquid, then drain. Purée the cucumber and strain through a fine sieve. Drain the gelatine leaves and squeeze out excess moisture. Put in a bowl with 2 tablespoons of warm water and stir to dissolve the gelatine leaves. Stir this into the strained cucumber juice. Refrigerate for at least 30 minutes before the next step. Warm the milk to blood temperature (test with your finger) and add the peppercorns to infuse for 30 minutes, then strain. Use a blender to emulsify the cucumber jelly with the milk and extra virgin olive oil. Season with salt to taste. Keep refrigerated.

PREPARE THE WHITE BEANS

Place the borlotti beans in a small saucepan, cover with cold water and bring to the boil. Take off the heat and refresh under cold running water. Remove the skins of the beans. Heat the oil in a frying pan over medium heat and fry the leek and garlic until softened. Stir in the borlotti beans and let the heat build up again. Add the cognac and let it cook out slightly. Add the bay leaf, thyme and tomato juice and 3–4 tablespoons of water and cook, covered with the lid slightly askew, for about 20 minutes until the beans are softened. Discard the bay leaf and thyme. Using a hand-held blender, purée the bean mixture. Add salt and white pepper to taste. Once the mixture is smooth, slowly drizzle in the extra virgin olive oil with the motor running. Stop adding oil when the mixture is very smooth, white and thick. Season again and strain through a fine sieve. Keep warm.

GRILL THE SQUID

Clean the squid by cutting off the head and removing the wings (but keep the skin on). Pull out the innards and rinse then dry the inside of the tubes. Cut the tentacles from the head and slice into individual tentacles. Marinate the tentacles in the cognac for 1 hour or so.

I'd suggest using a plancha (metal griddle plate) or a stainless steel frying pan for grilling the squid. Heat the pan on the highest flame until it's smoking hot. Scatter the salt on the pan, then add the squid and cook for about 10 seconds. Use a fish slice to keep the underneath of the squid flat against the pan so that it's golden and crusted. Turn the squid and repeat the process. Take out of the pan and season with white pepper.

Heat the peanut oil in a pan and fry the garlic and spring onion over medium–high heat until fragrant. Turn to high heat and add the tentacles. Fry for no more than 30 seconds until they turn pinkish. Season well with salt.

ASSEMBLE THE DISH

Place a spoonful of warm white bean purée on each plate. Add a few drops of the cucumber juice. Distribute the tentacles evenly among the plates. Serve each squid tube whole and arrange by the bean purée.

the TEMPTATION of PICKLED PEACHES

I remember that it was yet another hot and humid afternoon when my sister and I were asked to put on our nice dresses and sandals, for we were to go on an outing. My mother told me that we would be visiting one of her friends, another grown-up, who I was expected to call 'Auntie'. I guess I was feeling a little churlish or petulant at having my afternoon playtime interrupted, because the heat had either beaten me into languid submission or made me feel resentful about moving. It was simply one of those days when I was exhibiting resentment.

I have no recollection of how we arrived at this Auntie's house and what it might have looked like. But the interior is still imprinted in my memory. It appeared cavernous and darkened and there was a surprising coolness about it, even without air-conditioning. We were seated in a long space that might have been an enclosed verandah. I recall fidgeting on my chair while the adults exchanged greetings and what I felt was inconsequential small talk. The reward that I expected in making visits of this kind was either the opportunity to play with other children, an occasion to explore the curiosities of the house, or an amazing afternoon tea. And, with no children around, and being required to be on best behaviour as this was not an Auntie we knew well enough that I was likely to be let loose on the house, I was trying my best to wait patiently for refreshments to be offered.

The adults' conversation seemed like a dimly lit silent film until Auntie suddenly produced a huge glass jar filled with the most vividly green round objects. My attention was totally engaged with this jar, wondering whether it was something more than an ornamental object. The words that I did eventually catch were 'peaches' and 'pickled'. Auntie opened the jar in slow motion. The smell that escaped was so intense that it has remained in my memory: a seemingly incongruous combination of rain on the ground, a floral or fruity odour not quite fully developed and the overpowering vinegar smell that has always made my mouth water (and, who knows, that day may have been the first occasion I experienced that).

Auntie spooned some of the peaches onto a saucer and offered them to us to sample. I can't recall whether

I perhaps swiftly grabbed in my impatience to try these extraordinary objects (I very much hope I managed to retain some decorum). For, even to this day, I'm aware that there is a lot of gaucheness about my behaviour; that I can't bear to follow conventional politeness when I don't understand the reason for or significance of it. In my memory, those pickled peaches represented an impeccable moment when taste and sight were in faultless conjunction. The crisp crunch and the perfect balance of sweetness tempering sourness matched the green-ness of the fuzzy baby peaches.

I hope that on that day I learned a lesson not to be churlish and ungrateful, but to be open to experiences. Something amazing could be just around the corner, so why not let it come to you?

I almost don't have the heart to tell you, but I now suspect the pickled peaches that so impressed me were artificially coloured to maintain their intense green-ness. Acid and salt will cause the fresh colour to deteriorate, but just be happy that the texture of the pickled peach will be crisp and the taste deliciously sweet and tart.

Green Pickled peaches

Rub 1 kg (2 lb 3 oz) of unblemished green peaches with a handful of salt to remove the fuzz from their skins. Wash and rinse the peaches and dry them thoroughly. Keeping the fruit whole, place into a couple of large sterilised glass jars. Mix together 2 cupfuls of rice vinegar, 3 cups of cold water, ⅔ cup of sugar and 2 teaspoons of salt and pour over the peaches, ensuring they're covered with liquid. Weigh down with a saucer or some sort of weight to ensure this. Store in a cool place for at least a few days before using.

The intense colour of pickled radishes

I set out here with the intention of creating something to echo the intensity of the colour of those pickled peaches that I recall so clearly. I can't seem to stray from the pickling theme that's prevalent in this chapter. I'm following through with the logic of pickling: if there's an abundance of the stuff, preserve it. The quantity made here is a lot more than the recipe requires, but the pickle can be eaten by itself (it does have an addictive taste, as well as a very vivid colour). If you're keeping it for a longer time, store in sterilised preserving jars.

The intense colour of pickled radishes

SERVES 6

Ingredients

FOR THE PICKLED RADISHES

500 G (1 LB 2 OZ) RED RADISHES
2 TEASPOONS SALT
100 G (3½ OZ) CHILLI BEAN PASTE (DOU BAN JIANG)
1 TABLESPOON CHILLI OIL (SEE PAGE 280)
90 G (3 OZ) SUGAR
150 ML (5 FL OZ) RICE VINEGAR
1 TEASPOON SESAME OIL

FOR THE PICKLED FISH

PEANUT OIL FOR DEEP-FRYING
500 G (1 LB 2 OZ) WHOLE SARDINES, CLEANED AND GUTTED
55 G (2 OZ) GARLIC, THINLY SLICED
55 G (2 OZ) PIECE OF YOUNG GINGER, JULIENNED
125 ML (4 FL OZ) RICE VINEGAR
2 TABLESPOONS SUGAR
1 TEASPOON SALT

20 LOVAGE LEAVES TO GARNISH
1 TABLESPOON SNIPPED FENNEL FRONDS
2 TEASPOONS FENNEL POLLEN TO GARNISH

Method

PICKLE THE RADISHES

Wash the radishes. Remove the roots, trim off the tops, scrape off any imperfections and cut each one in half. Put in a bowl with the salt and leave for 3 hours or so to draw out the moisture. Drain and gently squeeze the radishes to get rid of excess liquid. Put in sterilised preserving jars. Purée the chilli bean paste and mix with the chilli oil, sugar, rice vinegar and sesame oil. Pour over the radishes in the jars. Store for at least 2 days in the refrigerator before using.

PICKLE THE FISH

Heat peanut oil in a deep-fryer to 180°C (350°F). Deep-fry the fish in a couple of batches until golden. Drain on paper towels and set aside. Heat 4 more tablespoons of peanut oil in a frying pan and fry the garlic and ginger until golden and crisp. Drain on paper towels. Cool the oil slightly and pour into a wide bowl. Stir in the vinegar, sugar and salt. Add the fish and the crisped ginger and garlic. Cover with plastic wrap and put in the refrigerator overnight to mature.

ASSEMBLE THE DISH

This dish is probably best served as a centrally shared plate. Bring the pickled fish to room temperature and serve with some of the pickling juice, ginger and garlic. Thinly slice some pickled radishes and drape the slices around the fish with the lovage, fennel fronds and a sprinkle of fennel pollen.

Fingers of purple potato

This dish started from a thought about the visual appeal of neatly aligned shapes. I then moved to thinking about the visual appeal of colour, and the choice of purple potato sprang from there. The technique for cooking the pork in this recipe is derived from a Hakka Chinese dish of taro and pork belly with fermented red bean curd, which, coincidentally, is all about the importance of moulding and alignment.

Fingers of purple potato

SERVES 4 AS A SMALL PLATE

Ingredients

FOR THE STEAMED PORK BELLY

500 G (1 LB 2 OZ) DEBONED PORK BELLY, SKIN ON
1 TABLESPOON LIGHT SOY SAUCE
1 TEASPOON DARK SOY SAUCE, PLUS 1 TABLESPOON
PEANUT OIL FOR DEEP-FRYING, PLUS 2 TABLESPOONS
6 GARLIC CLOVES, FINELY CHOPPED
2 CM (¾ IN) PIECE OF GINGER, FINELY CHOPPED
50 ML (1¾ FL OZ) BRANDY
2 PIECES OF PRESERVED RED BEAN CURD
1 TEASPOON FIVE SPICE POWDER
2 STAR ANISE
1 TABLESPOON SUGAR

FOR THE PURPLE POTATO DOUGH

300 G (10½ OZ) PURPLE CONGO POTATOES
90 ML (3 FL OZ) BOILING WATER
60 G (2 OZ) WHEAT STARCH
60 G (2 OZ) UNSALTED BUTTER, AT ROOM TEMPERATURE
½ TEASPOON BAKING POWDER
½ TEASPOON SALT
½ TEASPOON SUGAR
PEANUT OIL FOR DEEP-FRYING

FOR THE LEMON SALT

ZEST OF 3 LEMONS, GRATED ON A MICROPLANE
JUICE OF 3 LEMONS, STRAINED
70 G (2½ OZ) SALT

Method

STEAM THE PORK BELLY

Bring a large pan of water to the boil, remove from the heat and add the pork belly. Leave for 20 minutes. Refresh in iced water, dry thoroughly and prick the skin all over. Mix the light soy sauce with 1 teaspoon of dark soy sauce and rub all over the pork. Heat peanut oil in a deep-fryer to 200°C (400°F) and deep-fry the pork until golden. Drain on paper towels and then refresh again in cold water. Drain, dry and set aside.

Heat a frying pan over medium heat, pour in 2 tablespoons of peanut oil and fry the garlic and ginger until fragrant. Mash the brandy and red bean curd together and add to the frying pan with the five spice powder and star anise. Cook for long enough for the rawness of the alcohol in the brandy to evaporate a little. Add the 1 tablespoon dark soy sauce and sugar. Taste to see whether the sauce is salty and sweet and adjust if required. Cut the pork into 2 cm (¾ in) wide strips and mix with the sauce. Transfer to a heatproof container and cover with foil. Put in a steamer over high heat and steam for 45–55 minutes until the pork is tender and melting. Cool, then put in the refrigerator to cool completely before using.

MAKE THE PURPLE POTATO DOUGH

Peel the potatoes, cut into 1 cm (½ in) thick pieces and steam until cooked. Immediately pass through a potato ricer, or press through a drum sieve onto the workbench. Mix the boiling water and wheat starch together in a bowl to form a stiff paste. While still as hot as possible, break the starch into pieces over the pile of potato. Knead together, pressing the dough against the bench with the palm of your hand to ensure the potato and starch are mixed thoroughly. Break this mixture into pieces so it is easier to incorporate the next ingredients. The dough should only be warm at this stage; if it is too hot the butter will melt beyond control and be difficult to combine. Knead in the butter, baking powder, salt and sugar. The dough should be dry enough that it doesn't stick to your hands, but be smooth and tacky. Test by deep-frying a small sample ball in peanut oil at 180°C (350°F). It should form threads but not dissolve in the heat. If it does dissolve, increase the heat by 5°C (40°F) and try again. If it continues to dissolve, add more starch mixed with boiling water.

MAKE THE LEMON SALT

Blanch the lemon zest in boiling water and refresh under cold running water. Repeat this twice more to get rid of the bitter tasting oil. Place the lemon juice in a pan and heat to just below simmering point. Dissolve the salt in the juice. Mix in the drained, dried zest. Pour the near-saturated solution onto a non-reactive baking tray and place in a barely warm oven for about 6 hours to evaporate the solution. Grind the salt to a fine powder.

MAKE THE PORK FINGERS

Divide the dough into 8 pieces. Roll each into a 7 x 5 cm (2¾ x 2 in) rectangle. Put a strip of pork in the middle of each rectangle. Fold over the long sides to join and press all the cut sides together. Aim for a finished shape of 6.5 x 2.5 cm (2½ x 1 in). Ensure that the filling is fully covered and the pastry has not cracked. If there are cracks, seal with a little water as a last resort, but this will affect the formation of threads during deep-frying. Deep-fry in batches until golden. Drain on paper towels and serve immediately with lemon salt.

A jumble of shapes and colours masked by yellow

This recipe is the opposite of the orderliness found in the fingers of purple potato. The jumble of shapes and colours in the vegetables dressed with yellow spice paste creates a blend of textures and flavours, which in turn functions to complement the chicken liver parfait. The pickling method is derived from a traditional Malaysian vegetable dish called Achar — everyone has an opinion about its method and combination.

Ingredients

SERVES 6

FOR THE TURMERIC PICKLE

- 100 ML (3½ FL OZ) RICE VINEGAR
- 1 TABLESPOON GROUND TURMERIC
- 1 LEBANESE CUCUMBER, SEEDS SCRAPED OUT, CUT INTO 1 CM (½ IN) CHUNKS
- 1 CARROT, CUT INTO 1 CM (½ IN) PIECES
- 150 G (5½ OZ) CAULIFLOWER FLORETS, TRIMMED TO 1 CM (½ IN)
- 150 G (5½ OZ) YOUNG GREEN BEANS, CUT INTO 1 CM (½ IN) LENGTHS
- 20 DRIED RED CHILLIES, HALVED, DESEEDED, SOAKED IN HOT WATER
- 3 GARLIC CLOVES, CHOPPED
- 3 CM (1¼ IN) PIECE OF GINGER, PEELED AND CHOPPED
- 2 CM (¾ IN) PIECE OF GALANGAL, PEELED AND CHOPPED
- 2 LEMONGRASS STEMS, WHITE PART ONLY, MINCED
- 1 CM (½ IN) PIECE OF BLACHAN (SEE GLOSSARY), TOASTED
- 6 CANDLENUTS, ROASTED
- 125 ML (4 FL OZ) PEANUT OIL
- 2 TEASPOONS SALT
- 60 G (2 OZ) SUGAR

FOR THE CHICKEN LIVER PARFAIT

- 500 G (1 LB 2 OZ) CLEANED CHICKEN LIVERS
- ABOUT 125 ML (4 FL OZ) MILK
- 2 TABLESPOONS EXTRA VIRGIN OLIVE OIL
- 2 FRENCH SHALLOTS, THINLY SLICED
- 300 ML (10 FL OZ) DRY SHERRY
- 2 TABLESPOONS SALT
- 5 EGGS
- 300 G (10½ OZ) UNSALTED BUTTER, JUST MELTED, NOT CLEAR OR SEPARATED
- MELTED BUTTER TO SEAL (OPTIONAL)

Method

MAKE THE TURMERIC PICKLE

This pickle requires at least 2 days to mature so make it in advance. Combine 3 tablespoons of vinegar and 2 teaspoons of the turmeric in a saucepan with 2 litres (68 fl oz) of water and bring to the boil. Blanch the vegetables in boiling salted water for about 30 seconds, then refresh in cold water. Drain and squeeze the vegetables as dry as possible in muslin or a linen tea towel. Drain the chillies and then pound or blend them with the garlic, ginger, galangal, lemongrass, blachan, candlenuts and remaining 2 teaspoons of turmeric to make a smooth paste.

Heat the peanut oil in a frying pan over medium heat and fry the spice mixture until thoroughly cooked. The solids will darken and separate from the oil, which will take on a yellow colour. Take off the heat and cool. Mix in the remaining 2 tablespoons of vinegar, the salt and sugar and pour over the cooled vegetables. Mix thoroughly. Transfer to sterilised preserving jars and store in a cool dark spot.

TO MAKE THE CHICKEN LIVER PARFAIT

Soak the chicken livers overnight in milk to remove any bitterness. Drain well in a colander. Heat the oil in a sauté pan and fry the shallots for 3–5 minutes until starting to soften. Add the sherry and simmer until reduced by two-thirds then leave to cool slightly. Preheat the oven to 110°C (230°F). Line a 25 x 15 cm (10 x 6 in) terrine with baking paper. Put the chicken livers, shallot reduction, the salt and some white pepper in a blender and purée until smooth. Gradually add the eggs and then the butter. Pass through a fine sieve directly into the prepared terrine. Put this in a large roasting tin and pour very hot, but not boiling, water into the tin to come halfway up the sides of the terrine. Cover the terrine with foil and bake for 1 hour or so. Test if the parfait is ready by tilting the terrine: the parfait mix should just bulge slightly at the edge of the terrine and gently wobble in the middle when shaken. (Don't forget that it will continue cooking as it cools.) Remove the terrine from the tin, cool, then refrigerate for 4 hours until set. If desired, seal the surface of the parfait with melted butter. The parfait will keep in the fridge for up to 3 days.

TO ASSEMBLE THE DISH

Cut generous slices of parfait and dress with the turmeric pickle, including some of the oil. Eat with crackers or bread.

MY MUSHROOM AVERSION

Fungi and mushrooms seemed to grow in abundance around our home in Sandakan. They grew wherever I wandered, over rotting organic material, in the niches and recesses of structures and over the trunks of larger living plants. Grotesque shapes of orange and red popped out of tree trunks. Brown orbs might puff out a cloud of yellow powder when poked. Frilled caps and shapes aligned in an abundant collection following some sort of other-worldly order. These living things operated according to a logic of their own that I tried in vain to understand. They were thrilling to look at, prod at; curiosities to be dismantled and examined. So, in my head, the grotesquery of fungi and mushrooms was something to be observed and marvelled at. There was a repulsiveness about their appearance and they seemed slippery and viscous by nature. And, to my surprise, at home, I was expected to eat them?

The mushrooms we usually ate were dried shiitakes. In their plastic packaging (from extra-ordinary locales such as Hong Kong, China or Japan) they looked innocuous enough, like inactive elements. I liked scrunching up their plastic casing and peering at them in their dried-out and dusty-looking state. However, when reconstituted, those same entities transformed and took on a different demeanour. They had stems and gills and a certain glossy animation, which put me in mind of the fungi I tortuously examined on my wanderings. They were often featured in dishes that emphasised the viscosity in their nature, their slippery smoothness. In their cooked form they smelt amazing and alien, but I was still confounded by the repulsion I had for their appearance.

Revelation came soon enough ('everything in its own time' is perhaps a way to describe the development of my taste and gradual surrender to mature people's predilections). I recall being ill with some sort of bug that left me weak in bed, and subject to the blandest of foods. It happened late one evening; I had recovered some strength and wandered into the kitchen for something more substantial or exciting to eat and happened on the remnants of a family feast I'd missed. One of the mysterious delicacies that had fed my imaginings about the shiitake was a fragrant dish of slow-cooked chicken and shiitake with copious amounts of ginger. On this particular evening hunger led to an abandonment of my usual risk avoidance and the remnants of illness clouded my judgement ... I took the chance to pick at the mushrooms.

And, honestly, they weren't that bad: I survived to relive the memory here.

Chicken Braised with Dried Shiitake Mushrooms

Soak a large handful of dried shiitake mushrooms for a couple of hours until fully reconstituted. Drain, keeping the soaking water. Cut off the stems and fry the mushrooms in a couple of teaspoons of peanut oil until fragrant. Add a generous dash of sherry, a tablespoon of light soy sauce and a cupful of the soaking water and braise for 20 minutes or so until soft.

Now chop a small chicken into chopstick-friendly pieces. Thinly slice an onion, about 6 garlic cloves and a 3 cm (1¼ in) piece of ginger and fry in a hot wok with a tablespoon of oil until the aromats are fragrant and lightly coloured. Add the chicken and stir-fry until brown. Season with a little salt. Add the braised mushrooms and simmer, covered, for about 15 minutes, adding more soaking water to prevent the mixture drying out. Season with more salt if desired. The braise will have an intense mushroom flavour because the soaking water is used (if the flavour is considered too strong, use chicken stock or water instead).

Mushrooms with walnuts and chestnuts

I have in mind a luxurious version of a crouton with a texturally interesting accompaniment. The intent behind this recipe is to celebrate the texture of mushroom.

Mushrooms with walnuts and chestnuts

SERVES 4

Ingredients

FOR THE WALNUT PASTE

2 TABLESPOONS UNSALTED BUTTER
3 GARLIC CLOVES, PEELED BUT LEFT WHOLE
2 THYME SPRIGS
90 G (3 OZ) CUBES OF WHITE SOURDOUGH BREAD
1 FRENCH SHALLOT, FINELY DICED
60 G (2 OZ) WALNUT KERNELS, PEELED BY PLUNGING INTO BOILING WATER
2 TABLESPOONS FINELY DICED IBERIAN HAM
1 TEASPOON BRANDY
80 ML (2½ FL OZ) THICK (DOUBLE/HEAVY) CREAM

FOR THE 'CROUTON' BASE

100 G (3½ OZ) PLAIN (ALL-PURPOSE) FLOUR
75 G (2¾ OZ) UNSALTED BUTTER, COLD FROM THE REFRIGERATOR
25 ML (¾ FL OZ) ICED WATER

FOR THE WALNUT AND CHESTNUT GARNISH

250 G (9 OZ) UNSALTED BUTTER
300 G (10½ OZ) UNSHELLED CHESTNUTS
2 GREEN STEMS OF FRESH GARLIC, BULB AND STEM TRIMMED, THINLY SLICED
2 SPRING ONIONS (SCALLIONS), CUT INTO SHORT LENGTHS
1 TABLESPOON FLAT-LEAF (ITALIAN) PARSLEY LEAVES
75 G (2¾ OZ) OYSTER MUSHROOMS, STALKS REMOVED, CUT INTO 1.5 CM (½ IN) SLICES
75 G (2¾ OZ) KING BROWN MUSHROOMS, HALVED
50 G (1¾ OZ) WHOLE, FRESHLY SHELLED WALNUT KERNELS
JUICE OF ½ LEMON OR TO TASTE
FENNEL FRONDS TO GARNISH

TO SHELL CHESTNUTS

To shell chestnuts, make a slit with a sharp turning knife at the pointy end, ensuring that the inner skin is also pierced and exposing the yellow flesh. Next (a trick I learned from a Spanish chef who worked with me) is to put the chestnuts in the microwave for 2 minutes on High in a covered container and peel while they're hot and steaming (your hands will be scalded unless you hold the chestnuts with a dry tea towel). The alternative is to peel the husks off first, then fry the chestnuts in butter until the skins crisp up. Soften under hot water and then peel while hot.

Method

MAKE THE WALNUT PASTE

Melt the butter in a frying pan over medium heat and add the garlic and thyme. When the butter starts to separate and has a nutty flavour, drop in the bread. Fry until just golden and crisp. Remove the bread and drain on paper towels. Add the shallot to the pan and fry over low heat until softened. Transfer the contents of the pan to a food processor and add the bread, walnuts, ham and brandy. Blend to a smooth paste. Season to taste with salt and freshly ground black pepper. The flavour should be quite savoury and salty. Let the mixture cool then work in the cream.

MAKE THE 'CROUTON' BASE

Sift the flour and a good pinch of salt onto the workbench. Grate the cold butter onto the flour. Mix together with the heel of your hand and then use your fingers until the mixture resembles breadcrumbs. Add the water and quickly knead to a dough. Cover with plastic wrap and rest in the refrigerator for at least 30 minutes. Roll out the dough to 3 mm (⅛ in) thickness. Put on a tray, cover with plastic wrap and refrigerate again for at least 30 minutes. Cut the pastry into 8 rectangles each measuring 12 x 5 cm (5 x 2 in). There will be excess pastry, which can be rolled into one and frozen for use at another time. Rest the pastry again, covered, for 30 minutes or so. Preheat the oven to 200°C (400°F) and line a baking tray with baking paper. Spread 1½ teaspoons of walnut paste over each piece of pastry, leaving a few millimetres at the edges. Bake for 20–30 minutes until the pastry is golden on both the top and bottom. Serve warm.

MAKE THE WALNUT AND CHESTNUT GARNISH

Preheat the oven to 150°C (300°F). Shell the chestnuts (see box opposite). Melt 150 g (5½ oz) of the butter in a small ovenproof pot and, when hot, add the chestnuts. Cover the pot, put in the oven and confit or slow cook for 35–40 minutes or until soft. Set aside and, when ready to use, strain off the butter. Melt the remaining butter in a sauté pan over medium–high heat and cook until it has a nutty smell. Add the garlic, spring onion and parsley leaves and fry until everything has a wilted appearance and tastes cooked. Add the mushrooms and continue cooking until they are softened. If the mixture is sticking, add some water. Add the chestnuts and walnuts to warm through. Season to taste with lemon juice, salt and freshly ground black pepper. These seasoning ingredients are meant to accentuate the sweet and delicate balance of the ingredients.

ASSEMBLE THE DISH

Use a central platter so people can grab what they want. The pastries are the base and the sauté of walnut and mushroom is messily arranged over the top. Use the fennel fronds as garnish for the finished dish. If there's excess butter from the sauté, use it to dress the plate.

The gills of shiitake mushrooms

The cross-sections of fresh shiitake mushrooms remind me of the gills of fish or the feathers of birds. This recipe is about suspending those cross-sections in a sauce. However, I never intend to compromise taste purely to visualise my imaginings, so the sauce harnesses together many of what I consider to be umami elements.

The gills of shiitake mushrooms

SERVES 4

Ingredients

FOR THE SHIITAKE SAUCE

200 G (7 OZ) SHIITAKE MUSHROOMS, THICK CAPS PREFERRED
1 TEASPOON PEANUT OIL
50 ML (1¾ FL OZ) JAPANESE RICE WINE
1 TEASPOON GINGER JUICE (SEE GLOSSARY)
2 TEASPOONS SPRING ONION (SCALLION) JUICE (SEE GLOSSARY)
1 GARLIC CLOVE, PEELED AND BRUISED
400 ML (13½ FL OZ) BROWN CHICKEN STOCK
KUZU STARCH

FOR POACHING THE CRAYFISH

6 SPRING ONIONS (SCALLIONS)
3 GARLIC CLOVES, PEELED AND BRUISED
2.5 CM (1 IN) PIECE OF GINGER, CRUSHED
2 CELERY STALKS, ROUGHLY CHOPPED
75 ML (2½ FL OZ) SAKE
2 UNSHELLED FRESHWATER CRAYFISH (MARRON) TAILS, AROUND 170 G (6 OZ) EACH

FOR MAKING FRESH SOY MILK SHEETS

225 G (8 OZ) DRIED SOY BEANS, SOAKED IN WATER 3 TIMES THEIR VOLUME OVERNIGHT
850 ML (28 FL OZ) PURIFIED WATER

Method

MAKE THE SHIITAKE SAUCE

Remove the stalks from the shiitake mushrooms. Finely slice the mushrooms, using a very sharp knife so the cross-section isn't dragged and distorted. Heat the oil in a non-stick frying pan over high heat. Add the mushrooms in batches so that they spread out in the pan in a single layer (the point is to quickly colour and soften them, not steam them). Off the heat add the rice wine, the ginger and spring onion juices, and the garlic. Let the liquid in the pan reduce for 1 minute. Pour in the chicken stock and bring to a simmer. Season with salt and white pepper to taste. Take off the heat and cool. Measure the amount of liquid in the sauce. For every 300 ml (10 fl oz) of liquid, use 9 g (¼ oz) of kuzu. Dissolve the kuzu in a tablespoon of cold water and then introduce it to the sauce. Simmer for 2–3 minutes to allow the sauce to thicken.

POACH THE CRAYFISH

Put all the ingredients except the crayfish in a pot with 750 ml (25 fl oz) of water. Bring to the boil and simmer for about 30 minutes until the broth smells appetising and savoury. Strain it into another pan, as small in diameter as possible so that the volume of liquid will cover the crayfish tails. Skewer the tails straight. When the temperature of the broth cools to 60°C (140°F), add the tails. Leave off the heat for 15 minutes, or until the tails are just cooked. Fish out the tails and peel off the shells.

MAKE THE FRESH SOY MILK SHEETS

Process the drained soy beans and purified water in a food processor to make a fine sludge-like purée. Pour into a tall pot and cook over slow heat, stirring constantly to prevent the solids sticking. Bring to the boil and then cook for 5 minutes longer for the raw soy mixture to lose its green flavours and acquire a sweet nuttiness. Strain through muslin set over a strainer. Approximately 700 ml (24 fl oz) of soy milk will be produced.

When ready to make the soy milk sheets, choose a 20 cm (8 in) non-stick frying pan and pour soy milk into the pan to 1 cm (½ in) deep. Place over the lowest possible setting on the stove. The soy milk will heat up when left undisturbed and then form a skin after several minutes. Fan the skin and allow it to form visible wrinkles. Lift off using chopsticks and place on the serving dish. Repeat the process to make 4 sheets.

ASSEMBLE THE DISH

Cut the crayfish tails lengthways and then cut each half into three pieces. Arrange in a dish in which the wrinkled up soy milk sheets are already sitting. Spoon some of the shiitake sauce around the crayfish and over the pale colour of the soy milk sheets.

Spiced mushroom broth

The sight of slimy black-capped shiitakes was essentially what scared me as a child. A logical way to deal with this seems to be to remove any visual references and present the offending ingredient in an unrecognisable form. I couldn't help adding some black truffle. My grown-up self doesn't have any aversion to the appearance of truffles: there's a beauty about them and no evil potential in their look (to my eyes, anyway).

Ingredients

SERVES 4

FOR THE SPICED MUSHROOM PASTE

- 500 G (1 LB 2 OZ) SWISS BROWN OR OTHER STRONG-FLAVOURED MUSHROOMS
- 2 TEASPOONS SALT
- 1½ TEASPOONS BLACK PEPPERCORNS
- ¼ TEASPOON FENNEL SEEDS
- ¼ TEASPOON DILL SEEDS
- 190 ML (6½ FL OZ) APPLE CIDER VINEGAR
- 1 FRENCH SHALLOT, SLICED
- 1 LITRE (34 FL OZ) LIGHT CHICKEN STOCK

FOR THE SPICED MUSHROOM BROTH

- 1 LITRE (34 FL OZ) LIGHT CHICKEN STOCK
- 2 EGG YOLKS
- DRY SHERRY, TO TASTE
- 100 ML (3½ FL OZ) WHIPPING CREAM, LIGHTLY WHIPPED TO HOLD SHAPE
- 1 LARGE BLACK TRUFFLE, ABOUT 15 G (½ OZ) AN EXTRAVAGANCE I'D RECOMMEND FOR THE FULL IMPACT OF ITS FLAVOUR

Method

MAKE THE SPICED MUSHROOM PASTE

Slice the mushrooms thinly and mix with the salt in a bowl. Cover and marinate overnight. The next day, transfer the mushrooms and juices to a non-reactive saucepan. Grind the peppercorns, fennel and dill to a fine powder and add to the pan, along with the vinegar and shallot. Bring the mixture to the boil and cook for at least 30 minutes until reduced and syrupy. Add the chicken stock. Return to the boil and simmer slowly for about 1½ hours, until reduced by three-quarters. Take off the heat, cool slightly and purée to a fine paste with a blender. Pass through a sieve to get a more even texture. Taste for salt and black pepper. A mushroom flavour should be foremost when considering the balance of flavours and the paste will be quite a lot saltier than is usually edible. (There will be some left over after using 3–4 tablespoons in the broth. This can be stored in the refrigerator for a couple of weeks and used as a condiment.)

MAKE THE MUSHROOM BROTH

Bring the chicken stock to the boil. In a bowl, combine 3 heaped tablespoons of the mushroom paste with the egg yolks. Take a few spoonfuls of boiling stock and stir into the mushroom mixture. Quickly whisk this back into the pan of stock. Heat the broth slowly so the egg yolks slightly thicken the mixture. Season with sherry to taste. Pass the broth through a fine sieve for a lighter texture.

ASSEMBLE THE DISH

Serve the broth warm in bowls. Swirl the cream over the surface of the broth so that it melts and sits on top in the form of foam. Quickly shave a generous amount of truffle (if using) over each bowl and serve immediately.

SOU

UND

A BIRTHDAY TREAT of CLAWS and SHELLS

When I recall childhood days, it seems events just appeared on the horizon. Great celebrations such as Christmas seemed always to follow an interval of not having to go to school. (One day I would be at school, the next it was time to break from school and then suddenly there was a Christmas tree set up and we were opening presents.)

It also feels that my family made many impromptu trips. We seemingly just turned up at Sandakan's small airport, purchased tickets to fly out on the next plane and were transported to another place entirely. Perhaps it was simply that, from my point of view, big events held as much significance as small ones: the next visit to a favourite playground, or to see one of my grandmothers ... I don't know when I became aware of calendar, date and time, but a sure sign of the passing of time was the celebration feast of chilli crab, something that has been my favourite since I don't remember when.

I see this as a snapshot of what might have occurred on any birthday feast of my childhood. My sister, father and mother are the faces I recall sitting around the table, the centrepiece being a platter of orange-red crab claws and bodies covered with my favourite tomato-ey, faintly chilli hot sauce. For some reason (I would say I was parroting my parents' opinions), the most important consideration in my mind is that the sauce should be tasty but never overpower the sweet delicate flavour of the crab.

And so my family starts to methodically work its way through the pile of crabs, the shells knocking together with a high-pitched sound as we choose our favourite pieces. My sister and I have been shown how to take the sweet meat out of the various parts of the crab. My mother will have lightly cracked the harder, larger parts of the crabs such as the claws (depending on size, these would have been jointed and broken up into upper claws and the pincers). She will also have split the torso into quarters and included, for my father, the carapace with its tomalley. (I couldn't understand his taste for this at that time.) We snap open crab legs and are, hopefully, rewarded with a cylinder of leg meat (indicating perfectly cooked crab); break open the torso into the myriad chambers of translucent shell and tease out the rewarding pieces of flesh; shatter the large pincer and uncover the lode of meat hiding there. So there is much chomping,

crunching, cracking and smashing during this meal. It is all as messy as it sounded.

In thinking about the sounds of eating the birthday crab dish, my mind wanders to another favourite, a dish that we ate as an everyday meal: whole prawns, fried simply in oil and dressed with a few lines of oyster sauce. This also made for messy eating. I have always liked the intensified flavour that comes from cooking prawns in their shells; it does protect the prawn meat from excessive heat and preserves the delicate snappy texture. As a child, though, I didn't like getting oil and oyster sauce on my fingers as I detached segments of shell from the prawn tails. One solution was to suck off all the sauce before peeling, but then I'd lose the sauce that accompanied the prawn ... These were the sorts of perplexing thoughts that occupied me while I was trying to deal with these slippery objects, all the while silently hoping my mother or father would detect my mental difficulty and offer to peel the prawns for me.

A different kind of snap and crunch was the snatch and grab action my sister and I were involved in when presented with a bowl of hand-made prawn crackers. These are very different from the faintly pink, mock prawn crackers found around the edge of plates of crispy chicken and crispy noodles at many Chinese restaurants the world over. Although the restaurant variety are delicious in their own right, I wonder if you've ever been handed a bag of dehydrated prawn crackers, rattling full of promise? This was an occasional childhood delight: firstly watching the mysterious unravelling and puffing up in hot oil (the noise I'd use to describe the frying process is a quiet hiss); then seeing the crackers crisply piled on a plate for our consumption. There is quite a resistant crunch to these crackers; prawn meat ground up with tapioca flour makes for a rather dense paste.

The competition to get to the crackers could become aggressive and noisy, often accompanied by complaints from my sister or me that the other had helped herself to more than her fair allocation.

Birthday TOMATO & Chilli CRAB

This is a quickly cooked dish; the work is in the preparation and in finding the right crab. The preferred variety is the blue swimmer crab (known as the flower crab in Malaysia), but mud crab is also a good alternative. Take 4 blue swimmer crabs, split the torso with legs attached into quarters, remove the dead man's fingers (gills), separate the 2 front claws from the torso and lightly crack the hard shell, reserving the carapace. In a large pan or wok, heat a few tablespoons of peanut oil and fry 2 tablespoons of sliced ginger, 3 split and deseeded bird's eye chillies and 3 roughly chopped spring onions (scallions) until fragrant and lightly coloured. With the heat high, add the crab pieces and stir to distribute the heat. Add a little water and clamp on the lid to steam the crab for 5 minutes or so. Have ready a sauce base of a couple of tablespoons of tomato ketchup, 1 tablespoon of oyster sauce, ½ teaspoon malt vinegar, 2 teaspoons of sugar and a teaspoon of salt. Once the crab is almost cooked, pour in the sauce base and bring to a boil. Taste and adjust for seasoning (it should be briny, sweet, sour and a little hot).

HAND-MADE Prawn Crackers

Mince 500 g (1 lb 2 oz) prawn meat with a sharp cleaver to make a fine paste. Mix together with an equal mass of well-sifted tapioca flour. Season with 1 heaped teaspoon of salt, 1 teaspoon of sugar and 1 teaspoon of finely ground white pepper. Knead into a dough and keep kneading until the dough is smooth; the texture should be pliable but firm enough to hold its shape. At any time, if the dough is sticking, wet your hands and the work surface with water rather than flour. Divide the dough into four parts and shape into cylinders. Place in a bamboo steamer lined with fresh banana leaves and steam over medium heat for 1 hour until a skewer comes out clean when stuck into the middle of a roll. Don't try to hurry things along by increasing the heat: if the integrity of the dough is compromised it may crack and produce unsuccessful prawn crackers. Cool and chill overnight in the refrigerator. The next morning, using a very sharp knife, thinly slice the cylinders. Ideally, lay out on rattan mats and dry in the hot tropical sun for a couple of days. The alternative is to place on baking trays lined with baking paper and dry in the oven at the lowest setting until dried very much to a 'crisp'. Deep-fry at 190°C (375°F), keeping the cracker fully submerged in oil or else it won't puff up, and drain on paper towels. There's no need to advise serving them immediately ... I'm sure it will be a marvel to see how quickly they disappear.

Blue Swimmer
Crab

Three kinds of fish

Remembering past birthday feasts of claws and shells made me think about the different textures of seafood and how best I like to enjoy them. Coral trout is always on my wish list of favourite fish, although you could use any firm-fleshed white fish here. Have the fishmonger shuck the live abalone, then slice it yourself at home. A 400 g (14 oz) abalone with shell usually yields 30 slices and you will only need 12 slices here. A mature abalone is preferred over the smaller-sized ones because of its better developed flavour, so freeze the excess to use later in simple sautés or long braises.

Three kinds of fish

SERVES 4

Ingredients

FOR THE MARRON TAILS

50 G (1¾ OZ) UNSALTED BUTTER
2 GARLIC CLOVES, BRUISED
1 BIRD'S EYE CHILLI, LIGHTLY CRUSHED
2 MARRON (FRESHWATER CRAYFISH) TAILS, EACH 150 G (5½ OZ) SHELLED, DEVEINED
LEMON JUICE TO TASTE

FOR THE ABALONE

12 SLICES OF RAW GREEN-LIPPED ABALONE
50 G (1¾ OZ) UNSALTED BUTTER
3 CM (1¼ IN) PIECE OF GINGER, CRUSHED
2 CM (¾ IN) PIECE OF GALANGAL, CRUSHED
1 GARLIC CLOVE
2 THYME SPRIGS

FOR THE CORAL TROUT

1 TABLESPOON DRY SHERRY
1 TEASPOON LIGHT SOY SAUCE
½ TEASPOON SESAME OIL
400 G (14 OZ) CORAL TROUT FILLET, SKIN SCORED

A LITTLE OLIVE OIL FOR FRYING
4 SPRING ONIONS (SCALLIONS) OR BABY LEEKS
1 TABLESPOON COGNAC
100 ML (3½ FL OZ) BROWN CHICKEN STOCK
LEMON JUICE TO TASTE
4 LARGE SHISO LEAVES (SEE GLOSSARY), WILTED IN THE STOCK
1 TEASPOON OF MARRON (FRESHWATER CRAYFISH) ROE, EXTRACTED FROM THE HEAD

Method

ROAST THE MARRON TAILS

Preheat the oven to 200°C (400°F). Melt the butter with the garlic and chilli in an ovenproof frying pan. When the butter is nutty and redolent with garlic and chilli, turn down the heat and sear the marron tails for about 1 minute on each side. Season with lemon juice, salt and white pepper and finish in the oven for 5–10 minutes until just cooked through. Remove from the oven and take the marron out of the butter, reserving the butter.

PREPARE THE ABALONE

Place the abalone slices on a tray or in a shallow dish. In a frying pan melt the butter with the ginger, galangal, garlic and thyme until the mixture smells of the aromatics and the butter has an appetising nutty smell. Take off the heat and strain over the abalone. As soon as the butter hits the abalone, quickly take the slices out of the butter and check that they have become pliable. The abalone will toughen with too much heat but will remain with its raw tough-ish texture if not enough heat. Reserve the butter.

PREPARE THE CORAL TROUT

Combine the liquids, rub over the fish and leave for 30 minutes at room temperature. Steam over slowly simmering water for 10 minutes or so until the flesh easily flakes off. Leave to rest for about 5 minutes and then cut into 4 square portions for each person.

ASSEMBLE THE DISH

Heat a frying pan and sprinkle with salt. When hot, add a little oil. Add the spring onions and roll them around to pick up the heat. Add 1 teaspoon of water to the pan, put the lid on and let the spring onions soften a little for a couple of minutes. Place one on each serving plate. Combine the reserved marron and abalone butters in a saucepan and bring to a simmer. Add the cognac and let the alcohol dissipate, then add the chicken stock. Simmer for about 10 minutes until the mixture looks separated, like unemulsified salad dressing.

Season with salt, white pepper and lemon juice. Arrange the marron, abalone and trout on each plate over the spring onion and scatter some of the sauce on the plate. Decorate with some torn leaves of wilted shiso and marron roe extracted from the heads of the marron that have been blanched and dried.

Prawns out of their shells

This was conceived as a way to cook prawns out of their shells while maintaining the very integrity that's so nice about cooking them in their shells. I've used a frying oil flavoured with the shells to make for a more prawn-related flavour. And the synthesised prawn shells echo the sound of crunching on real shells. A note on the ingredients... Tomalley is the orange substance found in the head of prawns, also known as the 'liver' of shellfish. For the tomalley to be usable, the shellfish must be very fresh.

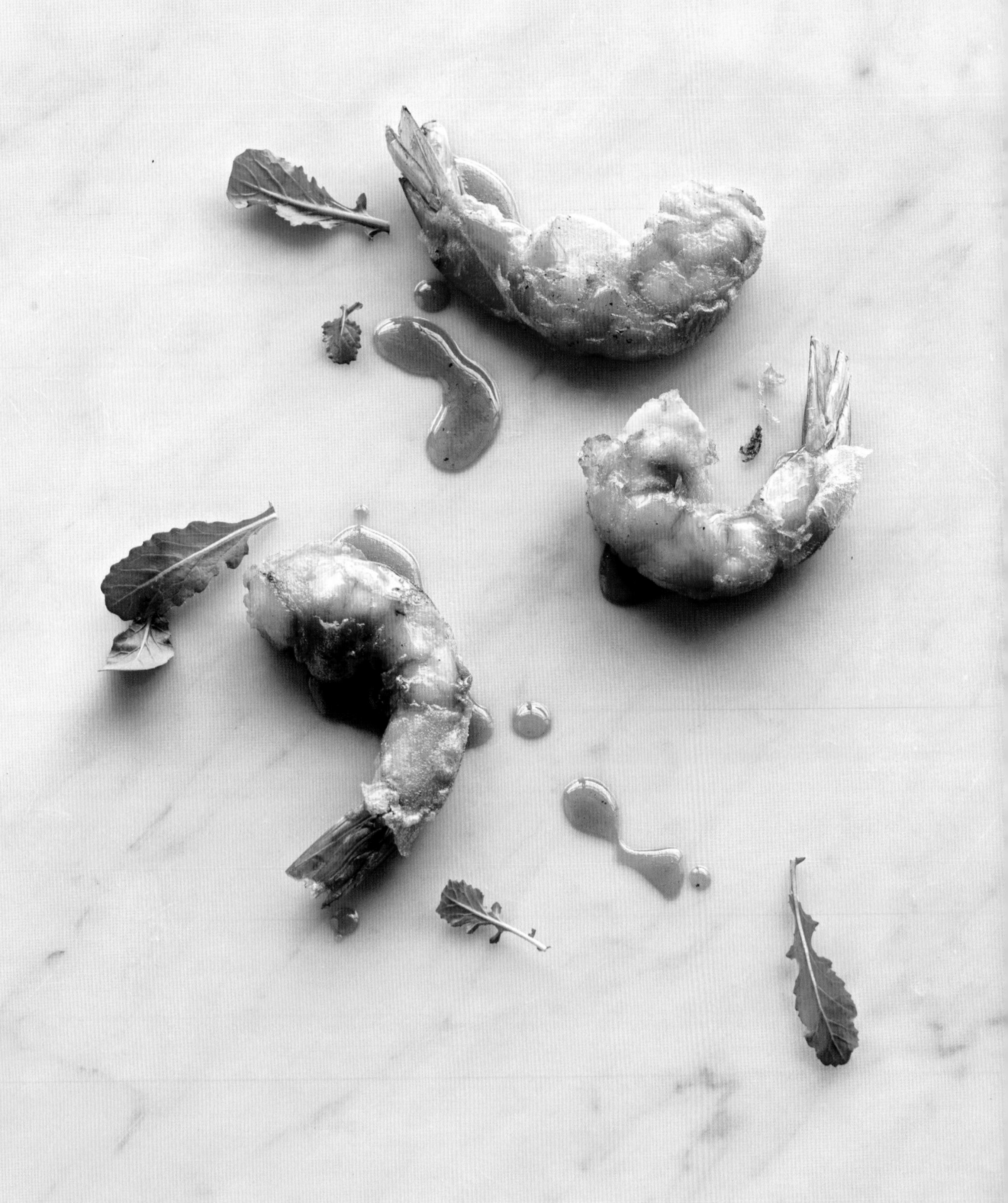

Prawns out of their shells

SERVES 3
OR 4 AS A SMALL PLATE

Ingredients

FOR THE PRAWNS

12 LARGE PRAWNS (SHRIMP)
300 ML (10 FL OZ) OLIVE OIL
1 RED ASIAN SHALLOT, CUT INTO QUARTERS
2 GARLIC CLOVES, SMASHED
4 CM (1½ IN) PIECE OF GINGER, SMASHED
2 BIRD'S EYE CHILLIES, SLIT IN THE MIDDLE TO PREVENT BURSTING DURING FRYING
½ CARROT, ROUGHLY CHOPPED

FOR THE HONEYED PRAWN SAUCE

50 ML (1¾ FL OZ) HONEY
2–3 TABLESPOONS TOMALLEY
2 TABLESPOONS GINGER JUICE (SEE BOX BELOW)
1 TABLESPOON SPRING ONION (SCALLION) JUICE (SEE BOX BELOW)
2 TEASPOONS GARLIC JUICE (SEE BOX BELOW)
LIME JUICE TO TASTE

6 SQUARE DRIED RICE PAPERS
SMALL ROCKET (ARUGULA) LEAVES TO GARNISH

Method

PREPARE THE PRAWNS

Remove the prawn heads and squeeze out the tomalley into a bowl set over ice so that it doesn't deteriorate. Remove the shells and set aside with the emptied heads. Devein the prawns with a skewer.

PREPARE THE PRAWN OIL

Pour a few spoonfuls of the olive oil into a saucepan over medium–high heat. When hot, add the shallot, garlic, ginger, chillies and carrot and cook until slightly softened. Add the prawn shells and heads. Let the mixture get hot, then add the rest of the oil. Initially the oil will be opaque and will acquire a reddish colour as the flavour is extracted from the prawns and vegetables and moisture is cooked out. The flavoursome stage is reached when the oil is clear and makes a crisp sizzling sound. Take off the heat, cool and strain through a fine sieve.

MAKE THE HONEYED PRAWN SAUCE

Bring the honey to the boil in a small saucepan. Let it caramelise over medium heat for about 15 minutes until it smells toasty and turns a darker colour. Combine the tomalley and juices. Heat 100 ml (3½ fl oz) prawn oil in a non-stick pan over medium–high heat. Add the tomalley mixture and fry until the raw eggy aroma has been cooked out. Add the caramelised honey and then taste: it should be very savoury and have some sourness, so adjust with salt and lime juice.

MAKE THE PRAWN PARCELS

Fill a large bowl with warm water. Dip the rice papers in the water for a few seconds until just pliable. Remove, cut in half and dry on a tea towel. Season the prawns with some salt and pepper and then loosely roll a rice paper half around each prawn. Heat a non-stick pan over medium–high heat, add 3 or 4 tablespoons of prawn oil and fry the prawn parcels for 2 minutes or so on each side until crisp. Drain and serve immediately, dressed with honeyed prawn sauce and garnished with rocket and drops of fragrant prawn oil.

TO MAKE GINGER, SPRING ONION AND GARLIC JUICES

Make ginger juice by pressing grated fresh ginger through a fine sieve and collecting the liquid. To make spring onion juice, roughly chop a couple of spring onions (scallions) and pound with a mortar and pestle with a pinch of salt, then press through a fine sieve to extract the juice. To make garlic juice, pound 4 garlic cloves with a little salt to make a paste, then pass through a fine sieve to extract the juice.

Early one morning I wandered into the garden. Curious things were usually discovered when one slowed down one's pace and looked a little more carefully, even in the familiar environment of the home: snails hatching eggs (which, I imagined, involved oozy, squishing sounds); fern-like plants folding themselves up almost as fast as the snap of a lock when touched; grotesquely patterned caterpillars feeding on leaves (with what I imagined to be systematic chomping noises).

On this particular day I was wandering past the pink-flowered oleander tree, holding my breath of course (because I'd been told it was poisonous but wasn't sure how, so thought it best just not to breathe in any of its noxious fumes). There was an unfamiliar sound of grass being torn up rapidly and a surprising bleat. I turned the corner and was speechless at the sight of a huge white goat tied to the fence. It towered over me, champing on the grass. I darted back to the house to fetch my parents.

Why was there a goat in the garden? It seemed that this was also a surprise to my parents. It was later revealed to be payment in kind to my father for his accounting services (for we were living in a Malaysia that still practised the barter system). The goat hung around for a few days. It wasn't a friendly creature; all it did was tear up the lawn and bleat. We were warned against going into the garden to play with it or to try to make friends. Just as suddenly as it had appeared, the goat disappeared.

Goat meat became a constant at our family meals for a while after that. My sister and I weren't told it was goat, although we did wonder why we were eating so much meat drowned in strong sauces. When we were told, it transpired that I wasn't one of those children who was upset to find out where dinner came from.

What did make me squeamish, however, was seeing chickens being slaughtered by my mother or grandmother. I wondered how they tolerated these tasks. I liked chickens (although they had beady eyes); the clucking sounds they made were rather reassuring and calming, in my opinion. A rooster crowing in the early dawn was a sound that I heard every morning of my life in Malaysia. It signalled the beginning of the day's adventures. There was always at least one family in the neighbourhood raising chickens.

Whenever my mother brought a live chicken home from market, it was quite evident what was going to happen to it that day. I hid as far away in the back of the house as I could, so I couldn't hear anything (a similar tactic to the one I now put into play when something violent or frightening appears on the TV).

I am anchored by these memories. If I've chosen to eat meat of any sort, I'm always mindful that an animal sacrificed its life for the meat to come into my kitchen or appear at the table where we eat. For me, keeping the integrity of the animal is a way of respecting the once living creature. There is something to appreciate in all aspects of living things; I know I can find it if I am persistent enough. One obvious example is the form of the fish. By keeping the beautiful line and shape of a fillet as much as possible and not trimming it down to a pre-determined shape in my head, I feel I'm respecting the living fish. Another form of appreciation is reflecting on the texture of flesh by savouring the raw, or by sometimes celebrating the toughness of flesh through minimal contact with heat. I believe in making use of all parts of the animal, exploring the limits of what's edible and making the (generally thought to be) less palatable, more palatable. These are some of the tributes I can make to celebrate the animal's life.

a Searingly hot Braise of Goat

This method is suitable for any cut of the goat. Trim 1 kg (2 lb 3 oz) of goat meat of all sinew and cut into 3 cm (1 inch) cubes. In a sand pot or a heavy-based pan, heat 3 tablespoons of peanut oil and lightly brown a whole head of peeled and lightly smashed garlic. Add a couple of star anise and 1 teaspoon of fennel seeds and the goat meat. Turn the meat around in the pan a few times until hints of garlic and spices can be sensed. Add 2 tablespoons of dark soy sauce, 1 teaspoon of sugar and 3 tablespoons of water, bring to a simmer and cover the pan. Cook over low heat for 2 hours, stirring and topping up with water from time to time, until the meat is tender, the water has evaporated and the mixture is a slick of oil and dark meat juices. Serve hot, straight off the stove.

Fish presented in its natural shape

I see this recipe as celebrating the natural shape of the fish, rather than trying to cut, shape, mince or add things to it in such a way as to fit the cook's vision. The plan is to serve half a side of dory per person. So, starting with two large fillets which are whole sides of the fish, these can both be separated out along the middle into two smaller pieces, essentially with your fingers. Take the skin off the fish for this purpose.

Fish presented in its natural shape

SERVES 4

Ingredients

FOR THE VADOUVAN SAUCE

1 BOILING CHICKEN, CHOPPED INTO SMALL PIECES
250 G (9 OZ) CHICKEN WINGS, CHOPPED
250 G (9 OZ) CHICKEN FEET, CHOPPED
2 TEASPOONS GROUND TURMERIC
OLIVE OIL FOR FRYING
100 G (3½ OZ) UNSALTED BUTTER FOR FRYING
1 BROWN ONION, CHOPPED
1 CARROT, CHOPPED
2 CELERY STALKS, CHOPPED
¼ GARLIC HEAD, CHOPPED AND BRUISED
2 CM (¾ INCH) PIECE OF GALANGAL, CHOPPED
3 CM (1¼ INCH) PIECE OF GINGER, CHOPPED
2 CM (¾ INCH) PIECE OF FRESH TURMERIC CHOPPED
2 TABLESPOONS VADOUVAN SPICE MIX (SEE BOX OPPOSITE)
2 TABLESPOONS BRANDY
1.5 LITRES (51 FL OZ) LIGHT CHICKEN STOCK
3 KAFFIR LIME LEAVES
20 G (¾ OZ) TAMARIND PULP, SOAKED IN 100 ML (3½ FL OZ) OF WATER, STRAINED
40 CURRY LEAVES, TAKEN OFF THE STEM
15 G (½ OZ) KUZU STARCH (SEE GLOSSARY)

FOR THE SPICED ONION MIXTURE

100 ML (3½ FL OZ) PEANUT OIL
10 CURRY LEAVES
1 BROWN ONION, THINLY SLICED
3 GARLIC CLOVES, THINLY SLICED
1 TEASPOON VADOUVAN SPICE MIX (SEE BOX OPPOSITE)
JUICE OF ½ LIME

FOR THE SEAFOOD

2 X 200 G (7 OZ) JOHN DORY FILLETS (EACH A WHOLE SIDE OF THE FISH)
100 G (3½ OZ) COOKED SPANNER CRAB OR MUD CRAB MEAT

MIXED FRESH SMALL BASIL LEAVES, CORIANDER (CILANTRO) LEAVES AND BORAGE FLOWERS TO GARNISH

Method

MAKE THE VADOUVAN SAUCE

Coat the chopped chicken, wings and feet with the ground turmeric and marinate overnight. Next day, heat some oil and butter in a large pot and fry the onion, carrot, celery and garlic with some salt until golden and soft. Add the galangal, ginger and turmeric and cook for about 5 minutes until fragrant. Add the spice mix.

In a separate pan sear the chicken in oil. Combine the brandy with 2 tablespoons of water and use to deglaze the pan, scraping up all the brown sticky bits. Transfer to the pot with the cooking vegetables. Add the chicken stock and bring to the boil. Add the kaffir lime leaves and simmer for 30 minutes. Add the tamarind water and simmer for another 30 minutes. Drop in the curry leaves and leave off the heat for about 30 minutes to infuse. Finally, press the contents of the pot through a coarse sieve, then pass this through a fine chinois.

MAKE THE SPICED ONION MIXTURE

Heat the peanut oil in a saucepan to 180°C (350°F). Put the curry leaves in a sieve and sit this over a heatproof container. Pour the oil over the leaves, into the container. Repeat this process two or three more times, until the leaves turn a dark translucent green. Drain on paper towels and set aside. Use this fragrant peanut oil to cook the onion in a pan over medium heat until golden and soft. Add the garlic and continue cooking until the garlic also turns golden. Add the spice mix and heat for a minute or so. Add salt and lime juice to taste, which should be distinctly tart.

COOK THE SEAFOOD

When ready to serve the dish, remove the skin from the dory fillets and divide each fillet in half along the natural 'spine' line, giving 4 pieces. Steam these over slowly simmering water for 8–10 minutes until the flesh would be soft enough to flake. Or brush the fillets with a little oil and bake in a preheated 160°C (320°F) oven for about 10 minutes. Before removing the fish from the pan or oven, spoon a quarter of the crab meat onto each fillet to warm the crab meat through before serving.

FINISH THE SAUCE

Start with 300 ml (10 fl oz) of the cooled vadouvan sauce in a saucepan. Take out 2 tablespoons and mix with the kuzu starch until it dissolves. Stir back into the sauce in the pan and bring to the boil. Simmer for a couple of minutes until the mixture is thickened, then keep it warm. Place a dory fillet with its crab on each plate, arrange some of the spiced onion on the plate and spoon the sauce over generously. Arrange some of the fresh herbs on each plate and serve at once.

TO MAKE VADOUVAN SPICE MIX

Combine 1 teaspoon of fenugreek seeds, ⅓ tablespoon of Indian coriander seeds, 1 teaspoon of fennel seeds, ⅓ tablespoon of dill seeds, 1 tablespoon of cumin seeds, 1 teaspoon of cardamom pods and 1 tablespoon of white peppercorns. Roast the spices until fragrant in a dry frying pan over medium-high heat, or in a preheated 180°C (350°F) oven. When cool, grind to a fine powder. Store the leftover mix in the freezer for up to 3 months.

Goat sausage and a spiced tomato sauce

This perhaps answers the obvious question of what to do with an excess of goat meat. I think the herbs and chilli flavours are great foils to any gamey meat. This will serve four people with leftover sausage. The rest of the sausage can be frozen and taken out gradually for use (I find it's a lot of effort otherwise to make a smaller amount of sausages).

Goat sausage and a spiced tomato sauce

SERVES 4

Ingredients

FOR THE GOAT SAUSAGE

200 G (7 OZ) CAUL FAT
1 LARGE HANDFUL OF SALT
100 ML (3½ FL OZ) VINEGAR
250 G (9 OZ) PORK BACK FAT
2 BROWN ONIONS, FINELY DICED
4 GARLIC CLOVES, FINELY CHOPPED
500 G (1 LB 2 OZ) LEAN GOAT MEAT (I USE LEG MEAT)
200 G (7 OZ) LEAN VEAL MEAT
1 TEASPOON THYME LEAVES, FINELY CHOPPED
1 LARGE HANDFUL OF PARSLEY LEAVES, FINELY CHOPPED
¼ BUNCH MARJORAM, LEAVES PICKED AND FINELY CHOPPED
4 BIRD'S EYE CHILLIES, BLACKENED AND MASHED (SEE BOX OPPOSITE)
50 ML (1¾ FL OZ) COGNAC
2 TEASPOONS FRESHLY GROUND BLACK PEPPER
15 G (½ OZ) SALT FOR EACH 1 KG (2 LB) OF SAUSAGE MIX
100 ML (3½ FL OZ) ICED WATER FOR EACH 1 KG (2 LB) OF SAUSAGE MIX

FOR THE SPICED TOMATO SAUCE

2 KG (4 LB 6 OZ) RIPE AND FLAVOURSOME TOMATOES, PEELED
1 TABLESPOON SALT
250 ML (8½ FL OZ) OLIVE OIL
½ BUNCH THYME
1 BROWN ONION, FINELY DICED
10 GARLIC CLOVES, FINELY CHOPPED
5 BIRD'S EYE CHILLIES, DESEEDED AND FINELY CHOPPED
100 G (3½ OZ) GINGER, PEELED AND FINELY CHOPPED
BROWN SUGAR TO TASTE

FOR THE EGGPLANT (AUBERGINE) RELISH

1 EGGPLANT (AUBERGINE)
PEANUT OIL FOR DEEP-FRYING
250 ML (8½ FL OZ) VEAL STOCK OR DARK BROWN CHICKEN STOCK

MIXED FINE-LEAFED SHISO, BASIL LEAVES AND MARSH SAMPHIRE (SEE GLOSSARY) TO GARNISH

Method

MAKE THE GOAT SAUSAGE

Prepare the caul fat by soaking in 5 litres (170 fl oz) of water with the salt and vinegar overnight. Check the caul fat is properly bleached before use, otherwise repeat the process. Finely chop 50 g (1¾ oz) of the pork back fat. Melt in a pan over medium–low heat and then add the onions. Cook until soft and golden. Add the garlic and cook for a minute or so until fragrant. Transfer to a tray to cool down, then cool in the refrigerator. Finely dice the remaining pork back fat with the goat and veal meat. It is important to keep all ingredients as cold as possible.

Combine the cooled onion mixture, diced meat, herbs, mashed chillies, cognac and pepper. Weigh the mixture and work out the amount of salt and iced water required. Mix in the salt and continue mixing until the ingredients emulsify (an electric mixer can be used here). Gradually add the iced water as you go. Use a sausage maker to pipe the filling into sausage skins, or wrap it in caul fat. Divide the mix into 5 portions. Make each sausage about 10 cm (4 in) long by 4 cm (1½ in) wide and 3 cm (1¼ in) high. Leave for at least a couple of hours before cooking, preferably overnight.

MAKE THE SPICED TOMATO SAUCE

Preheat the oven to 200°C (400°F). Halve the tomatoes and macerate with the salt for 30 minutes, then strain the juice and reserve. Toss the tomatoes with 150 ml (5 fl oz) of the olive oil, spread over two trays and roast for about 1½ hours, until dry and a nice caramel colour. You may need to turn the tomatoes during the cooking time.

Meanwhile, make a paste of the thyme, onion, garlic, chillies and ginger with the remaining 100 ml (3½ fl oz) of olive oil. In a large pan cook gently for around 30–40 minutes until the solids separate from the oil and it no longer tastes raw. Add the tomatoes and their oil to the cooking paste, along with the reserved tomato water. Cook gently until no liquid remains. Adjust the seasoning with salt and lots of freshly ground black pepper to taste; you may need to add a little brown sugar if the mixture tastes too acidic.

MAKE THE EGGPLANT RELISH

Trim the top off the eggplant and cut it lengthways into slices about 3 mm (⅛ in) thick. Heat the oil to 180°C (350°F) and deep-fry the slices a few at a time. Drain on paper towels. Spread a small spoonful of tomato sauce over each eggplant slice and fold in half. Heat the stock in a pan to simmering point. Gently add the eggplant and 2–3 spoonfuls of oil from the tomato sauce. Cook until the eggplant softens. Taste the sauce to check that it is slightly acidic. If not, add some of the tomato sauce.

ASSEMBLE THE DISH

Fry the sausages over medium–high heat. They should be browned all over but remain succulent inside (you can finish them in a hot oven for 10 minutes if you like). Rest for a few minutes before cutting into 3 cm (1¼ in) slices. Arrange on plates with some eggplant relish and spoon the sauce over. Serve garnished with mixed leaves.

TO MAKE BLACKENED MASHED CHILLIES

To prepare the chillies, hold them with tongs over an open flame or grill until the skins blacken all over. When cool enough to handle, peel away the skin. Finely chop the flesh, then mash finely with a little salt using the back of a knife.

Sirloin and accompaniments

This dish originated while I was considering how to make apparent leathery chewiness palatable. I generally prefer to eat meat that requires a lot of chewing: it's either a sign of a mature flavoursome animal, or a flavoursome secondary cut of meat. I also prefer not to cook meat so that it's 'falling-apart soft'. My solution here is to cook thinly sliced sirloin for the minimum amount of time, as gently as possible, to preserve its succulence and to make the accompaniments extremely flavoursome. In this way the sirloin texture becomes simply one of the numerous elements vying for attention in the dish.

PREPARING YOUNG BAMBOO

Choose a piece of young bamboo. Put in a pot, cover with water, add a handful of sugar and simmer for 40 minutes. The bamboo is done when it doesn't offer much resistance to a skewer. Leave to cool in the liquid. To use, remove the husk, cut off the tough base and slice cross-sections from it.

Ingredients

SERVES 4

FOR BRAISING INTERCOSTALS

- 100 G (3½ OZ) SUGAR
- 2 CARROTS, FINELY DICED
- 1 BROWN ONION, FINELY DICED
- 5 GARLIC CLOVES, FINELY CHOPPED
- 3 CELERY STALKS, FINELY DICED
- 1 BAY LEAF
- 2 THYME SPRIGS
- 1 TEASPOON BLACK PEPPERCORNS, LIGHTLY CRUSHED
- 300 ML (10 FL OZ) FULL-BODIED RED WINE
- 750 ML (25½ FL OZ) RICH VEAL STOCK OR RICH DARK CHICKEN STOCK
- 500 G (1 LB 2 OZ) WAGYU INTERCOSTALS (MEAT FROM BETWEEN THE RIBS)

FOR THE ACCOMPANIMENTS

- 1 TABLESPOON LIGHT SOY SAUCE
- 1 TEASPOON MIRIN
- 8 SLICES OF BAMBOO (SEE BOX OPPOSITE)
- 2 TABLESPOONS CLARIFIED BUTTER
- 80 G (2¾ OZ) ENOKI MUSHROOMS, SEPARATED
- 1 LEBANESE OR SMALLISH CUCUMBER
- 3 TABLESPOONS RICE VINEGAR
- 1½ TEASPOONS SUGAR
- 1 SHISO LEAF (SEE GLOSSARY), JULIENNED

- 4 ANGUS BEEF SIRLOINS, ABOUT 120 G (4½ OZ) EACH, TRIMMED OF EXCESS FAT AND SINEW

Method

BRAISE THE INTERCOSTALS

Heat a heavy-based ovenproof pan over medium–high heat. Add the sugar and leave it to turn a light colour caramel. Drop in the carrot, onion, garlic and celery and let the moisture coming off the vegetables gradually dissolve the caramel while they cook. Preheat the oven to 180°C (350°F). When the vegetables have coloured and softened, add the bay leaf, thyme, peppercorns and a little salt. Deglaze the pan with the red wine and then reduce until syrupy. Add the veal stock. Simmer for 10–15 minutes until the vegetables are done.

Meanwhile, brown the intercostals in a frying pan over medium–high heat to get a good caramelisation. Season with salt. Add to the simmering braising stock and place uncovered in the oven. Roast for 30 minutes, turning the intercostals over every 10 minutes so that they retain a certain amount of bite. Remove the intercostals (leave the oven on) and strain the stock (this is to be the liquid for cooking the sirloin). Slice each intercostal thinly along its length.

ROAST THE BAMBOO

Combine the soy sauce with the mirin. Pour it over the bamboo and marinate for 30 minutes. Place on a baking tray and bake for about 20 minutes at 200°C (400°F) until the edges are nicely browned.

CRISP THE ENOKI MUSHROOMS

Heat the butter in a pan over medium–high heat. Fry the mushrooms until lightly browned and crispy. Season with some salt and white pepper.

DRESS THE CUCUMBER

Peel the cucumber, trim the ends and cut in half. Hopefully each half is at least 8 cm (3¼ in) long. Cut away the seeds and slice the flesh into batons. Make the dressing by mixing the vinegar and sugar with some salt to taste. Mix the cucumber and shiso with the dressing and use within 30 minutes.

COOK THE SIRLOIN

Cook the sirloin only when you're ready to serve all the other elements. In a frying pan or shallow pan heat the stock retained from cooking the intercostals. If necessary, simmer to give a coating consistency. With the stock just at simmering temperature, add the sirloin and let it sit for a couple of minutes before fishing it out and transferring to a tray. To serve, put some of each vegetable accompaniment on one half of each slice of sirloin. Top with a couple of intercostal slices, then fold the sirloin slices over and lift onto individual plates.

EAVESDROPPING on adult CONVERSATIONS

My sister and I were included in most of my parents' restaurant excursions with friends, as is the way of Chinese families. It felt a privilege to be present at these events, which I viewed as the most sophisticated in my parents' lives. I loved nothing more than dressing up to attend. While I really can't recall how I conducted myself on these occasions, I imagine I would have been a very interested observer. Recalling the conversations that passed between the adults (looming way above my head height), some interesting things were said.

At large dinner gatherings, my parents and their friends would sit at a round table topped with a classic lazy susan. Appetisers were often already arranged at the table: saucers of boiled or deep-fried peanuts out of the shell, pickled chillies and vegetables. While everyone settled down in their place, snippets about what they had been up to recently created a background hubbub: 'Yes, just back from the rubber plantation; got back in the jeep yesterday'; 'Spent the past few days tidying up after the children left to go back to school in Australia.' I was often engrossed in honing my chopstick skills by picking up peanuts one by one.

As dinner progressed, adults clinked together their glasses of beer (or perhaps their glasses of tea; I couldn't tell the difference, just that they were varying shades of amber). These were sometimes slammed down onto the table and I would hear the thud of glass on wood, slightly muffled by a thin synthetic tablecloth. The pitch of the voices would grow louder: 'Well, I thought I'd ordered the terrapin soup; I said I wanted the field chicken and then they brought out this platter of frogs' legs!' 'They were for sale in the market the other day; the snake steaks were this wide.' 'It's great for building up resistance: I made a soup of it with the usual medicinal herbs.'

My eyes were probably bulging at the stories I was hearing as the adults started to relax amongst themselves. Dishes would be plonked down at regular intervals. When plates such as the steamed tropical fish with strips of pork came out, I knew the evening's excitement was coming to an end and I would soon be facing down my parents and their demands that I get to bed as soon as we arrived home. However, if I had been well behaved, perhaps I could prolong the excursion by being allowed to finish dinner with my favourite sago pudding with fresh coconut cream.

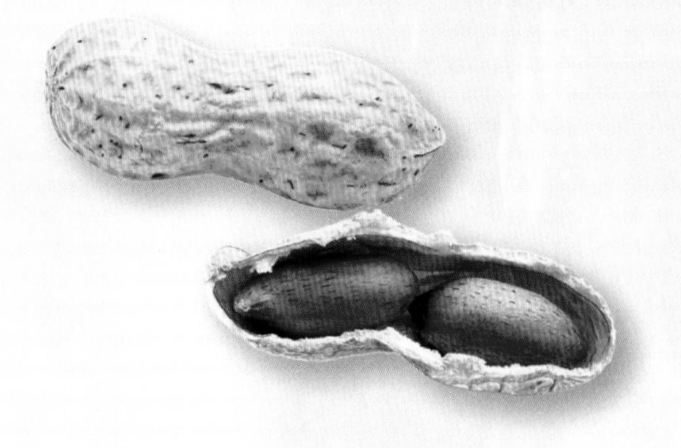

It was just as rewarding to visit other people's houses. A lot of the older houses in Sabah seemed cavernous and dark; some were quietly isolated on narrow roads, overlooked by tall trees trailing vines; others seemed to rest precariously on eroded hillsides that could only be reached by clunking steps up a series of outdoor staircases made of wood.

Up one such staircase, we would happen upon the house of a childhood friend of my father's, also our family doctor. He was a softly-spoken man with very gentle manners and his wife was the most elegantly made-up Chinese woman I knew. The usual course of an invitation to dinner at their house was a leisurely (read: interminable from the child's perspective) pre-dinner conversation over tea, reminiscing about boyhood days when he ran wild around the neighbourhood stirring up the adults' angst. The course of dinner had a similar unhurried feel to it ... course upon course was served, from braised wild boar to silken scrambled eggs incorporating local prawns. Here, at the table, conversation would turn to the men's experiences of studying overseas for their professional qualifications. Remembering now these visits to the doctor's house, I am more fully appreciative of the adult fondness for reminiscing.

One of my favourite houses was the one on the hill overlooking the old harbour. Everything was on a large scale at this place, and I'm sure everyone's voices echoed. It set the context for the tales of the interior of Sabah that I recall hearing. The resident of this house was the District Commissioner. He would settle himself back in one of those monumental rattan chairs with cushions sporting leaf motifs, and my head would be dizzied by the strange stories he'd relate of indigenous tribes he visited in the interior. Travelling upriver, he'd happened upon the structural magnificence of the longhouses, been greeted with fermented rice brimming with live weevils, seen the remnants of the headhunting culture and wondered whether it was still being practised. This other-worldly introduction would be followed by a more conventional dining experience (suckling pig never tasted so disconcerting).

Sago
PALM sugar

Sago Pudding

Soak 350 g (12½ oz) of small tapioca pearls in 1 litre (34 fl oz) of hot water until clear and soft but still holding their shape, then strain. Combine 200 ml (7 fl oz) of coconut milk and ½ teaspoon salt with the tapioca and let it thicken over low heat. Pour into moulds and chill. To make a syrup, combine 200 g (7 oz) of shaved gula melaka (Malaysian palm sugar) with 1 tablespoon of sugar and 125 ml (4 fl oz) of water in a pot over low heat. When the sugars dissolve, strain into a bowl and leave to cool. When ready to eat, unmould the puddings and serve with the syrup and a little coconut milk.

Sago with ginger milk pudding

With inspiration from the sago pudding that I tasted as a child, this dessert combines northern and southern Chinese traditions for a lighter and more subtle taste. This dish is also about my fascination with using ginger as a setting agent. And I thought creating a sauce of fermented rice wine made it seem all the more grown-up.

Sago with ginger milk pudding

SERVES 4

Ingredients

FOR THE GLUTINOUS RICE WINE

250 G (9 OZ) GLUTINOUS RICE
10 G (¼ OZ) WINE YEAST BALL (SEE GLOSSARY)

FOR THE SAGO AND RICE WINE SAUCE

70 G (2½ OZ) SMALL TAPIOCA SAGO
1 TABLESPOON SUGAR
2 TABLESPOONS UNSPRAYED JASMINE FLOWERS (SEE GLOSSARY)

FOR THE BLACK SESAME CROQUANT

100 G (3½ OZ) BLACK SESAME SEEDS
75 G (2¾ OZ) SUGAR

FOR THE GINGER MILK PUDDING

4 TEASPOONS GINGER JUICE (SEE GLOSSARY), FROM MATURE GINGER WHICH IS STRINGY AND STARCHY
2 TEASPOONS CASTER (SUPERFINE) SUGAR
240 ML (8 FL OZ) MILK

Method

MAKE THE GLUTINOUS RICE WINE

Put the rice in a strainer or colander and rinse with cold running water until the water running off the rice is clear. Transfer the rice to a steamer and stir in 450 ml (15 fl oz) water. Steam for about 30 minutes until just cooked. Spread on a large tray to cool to lukewarm. Crush the wine yeast ball to a fine powder with a mortar and pestle. Scatter over the rice and mix well. Put in an earthenware jar with a lid that is more than large enough to hold the amount of rice. (It shouldn't be airtight as the production of gas during the fermentation process will make an airtight container explode.) Place in a warm place and leave for 4 days. The glutinous rice wine is a mixture of broken down rice mixed with some liquid. You can also buy it ready-made from Chinese supermarkets and grocery shops.

MAKE THE SAGO AND RICE WINE SAUCE

Soak the sago in hot water to cover until softened. Drain. Meanwhile, take 200 g (7 oz) of the glutinous rice wine along with its rice. Strain into a jug, reserving the rice. Top up the wine with water to 200 ml (7 fl oz). Pour into a saucepan, add the sugar and heat to 80°C (170°F). Remove from the heat, drop in the jasmine flowers and leave to steep for 1 hour. Strain, then mix with the drained sago and the reserved rice.

MAKE THE BLACK SESAME CROQUANT

Preheat the oven to 160°C (320°F). Spread the sesame seeds on a baking tray and toast for 10 minutes in the oven until they smell toasty and refreshed. Combine the sugar and 1 tablespoon water in a heavy-based saucepan over medium heat. Heat until it liquefies and turns a light caramel. Don't attempt to stir or the sugar will crystallise and ruin any thought of it turning to caramel. Take off the heat, add the sesame seeds and leave in the pan for a minute. Lightly oil a baking tray. Pour the caramel onto it to give a thinnish sheet of croquant. Leave to cool, then crush to a fine powder with a mortar and pestle.

MAKE THE GINGER MILK PUDDING

Divide the ginger juice among four small but wide bowls, which you'd be happy to serve in. Dissolve the sugar into the milk and then divide the milk into four 60 ml (2 fl oz) portions. Heat one portion to around 75°C (165°F). Give the ginger juice in a bowl a good stir before pouring in the milk from a height of 15–20 cm (6–8 in) — this helps the ginger juice to mix through well. Make up three more puddings in this way. Put the bowls aside and don't disturb for 30 minutes until the puddings are set.

ASSEMBLE THE DISH

Serve the warm puddings with the sago and rice wine sauce and croquant as condiments, so those eating can choose how much sweetness and textural interest they add to their dessert.

Squid cooked in its own ink

The driving thought for me in this recipe is that a child's job is sometimes simply to make sense of what she sees and hears. This preoccupation doesn't end with childhood; I wanted to incorporate squid with pine mushrooms in some way and the following recipe was the result. If your squid doesn't yield enough ink, you might need to supplement with commercially sterilised ink from your fishmonger.

Squid cooked in its own ink

SERVES 4

Ingredients

FOR THE PICKLED PINE MUSHROOMS

250 G (9 OZ) PINE MUSHROOMS
JUICE OF 1 LEMON
200 ML (7 FL OZ) WHITE WINE VINEGAR
1 TABLESPOON SALT
2 RED ASIAN SHALLOTS, PEELED AND SLICED
2 GARLIC CLOVES, PEELED AND BRUISED
¼ TEASPOON CUMIN SEEDS
¼ TEASPOON WHITE PEPPERCORNS
4 JUNIPER BERRIES
1 SMALL BAY LEAF
3 THYME SPRIGS

FOR THE SQUID

500 G (1 LB 2 OZ) WHOLE SQUID OR MEDIUM CUTTLEFISH
1 TABLESPOON PEANUT OIL
1 GARLIC CLOVE, FINELY SHREDDED
½ CELERY STICK, FINELY SHREDDED
1 LARGE RED CHILLI, DESEEDED AND FINELY SHREDDED
2 CM (¾ IN) PIECE OF YOUNG GINGER, PEELED AND FINELY SHREDDED
1 TEASPOON DARK SOY SAUCE
½–1 TEASPOON SQUID INK

FOR THE SQUID STOCK

2 TABLESPOONS PEANUT OIL
2 RED ASIAN SHALLOTS, PEELED AND THINLY SLICED
4 GARLIC CLOVES, PEELED AND BRUISED
½ CARROT, PEELED AND THINLY SLICED
2 STEMS OF FLAT-LEAF (ITALIAN) PARSLEY
2 THYME SPRIGS
2 RIPE TOMATOES, PEELED AND ROUGHLY CHOPPED
1 TEASPOON SHERRY VINEGAR
500 ML (17 FL OZ) LIGHT FISH STOCK

2 TABLESPOONS FINELY SHREDDED GREEN PAPAYA
2 TEASPOONS ROCK SAMPHIRE STEMS (SEE GLOSSARY), BRIEFLY BLANCHED AND REFRESHED
CITRUS OIL (SEE BOX OPPOSITE)

Method

PICKLE THE PINE MUSHROOMS

Use a brush to clean the pine needles and dirt off the mushrooms. Trim the stems and cut the caps into quarters or halves, depending on their size. Put them in a bowl, sprinkle with the lemon juice and leave for an hour or so. Place the rest of the pickling ingredients into a pot with 500 ml (17 fl oz) water and bring to the boil. Cool the mixture to 80°C (175°F), then pour it over the mushrooms (the reduced heat helps preserve the colour). Leave at least overnight before using and place in a sterilised preserving jar if storing for a longer time.

PREPARE THE SQUID

Separate the head and tentacles from the body, reserving the tentacles for the stock. Remove and discard the guts and carefully extract the ink sac (this is a silvery pouch). Peel the skin off the body and cut it open. Wipe the inside surface with damp paper towels. Cut the squid into squares of about 2.5 cm (1 in). Squeeze the ink out of the sac into a bowl and add 1 teaspoon water. Set aside for 30 minutes, then strain. The rest of the squid preparation is done just before serving.

MAKE THE SQUID STOCK

Heat the oil in a saucepan over high heat, add the tentacles and cook so they colour quickly. Add the shallots, garlic and carrot and sauté until softened. Add the parsley, thyme and tomatoes and cook for 3–4 minutes until the tomatoes soften. Deglaze the pan with the vinegar, then add the fish stock. Simmer for about 30 minutes until the stock tastes of squid and has an extreme sweetness from the squid and tomatoes. Strain and set aside.

COOK THE SQUID

Heat the oil in a frying pan over high heat. Add the garlic, celery, chilli and ginger and fry quickly until just starting to become fragrant. Add 150 ml (5 fl oz) of the squid stock and bring quickly to a simmer. Add the squid pieces and cook for 1 minute. Fish out all the vegetables and squid and keep warm. Reduce the stock by half, add the soy sauce and squid ink and bring up to a simmer.

ASSEMBLE THE DISH

Arrange pieces of mushroom on each person's plate, then add some green papaya and samphire. Arrange a few pieces of squid and vegetables on top and spoon over some sauce. Finish with drops of citrus oil around the plate and serve immediately.

TO MAKE CITRUS OIL

Heat 100 ml (3½ fl oz) of grapeseed oil in a saucepan to 70°C (160°F). Put the zest of 1 lemon and 1 lime in a sterilised preserving jar and pour in the oil. Cover and leave overnight before use.

An alcoholic dumpling

I'm remembering the feeling of childhood awe at observing the unfamiliar behaviour of drunken adults at the dinner table. It all felt quite forbidden, since I wasn't allowed to participate. The idea then came of hiding away the alcohol (here, sherry and cognac) in the filling of an innocuous looking dumpling.

Ingredients

SERVES 4–6 AS A SHARED PLATE

FOR THE FILLING

- 125 G (4½ OZ) PORK BELLY, DICED
- 50 G (1¾ OZ) PRAWN MEAT, DICED
- 2 TABLESPOONS COGNAC
- 1½ TEASPOONS DRY SHERRY
- ½ TEASPOON SUGAR
- ½ TEASPOON FRESHLY GROUND WHITE PEPPER
- 1½ TEASPOONS CORN STARCH OR WHEAT STARCH
- 1 TEASPOON LIGHT SOY SAUCE
- 2 TABLESPOONS LIGHT CHICKEN STOCK
- 2 TEASPOONS PEANUT OIL
- 1 TEASPOON FINELY DICED GINGER
- 1 TEASPOON FINELY DICED GARLIC
- 1 SPRING ONION (SCALLION), FINELY SLICED
- 2 FRESH SHIITAKE MUSHROOMS, FINELY DICED

FOR THE DIPPING SAUCE

- 1 TABLESPOON SUGAR
- 1 TABLESPOON LIGHT SOY SAUCE
- 1 TEASPOON DARK SOY SAUCE
- ½ TEASPOON RICE VINEGAR
- 1 TABLESPOON PEANUT OIL
- 2 DROPS SESAME OIL
- 1 TABLESPOON CHILLI OIL (SEE PAGE 280)

FOR THE DUMPLINGS

- 165 G (6 OZ) GLUTINOUS RICE FLOUR
- 65 G (2¼ OZ) WHEAT STARCH
- 50 G (1¾ OZ) SOFT BROWN SUGAR
- ¼ TEASPOON SALT
- 60 G (2 OZ) LARD
- 160 ML (5½ FL OZ) BOILING WATER
- PEANUT OIL FOR DEEP-FRYING

Method

MAKE THE FILLING

Marinate the pork and prawn meat in the cognac for 30 minutes. Mix the sherry, sugar, pepper, starch, soy sauce and chicken stock together. Heat a frying pan over medium–high heat, add the peanut oil and fry the pork and prawns quickly as you would a stir-fry. Toss in the ginger, garlic, spring onion and mushrooms and let them heat through for a minute. Reduce to medium heat and then pour the soy mixture into the pan and cook until the mixture thickens. Spread over a plate to cool.

MAKE THE DIPPING SAUCE

Heat the sugar, light and dark soy sauces and rice vinegar in a little pot over low heat to dissolve the sugar. Add the oils. Adjust as necessary to your taste, with more light soy for saltiness or more sugar to reduce the chilli heat.

MAKE THE DUMPLINGS

Sift the rice flour, wheat starch, brown sugar and salt into a bowl. Quickly combine the lard and boiling water with the dry ingredients, firstly with a wooden spoon to roughly combine, and then with your hands to knead to a smooth dough. Cover and leave to cool. Divide the dough into 20 pieces of about 25 g (1 oz) each. Keep them covered with plastic wrap while working so they don't dry out. Roll a piece into a ball, press down the centre to form an indentation and work outwards from there with both hands to form a 6 cm (2½ in) bowl-like shape. Place 1 heaped teaspoon of filling in the centre. Press the sides of the dough together and roll it back into a ball. Try not to get any filling trapped in the seams (or the dumpling might explode). Put on a tray and cover with plastic wrap while working on the other dumplings.

Heat oil in a deep-fryer to 180°C (350°F). Fry the dumplings in batches until light golden and crisp. Serve hot, with the dipping sauce in a bowl on the side.

PAINSTAKING PREPARATIONS

I was always a keen helper in my parents' kitchen, but, like any other child with a developing mind, I lacked patience when the preparations became repetitious and took more time than my attention span could tolerate. The ritual involved in the preparation of everyday ingredients or the making of more elaborate culinary treats did, and still does, fascinate me. So while, as a child, I might have given up on finishing the small tasks given to me, I still lingered to watch and ask questions.

A favourite great aunt who lived in Singapore occasionally came to stay. She had an aura of glamour created by the fact that she was 'not from here'. She liked to inveigle her way into the kitchen, much to my mother's trepidation (perhaps it felt something like an invasion of territory). On one occasion my great aunt wanted to show my mother her method for making corn soup; I presume they'd found fresh corn at the market during a morning excursion. I was fascinated by the elaborate set-up of newspapers spread over the dining table and the array of large vessels for holding what seemed a somewhat small amount of corn kernels. The reason, explained my great aunt, was that a great amount of care was required to get the kernels off the cob. She demonstrated with a fork, which she drew along the cob away from herself. The fork raked roughly over the corn with a rasping, scratching noise and she said that if you pulled the fork towards yourself, it was likely that a kernel would get stuck in your ear. Then, as now, I was incredulous. But my fear and wonderment were reinforced one hundredfold because, although I insisted (and probably with a certain degree of whining) that I should have a go, she steadfastly stated that it was much too dangerous an activity for a child.

My mother has always insisted on what I used to consider an unmitigated amount of fastidiousness in the preparation of her favourite vegetables. It was only later that I understood the need for attention to detail: sometimes the detail is there only for one's own satisfaction.

I wondered why I should be asked to be neat and orderly about picking vegetables. Why would my mother insist on methodically separating out leaf and stem into two different piles? According to my parents' wisdom, the best species of matrimony vine is that which grows in Sabah. It has the most succulent of stems, so much so that the leaf is often ignored. One of my mother's favourite dishes is a soup of pork slices and the leaf from the sweetleaf. In preparing the bunches bought at market, she would separate the leaves from the asparagus-thick stems

with a whisper-soft 'tock tock' sound, laying leaves in one pile and stems in another. I recall later at dinner, slurping the liquid of the soup, that my progress would be impeded by the slightly bitter leaves sticking to my spoon. And I also recall crunching on the stir-fry of the stems, thinking all the while that this should be as tough as the privet stems I liked to cut up and mangle in the garden.

We often had kang kong (water spinach or swamp cabbage) at home. The words of my mother still ring in my ear: 'No one really takes the effort to pick kang kong properly; there shouldn't be any hint of stringiness when you eat it.' It was a matter of pride that only the youngest of the stems and leaves should be picked for cooking. I recall again the 'tock tock', a little more insistently loud though. And, sometimes, I'd hear a 'shuck shuck' noise, when my mother found it necessary to bruise and crush the hollow lower stem of the kang kong to make up a reasonable bulk of vegetable. No matter how the kang kong was served in our household — stir-fried with a variety of seasonings from blachan and chilli to fermented tofu, or cooked simply with garlic — there was never any hint of stringiness about the just wilted vegetable.

Something I really disliked having anything to do with was the bean sprout. It was a most excruciating activity to pick the hair-like roots from these sprouts, and there was no time lag before I lost patience with those wet hair-like threads sticking to my hands and creating such an inextricable mess. At that stage, I wondered at the necessity for all the fuss and most of the time it was unfortunately left to my mother to complete the task. She would gently snap the upper part of the root to leave a pristine example with only sprout adhering to the white stem. 'Patient preparation preparatory to a tortuous process of cooking,' as my mother would probably have observed to me.

However, the bean sprouts were a main ingredient of one of my favourite dishes: mee siam. Once prepared, they were blanched in the meticulously hand-ground sauce of salted soy bean, chilli and blachan, in combination with carefully shelled prawns and meehoon or rice vermicelli, which seemed to stick together unpleasantly at a moment's notice if the cook wasn't careful. The cooking process for this dish wasn't a spectacle to watch, but a quiet contemplative mixing and adjusting of flavours while adding more and more ingredients. And, after a few hours of preparation, we would all sit down to enjoy it. There really is a conspicuous disparity in the longer time taken to prepare dishes and the much shorter time taken to consume them, isn't there?

Stir-fried Kang Kong with Blachan

A couple of bunches of kang kong, once the tenderest parts are picked, will be enough for a dish in a multiple plate meal. The blachan paste should be prepared prior to contemplating the stir-frying of the vegetable: pound 3 bird's eye chillies, a couple of garlic cloves, 1 chopped red Asian shallot, 1 tablespoon of roasted blachan and 1 tablespoon of sugar to a fine paste. Heat a couple of tablespoons of peanut oil in a wok over medium heat and cook the paste. Remove and set aside in a bowl. Now, with a cleaned hot wok and another tablespoon of peanut oil, fry the kang kong until just wilted, then add the paste and toss together well. Serve immediately.

Corn and Egg Flower Soup

This soup requires a good base, namely a flavoursome rich chicken stock. This is simply made by simmering chicken bones and carcasses with ginger and spring onions (scallions) for about 3 hours. Place 1 litre (34 fl oz) of the chicken stock in a pot and have it at a simmer. Meanwhile, set a wok at high heat, swirl 1 tablespoon of peanut oil into the wok, add a teacup and a half of fresh corn kernels and half a teacup of fresh crab meat. Stir briskly to combine and then add 1 tablespoon of light soy sauce, ½ teaspoon of salt and 1 tablespoon or so of water, at which point the wok will explode with noise. Toss the contents around and then turn them over into the pot of stock. In a soup bowl, beat an egg with a few drops of sesame oil. Pour the egg into the just simmering soup in a slow stream, while stirring the pot with a chopstick so the egg forms threads. Season with more salt and some freshly ground white pepper. Place in a central serving vessel so everyone can help themselves.

Lobster siam

The original is a favourite dish of mine, presented here in a new context with new ingredients, but I do insist that you take the time to trim up the bean sprouts in the proper way, just as my mother would do.

Lobster siam

SERVES 4

Ingredients

FOR THE SAUCE

1 TEASPOON BLACHAN (MALAYSIAN SHRIMP PASTE), (SEE GLOSSARY)
250 ML (8½ FL OZ) COCONUT CREAM
PEANUT OIL FOR FRYING
10 RED ASIAN SHALLOTS, PEELED AND CHOPPED, THEN GROUND TO A PASTE
10 DRIED CHILLIES, TRIMMED AND DESEEDED, GROUND TO A POWDER
2 TABLESPOONS BRANDY
3 TABLESPOONS SALTED SOY BEAN, PUREED
125 ML (4 FL OZ) COCONUT MILK
250 ML (8½ FL OZ) TAMARIND WATER (STRAINED THROUGH 1½ TEASPOONS TAMARIND PULP)
½ TEASPOON SALT
¼ TEASPOON SUGAR

FOR THE LOBSTER AND EGG

1–1.5 KG (2 LB 3 OZ–3 LB 5 OZ) LOBSTER
ABOUT 2 TABLESPOONS PEANUT OIL
100 G (3½ OZ) BEAN SPROUTS, TOPPED AND TAILED (PATIENCE REQUIRED)
1 BUNCH FLOWERING GARLIC CHIVES, TRIMMED OF THE TOUGH ROOTS AND CUT IN HALF
3 EGGS
2–3 LIMES, HALVED, TO SERVE

Method

MAKE THE SAUCE

Preheat the oven to 160°C (320°F). Slightly flatten the blachan on a small baking tray and toast in the oven for 10 minutes until fragrant and crumbly. Grind to a powder. Meanwhile pour the coconut cream into a pan over medium heat and slowly bring to the boil, stirring. Keep stirring until the cream separates into oil and brown residue (the flavour changes as a result and the residue forms part of the sauce eventually).

Adding more peanut oil to the separated coconut cream if required, cook the ground shallots, chillies and blachan for about 10 minutes (the raw smell should have mellowed and the mixture taste sweet). Add the brandy and cook until the raw alcohol smell has evaporated, then add the salted soy bean purée. Add the coconut milk and tamarind water. Season with the salt and sugar and check that it's savoury but not overly sweet. Strain.

MAKE THE LOBSTER AND EGG

Cut the tail off the lobster. Leaving the shell on, cut the tail in half lengthways, then each half into quarters to give 8 segments. Heat 1 teaspoon of the oil in a hot frying pan and fry the bean sprouts quickly until they start to wilt. Season with salt and set aside. Toast the flowering garlic chives in a hot dry pan until they become a more intense green, then add 1 teaspoon of oil and a little salt. Stir-fry until cooked and sweet tasting (this method takes away the grassy flavour of the chive).

Beat the eggs together with some salt and white pepper, then pass them through a sieve. Brush a large non-stick pan with oil and put over medium–high heat. Pour the eggs in, swirling the pan to give an even, thin layer of egg. As soon as it is set, turn out onto a tray to cool. Cut into strips about 1cm (½ in) thick. Heat a frying pan to hot, add 1 tablespoon of oil and place the lobster into the pan, shell side down. Fry until the shell starts to turn red then turn the pieces onto the other shelled side. Fry until that side starts to turn red. Turn the heat down to medium–low and add the rest of the sauce base. Cover and steam the lobster for a few minutes until the meat is cooked.

ASSEMBLE THE DISH

Use a platter, as this is a celebration dish that should be shared and passed around the table. Transfer the lobster to the platter, arrange the bean sprouts, garlic chives and egg around the lobster pieces and spoon the sauce over the top. Serve with lime halves to add more acid if you like.

Stems and leaves treated meticulously

There is enjoyment to be found in the single-minded attentiveness devoted to picking only such part of that stem or only this leaf. Knowing how time consuming and painstaking the preparation of such ingredients can be, it's hoped that the elements of this dish are enjoyed at leisure rather than gulped down in seconds.

Stems and leaves treated meticulously

SERVES 4

Ingredients

FOR THE SYRUP

200 G (7 OZ) SUGAR
100 ML (3½ FL OZ) STRAINED LEMON JUICE
2 TABLESPOONS LIGHT SOY SAUCE
1 TEASPOON SALT
3 DROPS SESAME OIL

FOR THE STEMS, LEAVES, PODS AND ROOTS

¼ BUNCH UNMARKED CHRYSANTHEMUM LEAVES
4 SPRING ONIONS (SCALLIONS)
6 LARGE PODS OF BROAD (FAVA) BEANS
4 RADISHES, SCRUBBED AND THINLY SLICED
12 LARGE SORREL LEAVES
PEANUT OIL FOR DEEP-FRYING

FOR THE TOMATO BROTH

1.5 KG (3 LB 5 OZ) RIPE RED TOMATOES
50 ML (1¾ FL OZ) BALSAMIC VINEGAR
2 TEASPOONS SALT
1 TEASPOON SUGAR
2 TABLESPOONS DRIED LONGAN
6 DRIED RED DATES
2 TABLESPOONS DRIED GOJI (WOLFBERRIES)
½ STAR ANISE
½ TEASPOON CORIANDER SEEDS
2 CLOVES
1 TEASPOON WHITE PEPPERCORNS
½ TEASPOON FENNEL SEEDS
1 PIECE LIQUORICE ROOT
1 PIECE ANGELICA ROOT
2 CM (¾ IN) PIECE OF YOUNG GINGER, BRUISED
1 TABLESPOON COGNAC

Method

MAKE THE SYRUP

Place the sugar in a large heavy-based saucepan over medium heat and cook until caramelised. Add 100 ml (3½ fl oz) water and keep the heat on low until the caramel dissolves. Add the lemon juice and let the mixture reduce until syrupy. Remove from the heat and add the soy sauce, salt and sesame oil. Cool.

PREPARE THE STEMS, LEAVES, PODS AND ROOTS

Thoroughly wash and dry the chrysanthemum leaves as they can be very sandy. Trim the spring onions by cutting off the green tops and separate the stem into individual layers. Blanch in boiling water for 10 seconds. Refresh under cold water then dry. Shell the broad beans then blanch them in the boiling water for 10 seconds. Drain and refresh under cold water so the skins can be peeled off easily when cool enough to handle.

Preheat the oven to 50°C (120°F) and line two baking trays with baking paper. Dip the chrysanthemum leaves, scallions, radish slices and sorrel in the syrup and lay on the prepared trays. (Keep the syrup as you'll need it later.) Put the trays in the oven to dry for 8 hours or overnight (ideally, this should be done in intense sunlight for a day). The leaves should be crunchy and the more hardy items such as radish should be chewy.

MAKE THE TOMATO BROTH

Preheat the oven to 200°C (400°F). Cut the tomatoes into quarters, place in a bowl and mix with the balsamic vinegar, salt and sugar. Marinate for 30 minutes. Spread them in a single layer on a large enough baking tray and roast for up to 1 hour, when the tomatoes should be caramelised and charred on the edges. Use any juices from the marinating to baste the tomatoes occasionally. Remove from the oven and put the tomatoes in a pan.

Meanwhile soak the longan, red dates and gojis in cold water for 30–40 minutes until softened. Drain and add to the tomatoes. Spread the star anise, coriander seeds, cloves, peppercorns and fennel seeds on a baking tray and roast in the oven until fragrant. Add to the tomatoes. Now add all the remaining ingredients to the tomato pot and cover with water. Simmer gently for 30 minutes, or until the taste and smell tells you that everything has been extracted into the infusion. Taste for salt. The broth should be slightly acid, quite sweet but also very savoury. Strain through a fine sieve.

ASSEMBLE THE DISH

Quickly deep-fry the broad beans in peanut oil and then dip them in the syrup. Arrange the vegetables in individual bowls and pour in hot broth to drown them like soup. Serve immediately.

A different type of tuile

The traditional kuih lapis is a cake that takes a lot of patience to make. Why not take a painstaking preparation to its logical end and transform the rich cake into a fanciful wafer-like biscuit?

Ingredients

MAKES 1 LARGE CAKE

- 250 G (9 OZ) UNSALTED BUTTER, AT ROOM TEMPERATURE
- 15 EGG YOLKS AND 8 EGG WHITES
- 225 G (8 OZ) ICING (CONFECTIONERS') SUGAR, SIFTED
- 1½ TEASPOONS MIXED SPICE
- 80 G (2¾ OZ) PLAIN (ALL-PURPOSE) FLOUR
- 1½ TABLESPOONS GROUND CASHEW OR ALMOND MEAL
- 1 TABLESPOON COGNAC
- ½ TEASPOON VANILLA EXTRACT

Method

MAKE THE CAKE

Preheat the oven to 180°C (350°F). Line a 20 cm (8 in) square cake tin with baking paper and butter the base and sides. Using electric beaters, cream the butter until light and white. In a separate bowl beat the egg yolks with the icing sugar for 10 minutes. Add the mixed spice. In another bowl whisk the egg whites until stiff peaks form. Fold the whites and flour alternately into the egg yolk mixture. Fold in the nut meal, then the creamed butter and finally the cognac and vanilla.

Preheat the baking tin by placing in the oven for a couple of minutes. Heat a grill or salamander at the same time. Spread 3 tablespoons of batter over the tin and bake for about 5 minutes until it's set. Remove the tin from the oven and transfer to the grill to colour the cake until it's quite dark. Remove from the grill and use a large buttered spoon to press out any air bubbles forming under the cake. Spread another 3 tablespoons of uncooked batter over the top of this cake to make another thin layer. Bake and grill in the same way and push out any air bubbles. Repeat until the batter is used up (a laborious process as there will be about 20 layers to complete).

When the mixture has been used up and the last layer cooked, cover the cake with foil and place in the oven for 5 minutes. Cool in the tin before turning out. It can be eaten now, or you can follow the next steps to participate in this fanciful vision for taking painstaking preparations to extremes.

Store the cake overnight. Preheat the oven to 150°C (300°F) and line a baking tray with baking paper. Cut the cake in half and slice thin pieces from the short width of cake to reveal its many horizontal layers. Working in batches, spread slices on the tray and bake in the oven for 10–15 minutes until the cake acquires a biscuity texture. Serve as you would biscuits.

DOWN the LONG PEBBLY PATHWAY

When I got home from school that afternoon, it was surprisingly quiet. My sister wasn't there to pester me as soon as I opened the door, nor was my mother in one of her usual haunts in the house. I ran from room to room with an increasing feeling of panic at the unrelenting quiet. I asked our maid where they all were. How frustrated did I feel when I was told that everyone had gone to the birthday party of a girl slightly older than me whom I idolised for her superior dress sense and overall sophistication (she favoured frilly, knee-length socks and peter pan-collared dresses tied with bows). I was distressed at missing out and was incredulous that my sister and mother would have gone without me. I expressed all this to our maid in fluent Malay while changing into my version of 'party best'. (Now, having no memory of the Malay language, I recall this conversation with some wonder.)

On that humid and hot afternoon I insisted that we walk quickly to my older friend's house. My little girl sandals made a soft sound against the bitumen of the road. The air was heavy, as it usually was during the tropical mid-afternoon, and it seemed that with this oppressiveness the environmental sounds were somewhat muted: birds and animals were not very active and the incessant noise of the cicadas dominated, although I felt there was a querulous tired edge to it. It seemed a long walk but eventually we approached her house. I recall what seemed truly large pebbles lining the driveway; our feet made a crisp crunching sound as we made our way across them and, not only were they noisy, but they impeded fast progress. The anticipation of what to expect on our arrival was killing me. The pilgrimage was finally over when we entered her house and I was overjoyed to discover I hadn't missed out on the birthday tea.

Amid the joy of noisy chatter and play with this older group of children, I found something new to worry about. The large table was laden with sweet and savoury treats and I discovered, with some satisfaction, a platter of my favourite party delicacies: deep-fried crab claws. However, I was prevented from wholeheartedly enjoying my too-infrequent indulgence in this dish by the number of beautifully decorated cakes also on the table. Moreover, in the corner was the birthday cake, with bright accessories and colourful writing to acknowledge the older girl's special day. At that point I suffered cake envy.

Stuffed Crab Claws

Acquire 8 fresh crab claws. Crack the shell, keeping the pincer part of the claw attached to the meat. Carefully remove the shell from the main part of the claw, keeping the meat intact. Set these aside in a cold place while preparing the 'stuffing'. With a cleaver, mince 300 g (10½ oz) of prawn meat and then, using the flat of the cleaver, work into a paste on the chopping board. Mix in ½ teaspoon of salt, ½ teaspoon of light soy sauce, a few drops of sesame oil and a few grinds of white pepper. Mould the prawn paste around the claw meat, being sure to leave the pincers exposed. Dust with a little flour, before deep-frying in hot oil for about 5 minutes until golden brown. Drain and serve immediately with some red vinegar.

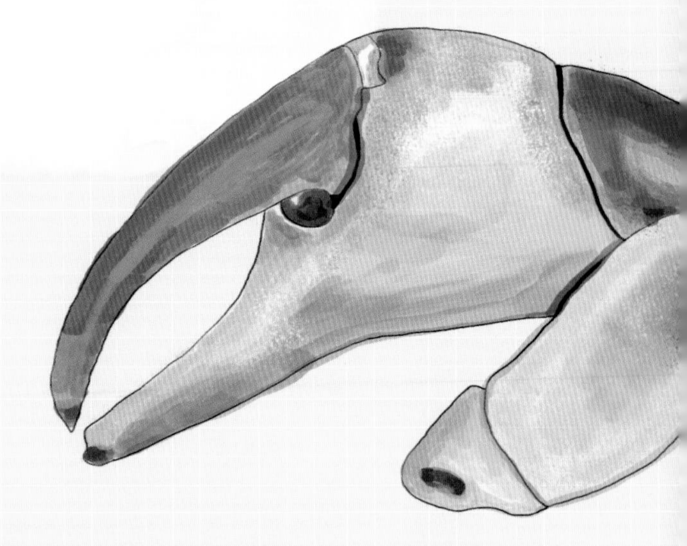

Ants' nest cake

This recipe celebrates plain-ness. The traditional recipe from Malaysia and Indonesia turns out an unassuming brown cake. However, the technique employed in beating air bubbles into the batter and allowing the baking soda to do its work creates holes in the structure of the cake. So, the plain-looking cake actually has a very unusual texture. This is an aesthetic that characterises the way I like to work.

Ants' nest cake

SERVES 4

Ingredients

FOR THE CAKE

250 G (9 OZ) SUGAR
100 G (3½ OZ) UNSALTED BUTTER
250 G (9 OZ) PLAIN (ALL-PURPOSE) FLOUR
6 LARGE EGGS
180 G (6½ OZ) CONDENSED MILK
1½ TEASPOONS BICARBONATE OF SODA (BAKING SODA)

FOR THE HONEY-SPICED FIGS

4 PURPLE FIGS
300 ML (10 FL OZ) PORT
1 TABLESPOON HONEY
2 CM (¾ IN) CASSIA BARK
1 STAR ANISE
½ VANILLA BEAN, SPLIT, SEEDS SCRAPED

FOR THE CUMIN CREAM

1 TABLESPOON CUMIN SEEDS
4 EGG YOLKS
100 G (3½ OZ) SUGAR
250 ML (8½ FL OZ) MILK
250 ML (8½ FL OZ) THICK (DOUBLE/HEAVY) CREAM

Method

MAKE THE CAKE

Put the sugar in a wide heavy-based saucepan over low heat. Heat until it melts and then caramelises to golden brown. Add 250 ml (8½ fl oz) water a little at a time to dissolve the caramel (it will help if you turn up the heat, but avoid disturbing the sugar by stirring or it will crystallise and become useless). When you have a smooth, thin caramel syrup, add the butter to stabilise the mixture. Cool for 5 minutes.

Sift together the flour and a pinch of salt. Gradually whisk the caramel into the flour with an electric mixer. Give the batter a good whisk for a couple of minutes after adding the caramel to create more structure in the cake. Let it rest for 10–15 minutes. Beat the eggs and condensed milk together until light, thick and foamy. Beat the egg mixture into the caramel batter with the baking soda.

Line a 20 cm (8 in) square cake tin with baking paper and butter the baking paper. Strain the cake batter into the tin. Leave in a cold oven for 30 minutes to allow the baking soda to start acting. Turn the oven to 150°C (300°F) and bake the cake for 1 hour until a metal skewer inserted into the middle of the cake comes out clean and the cake is firm to the touch. Cool before turning out.

POACH THE FIGS

Prick the figs all over with a skewer so that they are better able to absorb flavours. Combine the port, honey, cassia, star anise and vanilla pod with its seeds in a saucepan with 100 ml (3½ fl oz) water. Bring to simmering point. Add the figs and bring back to a simmer, then remove the pan from the heat. Leave the figs for 1 hour to steep; they should be soft but not mushy. Remove the figs from the syrup and reduce the syrup by half.

MAKE THE CUMIN CREAM

Preheat the oven to 160°C (320°F). Toast the cumin seeds in the oven for 10 minutes. Beat the egg yolks with half the sugar until pale and foamy. Transfer the cumin seeds to a saucepan and add the milk and remaining sugar. Bring to simmering point, then whisk the hot milk into the egg yolks. Pour the mixture back into the saucepan and return to low heat. Cook, stirring, until thickened enough to coat the back of a spoon. Strain into a bowl set over iced water. When cold, mix the cream through.

ASSEMBLE THE DISH

Serve a thin slice of cake for each person. Slice each fig from top to bottom and arrange by the cake. Drizzle a few small spoonfuls of cumin cream beside the cake and fig.

An unassuming dish of scallops

This recipe continues an exploration of the unassuming nature of my aesthetic as a cook. Here, I try to harvest the briny taste of the sea and contrast that with the sweetness of scallops. The focus is on the taste, rather than trying to create a spectacle on the plate. The look is minimalistic, as I want the ingredients to speak for themselves as unpretentiously as possible.

An unassuming dish of scallops

SERVES 4

Ingredients

FOR THE BRINY CONCOCTION

1 TEASPOON GRAPESEED OIL
300 G (10½ OZ) SMALL CLAMS (VONGOLE TYPE ARE MORE FLAVOURSOME)
50 ML (1¾ FL OZ) DRY WHITE WINE
100 G (3½ OZ) SUMMER PURSLANE LEAVES (SEE GLOSSARY), PLUS EXTRA TO SERVE
2 G (1/16 OZ) AGAR-AGAR POWDER

FOR THE WILTED WATERCRESS

1 TABLESPOON UNSALTED BUTTER
1 GARLIC CLOVE, UNPEELED, BRUISED
150 G (5½ OZ) LARGE SPRIGS OF WATERCRESS
A FEW CHIVES

FOR THE SCALLOPS

12 LARGE SCALLOPS
GRAPESEED OIL FOR BRUSHING

Method

MAKE THE BRINY CONCOCTION

Heat the oil in a saucepan over high heat and throw in the clams with the white wine. Cook, covered, until the shells open. Strain the juice through a fine sieve into a jug. You can use the clams for another dish. Purée the purslane, strain the juice through muslin into a jug, combine with the clam juice and measure the amount of liquid: you need 200 ml (7 fl oz) of liquid to be set by 2 g of agar-agar powder. Pour half the liquid into a little saucepan and dissolve the agar-agar in it. Bring to the boil and then simmer for 1 minute. Strain and combine with the rest of the liquid. Cool, then put in the refrigerator to set. When ready to use, blend or whisk until creamy like mayonnaise. Add salt to taste.

WILT THE WATERCRESS

Put the butter and garlic in a saucepan over medium heat and heat until the butter melts and separates and becomes nutty in flavour. Add the watercress and chives to the pan and leave them in long enough to wilt but not brown. The watercress takes on an aromatic muddy smell that's quite pleasant. Season to taste with salt and white pepper and set aside, keeping the leaves warm.

COOK THE SCALLOPS

Prepare these at the last moment. Preheat the oven to 150°C (300°F). Slice horizontally through the middle of 4 scallops. Season with some salt and white pepper, place on a plate and put in the oven for a few minutes to heat through. Brush a non-stick frying pan with oil and heat up. Sear the remaining 8 scallops in the pan for 1 minute on each side. Season with salt and white pepper.

ASSEMBLE THE DISH

Spoon the wilted watercress mixture in long strands on each plate. Scatter with pieces of baked scallop and place a spoonful of the briny concoction on each plate. Divide the seared scallops among the plates. Garnish with fresh purslane if you like and serve at once.

UCH

MORTAR & PESTLE COOKING

My mother was concentrating hard as she stood at the kitchen bench. She was grinding a fragrant paste with the mortar and pestle. I wondered if she was trying to ignore my question, but I repeated it anyway: how would she know when the paste was ground up enough? At last, with a sigh, she answered: 'You shouldn't be able to taste any fibre in the sauce. That's the thing I take pride in.' This left me wondering how that could be achieved. Yet again, I'd insisted on giving a helping hand, but found this hard to follow through with my little girl's fingers and lack of endurance and coordination. My mother had decided to make a laksa lemak that day. The ingredients for the spice paste, or rempah, were before us. There were the soft, manageably sized ingredients: roasted blachan, fresh and dried chillies, peppercorns. There were the larger ingredients such as shallots and garlic. And then there were the stubborn, hard ingredients which I'd grown to dislike because there was no way of taming them into becoming fibre-less: galangal, lemongrass and turmeric.

My mother had to be doubly patient while I was in the kitchen. She had to slowly render these ingredients to a paste in a painstaking way, all the while fielding my questions and supervising my attempts to help.

Mother: Would you just keep the ingredients separate while I peel them? No, I can't let you use the knife yet, just watch. You can't simply push the galangal around in the mortar, it doesn't do anything. Be careful of your fingers. I need to chop everything up so it's easier to grind down. Yes, the chopped galangal first. Don't add the lemongrass yet, let me pound the galangal a bit more to a paste first. So, do you understand now: hard ingredients, then soft ingredients? I know the mortar is a small one; I'll just take out some of the paste so it doesn't spill over the side. That's the solution isn't it? Well, it's the only mortar we have here, so we just have to deal with it ...

The time and patience required to make paste in such a way with the mortar and pestle is perhaps not practicable for the preparation of an everyday meal, but is more an expression of interest in cooking as a hobby. My mother's words have made me question the efficacy of making pastes in blenders and food processors. These instruments chop ingredients to the finest consistency and produce a different result from a mortar and pestle, which bruises and softens ingredients to a paste. Today, when I wish to make a spice paste (or any purée or paste which follows my mother's precept), I choose the option that requires more patience, physical strength and stamina.

Laksa Lemak

To make the laksa broth, first make the spice paste by pounding together, as finely as you can, 10 red Asian shallots, 1 stem of lemongrass, half a finger of galangal and a third of a finger of turmeric, 1 teaspoon of powdered coriander seed, 8 dried chillies and 1 tablespoon of toasted blachan. Fry the spice paste in some peanut oil until fragrant and separated. Add 12 shelled prawns and 200 g (7 oz) of trimmed bean sprouts and stir around until the prawns are cooked. Remove the prawns and bean sprouts and add a cupful of fresh coconut milk. Bring to a gentle simmer and season with salt, sugar and lime juice. Spoon the broth over rice vermicelli (softened in hot water) and shredded poached chicken, then add the prawns and bean sprouts. Garnish with laksa leaf and serve with limes, should you wish for more acid.

The softest, smoothest spice paste

This recipe is partly a response to the challenge of making the smoothest spice paste possible. And, if the texture of the paste is softened, I asked myself, should the flavour also be correspondingly softened and more subtle?

The softest, smoothest spice paste

SERVES 4

Ingredients

FOR THE PEANUT PASTE

- 3 CM (1¼ IN) PIECE OF GINGER, SLICED
- 6 RED ASIAN SHALLOTS, CHOPPED
- 1 GARLIC CLOVE, CHOPPED
- 2 DRIED RED CHILLIES, DESEEDED, SOFTENED IN HOT WATER THEN CHOPPED
- 2 TABLESPOONS PEANUT OIL
- 1 TABLESPOON TOMATO PASTE
- 120 ML (4 FL OZ) COCONUT MILK
- 100 G (3½ OZ) PUREED PEANUTS (SEE BOX BELOW)
- 1 TEASPOON SUGAR
- 1 TEASPOON SALT
- LEMON JUICE TO TASTE

FOR THE ACCOMPANIMENTS

- 1 BROWN ONION
- 50 ML (1¾ FL OZ) PEANUT OIL, PLUS EXTRA FOR BRUSHING
- 4 GREEN CHILLIES
- 100 G (3½ OZ) CHINESE CABBAGE STEM, CUT INTO MATCHSTICKS
- 4 EGGS AT ROOM TEMPERATURE

Method

MAKE THE PEANUT PASTE

Pound the ginger, shallots, garlic and red chillies to as fine a paste as possible with a mortar and pestle. Heat the oil in a saucepan over medium heat and add the paste. Cook until the oil separates from the main mass. Remove from the heat and mix in the tomato paste. Return to the heat and cook until the mixture starts to darken, making sure the paste doesn't burn. Add the coconut milk and simmer for 5 minutes. Cool and pass through a fine sieve. Stir in the puréed peanuts, add the sugar and salt and season to taste with lemon juice. If the mixture is too thin, gently simmer in a saucepan until it holds a line when a spoon is run through the middle of the mixture. Keep warm and covered.

PREPARE THE ACCOMPANIMENTS

Peel the onion, cut in half and slice thinly and evenly. Heat a pan over medium–low heat, add the oil and slowly sweat the onion until caramelised. Drain off the oil and season the onion with a little salt. Keep warm. Brush the green chillies with a little oil, season with salt and grill until slightly scorched all over. Heat a frying pan over medium heat and brush with a little oil. Add the cabbage matchsticks and fry gently with some salt until slightly softened but still retaining a bite. Remove from the pan and keep warm. Bring a saucepan of water to a rolling boil. Add the eggs and cook for 5 minutes. Drain and refresh under cold water. Peel the eggs and then place in water at 65°C (150°F) until ready to use.

ASSEMBLE THE DISH

Place a spoonful of the warm peanut paste in each serving bowl. Arrange the onion, chillies and cabbage around the paste and place an egg amongst the arrangement.

TO PUREE PEANUTS

Lightly roast 120 g (4½ oz) peanuts to refresh them. Make a poaching liquid with 500 ml (17 fl oz) water, some ginger peelings, a red Asian shallot split in half and a clove of garlic. Bring to the boil and then simmer for about 15 minutes until the shallot smells mellow and cooked. Add the peanuts and simmer for about 1 hour until softened, topping up with water if necessary. Drain and set aside liquid. Fish out the peanuts, puree with a blender until a fine paste, adding the poaching liquid to help make a smooth paste if needed.

A gritty, fibrous shrimp paste

Taking things to the other extreme, this recipe uses the cutting action of a food processor to create a rough paste from the most fibrous of the traditional spice paste ingredients. The paste is then cooked in such a way that it's intentionally crunchy and dry and gritty.

Ingredients

MAKES ENOUGH CONDIMENT FOR 10 SERVINGS

- 150 G (5½ OZ) DRIED SHRIMP, SOAKED IN WATER FOR 1 HOUR, DRAINED
- 100 G (3½ OZ) RED ASIAN SHALLOTS, CHOPPED
- 75 G (2¾ OZ) LARGE RED CHILLIES, DESEEDED AND CHOPPED
- 2 GARLIC CLOVES, CHOPPED
- 2 CM (¾ IN) PIECE OF GALANGAL, SLICED
- 2 LEMONGRASS STEMS, SLICED
- 75 ML (2½ FL OZ) PEANUT OIL
- ¼ MATURE COCONUT, FLESH COARSELY GRATED
- ½ TEASPOON CORIANDER SEEDS, TOASTED AND GROUND
- 5 KAFFIR LIME LEAVES, FINELY SLICED
- LIME JUICE TO TASTE
- SUGAR TO TASTE
- PRAWNS (SHRIMP) TO SERVE, IF YOU LIKE

Method

Shred the shrimp in a food processor and then set aside. Make the spice paste by processing the shallots, chillies, garlic, galangal, lemongrass and oil in the food processor until blended to a paste. In a dry frying pan sauté the paste over medium heat until aromatic. Add the coconut, coriander seeds and shredded shrimp and keep frying over low heat until the mixture is dry and crumbly. Ensure that all moisture has evaporated: the aim is to make the mixture crispy. Sprinkle in the lime leaves. Season to taste with lime juice, sugar, salt and white pepper. The paste can be kept in a sterilised jar for a couple of weeks.

I'd suggest serving this with prawns. Peel large prawns, keeping the heads and tails intact. Take out the intestinal tracts with a toothpick. Brush with coconut or peanut oil and grill over very high heat. The aim is to get some crunchy parts to the prawn meat. Sprinkle generously with the shrimp spice paste and serve with additional lime juice.

Reworking laksa lemak into a spiced bouillon

This came about from contemplating the gritty solids that gather at the bottom of a bowl of traditional laksa when the soup has been almost completely drunk. It led to this alternative of a light, clear and flavoursome bouillon.

Reworking laksa lemak into a spiced bouillon

SERVES 4

Ingredients

FOR THE SPICED BOUILLON

1 LITRE (34 FL OZ) LIGHT CHICKEN STOCK
SUGAR TO TASTE
10 FRENCH SHALLOTS, CHOPPED
1 LEMONGRASS STEM, TRIMMED OF TOUGH OUTER LEAVES, BRUISED AND SLICED
3 CM (1¼ IN) PIECE OF GALANGAL, BRUISED AND SLICED
2 CM (¾ IN) PIECE OF FRESH TURMERIC, BRUISED AND SLICED
1 TABLESPOON CORIANDER SEEDS, ROASTED AND GROUND
8 DRIED CHILLIES, DESEEDED
6 MEDIUM PRAWNS (SHRIMP), UNSHELLED
LIME JUICE TO TASTE

FOR THE PRAWN RELISH

3 TABLESPOONS VEGETABLE OIL
FISH SAUCE TO TASTE
LIME JUICE TO TASTE

FOR THE ACCOMPANIMENTS

OIL FOR DEEP-FRYING
25 G (1 OZ) DRIED FISH MAW (SEE GLOSSARY)
100 G (3½ OZ) SPANNER CRAB MEAT
10 G (¼ OZ) LAKSA (VIETNAMESE MINT) LEAVES
1 LEBANESE (SHORT) CUCUMBER, PEELED AND SLICED

Method

MAKE THE SPICED BOUILLON

Bring the chicken stock to the boil. Season with salt and sugar. Add the shallots, lemongrass, galangal, turmeric, coriander seeds and dried chillies and simmer for 10 minutes. Peel the prawns, reserving all the shells. Drop the prawns into the stock and poach for 5 minutes, then remove and set aside. Add the shells and simmer for another 5 minutes. Remvoe from the heat, cover and leave to infuse for 30 minutes. Strain and set aside. When ready to use, season with lime juice and additional salt and sugar if you like.

MAKE THE PRAWN RELISH

Devein the poached prawns and shred the meat as finely as possible. Heat the oil in a frying pan and add the prawn meat and cook for around 30 minutes. While it is frying, use the wooden spoon to press the meat against the side of the pan to shred it to floss. Add a little water if the mixture starts to stick. It's ready when the meat is evenly shredded into a dried floss (although the floss should not be overly dry). Season with fish sauce, salt and lime juice.

ASSEMBLE THE DISH

Heat the oil to 180°C (350°F) and deep-fry the fish maw until puffed up and golden. Rinse in cold water. Pour 100 ml (3½ fl oz) of the spiced bouillon and 250 ml (8½ fl oz) of water into a pan, add the maw and simmer for 30 minutes until very soft. Take out of the stock and cut into small chunks. Use the hot chicken stock to steep the crab meat until just cooked. Place a laksa leaf, piece of cucumber, some fish maw and crab meat into each person's bowl and pour the broth over until the objects are semi-submerged. Sprinkle with prawn relish.

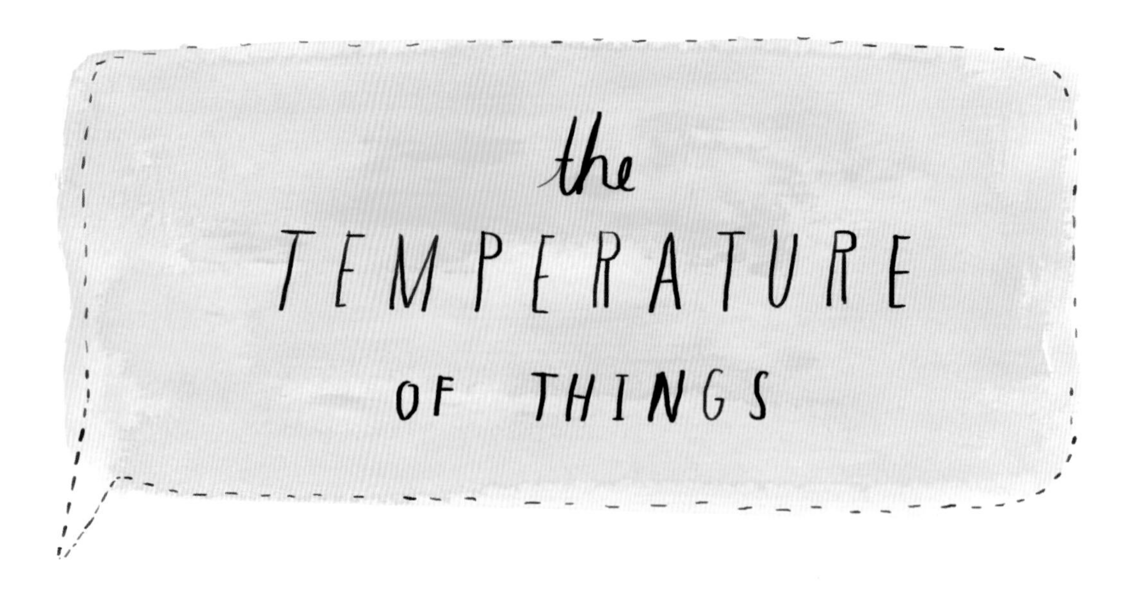

Here's my question: I wonder if you can recall the same confusion I felt, growing up, when trying to differentiate between temperature and taste? (I may simply be dragging others into my own confusion by revisiting it here, but I'd like to think some inspiration can come from examining old memories, which, after all, is why I'm writing this book.)

The confusion became apparent once I'd grown accustomed to spicy heat and was no longer so tentative about trying the fieriest dishes that could be conjured up with peppercorns and chillies. It was obviously very hot and humid where we lived and that's an immutable environmental issue (to be fixed only by sitting in a room blasted with icy air-conditioning). I remember sitting down with my family to a new version of a pork dish that my mother had come up with: hock braised with chilli, black beans and pineapple. There was a delicious new intensity to this dish that I wasn't used to. It was much sourer, more spicy and the dish was served scalding hot. I blew on a piece of pineapple to cool it, as advised by my parents. The explosion of heat in my mouth made me break out in a sweat, and then keep sweating profusely. It was a wonder that a piece of pineapple could retain so much heat and absorb so much chilli spiciness. I can now describe that combination of temperature and spicy heat as making me feel as though I were in a furnace. However, at that time, confusion and puzzlement led to distrust of foodstuffs (and parents).

It was confusing at other times also. Because of the constant tropical heat I had rarely shivered with cold. Even when I got out of swimming pools, or the sea, the water was warm and the ambient temperature balmy enough that any breeze was soothing rather than cooling. I knew of shivering with cold through stories of colder lands and from what I could see on television or films. So, how was it that I only had to look at the plate of mango pickles to shiver? And shivered again when I tasted them? Those pickles weren't chilled; they were room temperature, but I felt as if I were experiencing cold.

It might be annoying for you, but I'm not seeking to explain the physiological factors behind the reactions above. I'm trying to draw a conclusion as to how I can design dishes that make people physically react; not simply sit there, chewing and swallowing and perhaps being interested or amazed by the taste sensation. Cooking creates an ephemeral experience and there is only a very limited opportunity to elicit a reaction from the eater so that the dish becomes part of their memory (if that's to be considered the point of the experience). Another way to capture the imagination of the eater is to proceed beyond the bounds of the sense of taste and draw responses from one of the other senses. A non-conventional combination of taste and temperature is initially weird and will make the eater think and wonder. A sense of ease and well-being can come from something sweet and comfortingly warm. Those are the issues I'm trying to explore in revisiting my memories of confusion.

Green Mango Pickles

Peel 500 g (1 lb) green mangoes (being careful if your skin is sensitive to sap) and cut into small rectangles. Place in a bowl and rub 200 g (7 oz) crystallised sugar and 2 teaspoons salt through the mango. Cover the bowl and refrigerate overnight. Stir and store in a sterilised container. These are ready to eat on the second day but will keep for 2–4 weeks. Eat as a snack or use in recipes.

Hot and Sour Pork Hock

The pork hock is kept whole for this recipe. First blanch it in boiling water for about 30 minutes for a clearer sauce, rinse under cold water and pat dry. Prepare a pineapple by taking off the spiky skin, quartering it and then taking the core from each quarter. Cut the pineapple flesh into smaller pieces at angles across the grain (each piece will now be much tenderer to the bite as a result). Stir-fry 4 thick pieces of peeled ginger with 1 tablespoon of unrinsed fermented black beans and 4 deseeded bird's eye chillies until fragrant. Add the pork hock, pineapple pieces, a few tablespoons of dark soy sauce and salt and sugar to taste. Make sure the pork hock is covered with water, bring to the boil and cook gently for about 40 minutes until the hock is spoon soft. It's essential to keep the pork skin under the protection of liquid so it won't dry out and become tough. It also ensures you have plenty of sauce to serve with rice.

Green mango pickles with other things that make me shiver

I was speculating what might be a good foil if these disparate things were brought together in one place. I decided it would have to be something very salty and something sweet-fleshed.

Make a dressing by frying 4 thin slices of pancetta in 1 tablespoon extra virgin olive oil until crisp. Drain the pancetta, keeping the oil. Scrunch up the pancetta and mix with ¼ teaspoon of finely chopped salted preserved plum, 1 teaspoon of ground black pepper and the oil. If it needs more acidity, mix in a little liquid from your mango pickles.

Dredge 3 scaled, cleaned, whole sand whiting in rice flour seasoned with salt and pepper. Shallow-fry for 4 minutes on each side until golden, drain on paper, then lift the meat off the fish. Blanch a large handful of spinach leaves in salted boiling water until just wilted but still crunchy, then refresh in iced water and wring dry. Deep-fry 8 medium-sized betel leaves. Cut 4 pieces of pickled mango into long thin slices. Mix the spinach leaves and mango with a little dressing. Arrange on plates with the betel leaves and fish and dress with the rest of the dressing.

Numbing ox tongue

This is intended as a non-scientific illustration of how temperature might affect perception of spicy heat. My feeling is that, when tasted cold, spicy heat seems to numb rather than burn the tongue.

TO CANDY WALNUTS

To candy walnuts, drop 100 g (3½ oz) of walnut halves into boiling water. Wait for the water to come back to the boil, then scoop out the walnuts, drain and place in a large bowl. Scatter 30 g (1 oz) of icing (confectioner's) sugar over the walnuts and toss them around to coat well. Heat oil in a deep-fryer to 180°C (350°F) and carefully deep-fry the walnuts in batches until light golden. Spread over generously oiled foil, separated so they don't clump together. Quickly make a spice mix from 1 teaspoon each of freshly ground sichuan pepper, black pepper and salt and sprinkle over the walnuts. This will make more candied walnuts than you'll need for the recipe but they can be eaten as a snack.

Ingredients

SERVES 4

FOR THE OX TONGUE

- 4 CM (1½ IN) PIECE OF GINGER, CRUSHED WITH THE SIDE OF A KNIFE
- 6 GARLIC CLOVES, CRUSHED
- 4 SPRING ONIONS (SCALLIONS), BRUISED
- 3 FRENCH SHALLOTS, QUARTERED
- 5 DRIED SHIITAKE MUSHROOMS, SOAKED IN WATER FOR 2 HOURS
- 2 PIECES ANGELICA ROOT, SLICED
- 5 CM (2 IN) PIECE OF CASSIA BARK
- ½ TEASPOON FIVE SPICE POWDER
- ½ TEASPOON CLOVES
- 1 TABLESPOON CORIANDER SEEDS
- 1 TEASPOON FENNEL SEEDS
- 4 GREEN CARDAMOM PODS
- 1 TEASPOON DILL SEEDS
- 1 TEASPOON BLACK PEPPERCORNS
- DRIED PEEL FROM ½ MANDARIN
- 150 G (5½ OZ) ROCK SUGAR
- 60 ML (2 FL OZ) DARK SOY SAUCE
- 1 OX TONGUE, USUALLY 1.5–2 KG (ABOUT 4 LB)

FOR THE DRESSING

- 30 G (1 OZ) CANDIED WALNUTS (SEE BOX OPPOSITE), CHOPPED OR CRUSHED ROUGHLY
- 1 CELERY STALK, FINELY DICED
- 50 G (1¾ OZ) PICKLED MUSTARD GREENS OR TIANJIN PRESERVED VEGETABLE
- 50 ML (1¾ FL OZ) CHILLI OIL (SEE PAGE 280), USE SOME OF THE CHILLI SEDIMENT IF DESIRED
- LEMON JUICE OR RICE VINEGAR TO TASTE

- 200 G (7 OZ) SILKEN TOFU, DRAINED AND CUT INTO THIN SLICES, TO SERVE

Method

POACH THE OX TONGUE

Into a large pot put all the ingredients except the rock sugar, soy sauce and tongue. Cover with cold water and bring to the boil. Simmer for 30 minutes until the aromats are cooked. Meanwhile, dissolve the rock sugar in some of the hot liquid. Add the soy sauce, which will increase the colour of the stock. Set aside.

Preheat the oven to 160°C (320°F). Rinse the tongue under cold running water. Place in a large pan and cover with cold water. Bring to the boil, skimming off the scum which floats to the surface. Turn down to simmering point. Simmer for 30 minutes or until scum no longer rises to the surface. Place the poaching liquid and the sugar and soy sauce mixture in a flameproof casserole. Add a good amount of salt so there's an exchange of savouriness between the meat and the stock. Add the tongue and bring to a simmer. Semi-cover and transfer to the oven for about 3 hours until the tongue is tender but not falling apart. Take from the oven and cool until the tongue is cold enough to handle. Strain the poaching liquid and put aside. Peel the skin from the tongue and keep it in the poaching liquid until cooled and ready for use.

MAKE THE DRESSING

Mix the walnuts, celery and mustard greens together. Toss with the chilli oil and add some lemon juice or rice vinegar, if you like. If a looser dressing is desired, add some of the ox tongue poaching stock. Keep in the refrigerator until required.

ASSEMBLE THE DISH

Thinly slice 300 g (10½ oz) of the cold ox tongue. Arrange on a serving plate with the tofu and spoon the dressing on top.

Ox tongue with five tastes

This is a study in taste and temperature. The aim is to try the ox tongue slices cold and hot, adding one or more elements of the seasoning ingredients that represent the five basic tastes to create something you can enjoy eating. (And, if not, then to learn about tempering taste by proportions.)

Ox tongue with five tastes

SERVES 4

Ingredients

FOR THE SOUR TASTE	JUICE AND ZEST OF 3 LEMONS 70 G (2½ OZ) SALT
FOR THE BITTER TASTE	50 G (1¾ OZ) GREEN BITTER MELON, NO PITH 20 G (¾ OZ) CELERY
FOR THE SALTY TASTE	50 G (1¾ OZ) TOASTED CASHEW NUTS 10 G (¼ OZ) SALT 10 G (¼ OZ) SALT FLAKES
FOR THE HOT TASTE	50 G (1¾ OZ) FRESH GREEN PEPPERCORNS 10 G (¼ OZ) BIRD'S EYE CHILLIES, DESEEDED AND CHOPPED 10 G (¼ OZ) UNRIPE BIRD'S EYE CHILLIES (SCUD CHILLIES), DESEEDED AND CHOPPED 1 TABLESPOON PEANUT OIL
FOR THE SWEET TASTE	50 G (1¾ OZ) MERINGUE (SEE BOX OPPOSITE) 2 TEASPOONS CASTER (SUPERFINE) SUGAR
FOR THE HOT OIL	1 LITRE (34 FL OZ) VEGETABLE OIL 2 CM (¾ IN) PIECE OF GINGER, SMASHED 3 STEMS OF GREEN GARLIC, CRUSHED 3 SPRING ONIONS (SCALLIONS), BRUISED 1 TEASPOON BLACK PEPPERCORNS
	400 G (14 OZ) POACHED OX TONGUE (SEE PAGE 227), THINLY SLICED

Method

MAKE THE SOUR TASTE

Blanch the zest in boiling water and refresh under cold running water. Repeat this twice more to get rid of the bitter tasting oil. Place the lemon juice in a pan and heat to just below simmering point. Dissolve the salt in the juice. Mix in the drained, dried zest. Pour the near-saturated solution onto a non-reactive baking tray and place in a barely warm oven for about 6 hours to evaporate the solution. Grind the lemon salt to a fine powder.

MAKE THE BITTER TASTE

Dice the bitter melon, finely chop the celery and toss together. Dry-fry in a small pan until bright green.

MAKE THE SALTY TASTE

Grate the cashew nuts with a fine microplane. Grind the salt to a powder. Mix the two together.

MAKE THE HOT TASTE

Grind the peppercorns with a mortar and pestle. Add the two lots of chillies separately, pounding each one in thoroughly before adding the next. When you have a fine paste, mix with the oil.

MAKE THE SWEET TASTE

Grind the meringue to a powder. Grind the sugar to a powder. Mix the two together.

PREPARE THE OIL

Pour the oil into a saucepan and heat to 70°C (160°F). Throw in the aromats and keep at 70°C (160°F) to infuse for 30 minutes. Strain the oil.

ASSEMBLE THE DISH

At the table, serve the oil at 70°C (160°F); sitting it on a portable burner such as a fondue burner is ideal. To start, taste a slice of cold tongue so you are familiar with its flavours. Dip a slice into the oil to heat. Season it with one or more of the five tastes and try it. Proceed in this way, trying different tastes or combinations until you discover what you like. When you tire of this exercise just go ahead and enjoy the flavours rather than thinking too much about it.

TO MAKE MERINGUE

Beat 6 egg whites until soft peaks form. Gradually beat in 350 g (12½ oz) of caster (superfine) sugar and continue beating until stiff peaks form. Fold in 100 g (3½ oz) of walnut meal. Pipe 1.5 cm (½ in) discs onto a baking tray lined with baking paper. Bake at 110°C (220°F) for 30 minutes, then at 100°C (210°F) for about 1 hour.

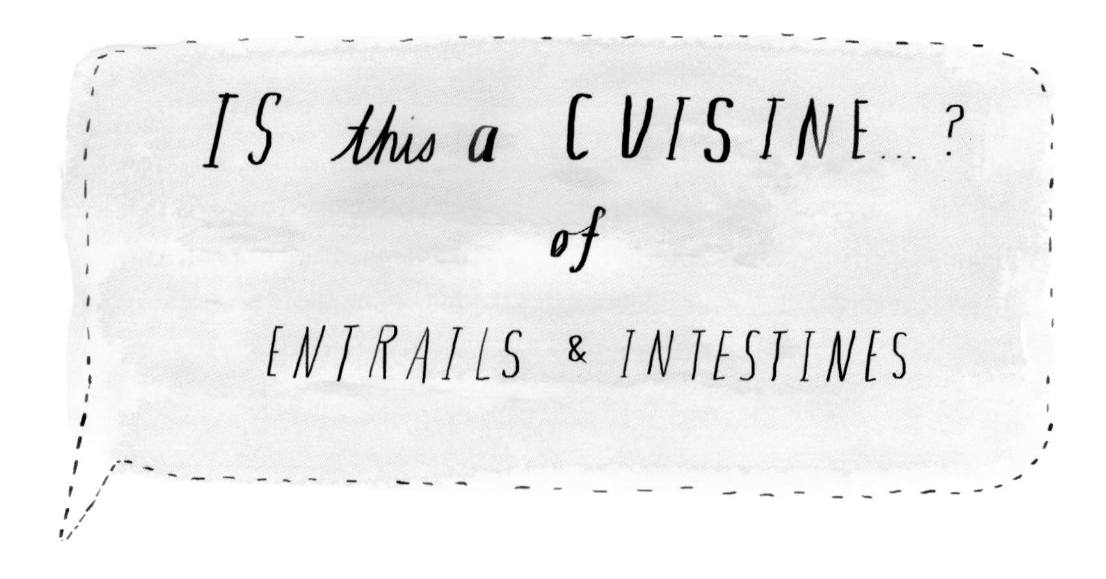

The Chinese sand pots at home held such a lot of promise. Those pots with their coarsely textured sloping sides that graduated from a narrow base and were covered tightly with a (probably mismatched) lid from the family's motley collection of kitchenware ... There was no indication of what they might hold. The sides were sometimes stained with the overflow of a sauce that had been cooked within, lending mystique and the threat of volcanic heat. However, for all the show of promise as it sat on the stove or at the table, it was always ill-advised to touch one of these pots, for the promise it did keep was that it radiated as well as retained heat.

I had an obsession with one particular recipe. This was a dish that, in my childhood experience, could be presented on a large platter, but was more often served in one of my mother's sand pots. It has a place in Chinese cuisine as signifying good luck, but was the cause of slight alarm on my part whenever the lid was lifted. The dish was a slithery braise of dried oyster and black moss, the rich darkness, the intense smell and the highly savoury taste of which attracted the admiration of all the adults. The dismay I felt was caused by imagining the feel of the dish: smooth, slippery pieces of unidentifiable animal parts (given the intense shellfish-iness of the smell, I concluded this to be some sort of sea-based animal) and fine tresses of black moss fungus snagged through the darkly thick mixture. There was always something threatening in its imagined texture; the eating, too, seemed to come with a veiled threat and I couldn't guess whether I might love or hate what was about to be offered. (Unidentified animal parts being something that yielded a response of visceral disgust and fear at that time.)

When I dared taste this dish, the oysters had a combination of chewiness and softness which didn't do anything to relieve my apprehension about dismembered body parts. And the black moss seemed to be simply another aspect supporting my conclusions about its gruesome composition. But, for all the disgust I felt, the taste was intensely fulfilling and tantalising. It felt as if I were participating in something dangerous and mysterious.

The texture of offal is fascinating, but to have any appreciation of its variety and breadth and versatility as a child I had to navigate my way out of my prejudices and come to a place where I could tolerate understanding where different organs came from. I had to relieve myself of fear in the association of bloodied parts and innards with something to eat.

So, while I later saw that there was a similar thick darkness in the glaze for duck and chicken livers, the threat was gone once I knew exactly what it was all about. I still saw a mass of oddly shaped items on a plate, but my imagination wasn't working itself to the extreme in an attempt to draw the most horrific conclusions it could. They appeared more like candied pieces arranged for delicate tasting.

Another ingredient that never repulsed me, although it potentially could have done, was the slippery swallow's nest. In the first place, this was ideologically unsound for us to have indulged in, for the nests were stolen from swallows who'd built them precariously high in Malaysia's rock caverns. What's more, the nests are actually the hardened saliva of swallows, making me wonder if anyone has tried to make something edible from spiders' webs or the cocoons of moths and caterpillars?

I saw the painstaking way my mother prepared these for soup. The nest had to be soaked in water to soften it. When draining, she had to be careful not to let any filaments escape down the sink (these were expensive titbits). Once softened, the nest would expand greatly in size. My mother would then take tweezers and set to the task of picking out the twigs, splinters, feathers and unidentifiable fragments from the mass of filaments. I have to confess, I was entranced by the transformation process I saw in the cooking of these nests. She placed the nest with water and rock sugar in a ceramic jar with a lid, which was then placed inside a pot partially filled with water. The hot water bubbling around the jar made a comforting noise. In the end, the bird's nest became a pure and pale concoction that we happily snacked on.

Texture seems to have been my initial problem with certain dishes and was something I overcame with time as a child. On the other hand, sometimes smell overrode everything else. When we were sick, my sister and I were sometimes given a restorative soup of pig's liver and sweet leaf or matrimony vine. The sharp, iron smell of the slices of poached liver, cooked until floury and chewy, confounded me. And, in the instance of a delicacy — pig's kidneys stir-fried with slices of ginger, preserved mustard greens and spring onions — no amount of complementary and contrasting aromats could reduce the high stink of the kidney. Included in this collection of bits and pieces — of tripe, glands, jellyfish, tendon, birds' tongues, animal and bird hearts — eyeballs may be added! It's all an eccentric and subjective view; there's no logical or rational reason why I did and do find certain things threatening or inedible. I do still harbour a fear of offal and other slimy and smelly organs. However, I set challenges for myself, to devise ways of cooking animal parts of which I'm not absolutely fond. In this way I can trick myself, whether it's by playing with texture or taste or smell.

braised DRIED Oysters with BLACK moss

Obtain the plumpest dried oysters, calculating 3 or 4 per person. Rinse of any grit or broken shells and soak overnight in fresh water. The following day, drain the oysters and pat dry. Fry 1 tablespoon of thinly sliced ginger with ¾ tablespoon of fermented red bean curd with the oysters in an explosively hot wok until everything smells really fragrant. Add ½ cupful of chopped roast pork (bought from the local Chinese barbecued duck shop), a few leaves of Chinese cabbage cut to bite-sized pieces, and a cupful of water. Simmer gently with the lid on until the cabbage starts to wilt then introduce 50 g (1¾ oz) of dried black moss which should have been reconstituted in water and had any twigs and other impurities removed. Season with oyster sauce and salt.

Chicken and other bits

You might be like me: I am still rather wary of eating offal although I work with it on a constant basis. This dish is designed as an opportunity to sample many different textures without having to commit to a large portion of offal.

Chicken and other bits

SERVES 4

Ingredients

FOR THE SAUCE

1 TEASPOON WHEAT STARCH OR POTATO FLOUR
2 TEASPOONS DARK SOY SAUCE
2 TEASPOONS LIGHT SOY SAUCE
2 TABLESPOONS CHINKIANG VINEGAR
150 ML (5 FL OZ) LIGHT CHICKEN STOCK
SUGAR TO TASTE

FOR THE CHICKEN AND OTHER BITS

150 G (5½ OZ) CHICKEN GIZZARDS
POACHING LIQUID (SEE BOX OPPOSITE)
200 G (7 OZ) DUCK TONGUES
1 TEASPOON CASTER (SUPERFINE) SUGAR
½ TEASPOON SALT
1 TEASPOON SOY SAUCE
1 TEASPOON WHEAT STARCH OR POTATO FLOUR
1 CHICKEN BREAST FILLET, ABOUT 200 G (7 OZ), CUT INTO 2 CM (¾ IN) CUBES
150 G (5½ OZ) CHICKEN HEARTS
GINGER JUICE (SEE GLOSSARY) FROM A 5 CM (2 IN) PIECE OF GINGER
SPRING ONION (SCALLION) JUICE (SEE GLOSSARY) FROM 5–6 SCALLIONS
2½ TABLESPOONS PEANUT OIL
5 GARLIC CLOVES, THINLY SLICED
5 CM (2 IN) PIECE OF GINGER, THINLY SLICED
5 DRIED RED CHILLIES, CUT IN HALF AND SEEDS SHAKEN OUT, LEFT WHOLE
1 TEASPOON SICHUAN PEPPERCORNS, LEFT WHOLE
4 SPRING ONIONS (SCALLIONS), CUT INTO 2.5 CM (1 IN) LENGTHS
100 G (3½ OZ) FRESHLY ROASTED PEANUTS
1 TEASPOON SESAME OIL
SUGAR TO TASTE

Method

MAKE THE SAUCE

Mix together all the ingredients except the sugar. Taste, then add sugar if you think necessary.

PREPARE THE CHICKEN AND OTHER BITS

Trim the chicken gizzards to get rid of the tough white inner lining, trying not to split the sac which contains seeds and grit. Wash in salted water and poach in half the poaching liquid at a gentle simmer for 2–3 hours until the gizzards are tender. Cut into thin, attractive slices and set aside.

Blanch the duck tongues in boiling water for a few seconds, then refresh in cold water. Put in a saucepan with the remaining poaching liquid and bring to the boil. Simmer for 30 minutes or until the tongues are soft but not falling apart. Take out of the liquid and reserve.

Mix together the caster sugar, salt, soy sauce and starch to make a marinade. Add the chicken breast pieces, toss well to coat and leave for 30 minutes. Split the chicken hearts in half and clean of any blood clots. Slice each one into 4 pieces. Put in a bowl with the ginger juice and spring onion juice and leave to marinate.

Heat a frying pan or wok over high heat. Add the oil and quickly fry the chicken breast until coloured then remove. Add the chicken hearts to the pan and stir-fry for 1–2 minutes until just cooked, then remove. Reduce the heat to medium, add the garlic and ginger and fry until starting to colour. Add the chillies and peppercorns and fry until the chillies become dark red and smell toasty. Add the spring onions and let the mixture come back up to heat. Add the sauce, bring to the boil and simmer until it begins to thicken. Toss in the chicken breast and warm through. Stir in the duck tongues, chicken hearts and gizzards, the peanuts and lastly the sesame oil. Taste to see if you need to add sugar or salt, then serve immediately.

TO MAKE POACHING LIQUID

To make the poaching liquid, put 1 litre (34 fl oz) of water, 1 tablespoon of crushed rock sugar, a 2 cm (¾ in) piece of bruised ginger, 2 lightly crushed garlic cloves, 1 red Asian shallot (sliced in half), 1 star anise, 2 cloves, 1 teaspoon of black peppercorns, 2 teaspoons of light soy sauce, 2 teaspoons of dark soy sauce and 2 teaspoons of shaoxing wine in a large pan. Bring to the boil and simmer until the aromats smell appetising.

Oysters and black fungus with pigeon

This is my response to the traditional New Year celebratory dish of dried oyster and black hair seaweed. I wanted to capture the essence of what the dish means to me, through inspiration and reinvention, rather than presenting it in its original form. I've included succulents from the seaside for clean and briny freshness and to contrast with the very rich overtones of the original dish.

Oysters and black fungus with pigeon

SERVES 4

Ingredients

FOR THE OYSTER SAUCE

1 TABLESPOON PEANUT OIL
2 GARLIC CLOVES, SMASHED THEN SLICED
3 CM (1¼ IN) PIECE OF GINGER, PEELED AND SLICED
3 SPRING ONIONS (SCALLIONS), WHITE PART ONLY, SMASHED, CUT INTO 5 CM (2 IN) LENGTHS
4 LARGE DRIED OYSTERS, RINSED, SOAKED OVERNIGHT IN 100 ML (3½ FL OZ) WATER
2 MEDIUM DRIED SHIITAKES, SOAKED IN 100 ML (3½ FL OZ) WATER FOR AT LEAST 1 HOUR
25 ML (¾ FL OZ) SHAOXING WINE OR SAKE
500 ML (17 FL OZ) LIGHT CHICKEN STOCK
1 TABLESPOON LIGHT SOY SAUCE
½ TEASPOON ROCK SUGAR

FOR THE BLACK FUNGUS RELISH

1 TABLESPOON SUGAR
4 RED ASIAN SHALLOTS, HALVED AND FINELY SLICED
2 GARLIC CLOVES, FINELY GRATED
1 TABLESPOON UNSALTED BUTTER
2 TEASPOONS NOILLY PRAT OR OTHER DRY VERMOUTH
200 ML (7 FL OZ) LIGHT BROWN CHICKEN STOCK
100 G (3½ OZ) BLACK FUNGUS, FINELY JULIENNED

FOR THE PIGEONS

125 ML (4 FL OZ) DARK SOY SAUCE
125 ML (4 FL OZ) LIGHT SOY SAUCE
1 TABLESPOON ROCK SUGAR
1 STAR ANISE
½ TEASPOON CORIANDER SEEDS
½ TEASPOON FENNEL SEEDS
2 CM (¾ IN) PIECE OF GINGER, SMASHED
3 TABLESPOONS SHAOXING WINE
2 PIGEONS
VEGETABLE OIL FOR DEEP-FRYING

FOR THE ACCOMPANIMENTS

8 ROCK OYSTERS, FRESHLY SHUCKED (STRAIN THE LIQUID FROM THE SHELLS AND KEEP)
3 TABLESPOONS YOUNG PEAS
2 TABLESPOONS SEA BANANA (SEE GLOSSARY)
3 TEASPOONS SAMPHIRE (SEE GLOSSARY)
10 FENNEL FRONDS

Method

MAKE THE OYSTER SAUCE

Heat a wok over high heat, add the peanut oil and swirl until very hot. Add the garlic, ginger and spring onions, one after the other, allowing each to get hot before adding the next. They should be slightly charred. Keeping the soaking liquids, drain the oysters and mushrooms and pat dry. Add them to the wok and stir until they heat through. Add the wine. Once the raw alcohol smell has disappeared, add the stock, soy sauce, rock sugar, and 2 tablespoons each of the reserved oyster and mushroom soaking liquids. Bring back to the boil and simmer for about 30 minutes. There should be a balance of oyster and mushroom savouriness and the liquid should have reduced enough to coat the back of a spoon. Strain, discarding the solids, and check the seasoning. Reduce in a frying pan to slightly thicken. Add salt or soy sauce to taste.

MAKE THE BLACK FUNGUS RELISH

Melt the sugar without stirring in a heavy-based pan over medium heat. Continue heating until caramelised to a golden brown. Add the shallots and cook until the moisture from them dissolves the caramel, reducing the heat if necessary to prevent burning. Add the garlic and sauté for 1–2 minutes until fragrant. Remove from the heat and add the butter. When it foams and looks nutty, stir in the vermouth and simmer until the raw alcohol smell has disappeared. Add the stock and simmer until the mixture becomes syrupy. Stir in the fungus, but don't cook it for too long or it will lose its texture. The end result should be like a paste and salty enough to be considered a relish. Season with salt and black pepper.

POACH THE PIGEONS

Put all the ingredients except the pigeons and oil in a large pot with 500 ml (17 fl oz) water and bring to the boil, then take off the heat and let the liquid cool to 70°C (160°F). Tuck the pigeons' wings behind their backs so they don't impede the cooking of the breasts. Drop the pigeons into the pot and submerge them, making sure their cavities are filled with the poaching liquid. Leave for 30 minutes for the pigeons to steep. They will be coloured by the liquid but the flesh should be quite rare. Hang to dry for at least 1 hour. Just prior to serving, heat oil in a deep-fryer to 180°C (350°F). Add the pigeons and deep-fry for about 5 minutes until the skin is browned. For serving, carve each breast in half and remove the bones from the leg and thigh pieces.

PREPARE THE ACCOMPANIMENTS

Season a pot of water with enough salt to match the saltiness of the sea and bring to the boil. Drop in the oysters and poach for just 2–3 seconds. Scoop out and reserve. Blanch the peas, sea banana and samphire in the boiling water and refresh under cold water. Peel the peas and split in half. Dress the peas, sea banana, samphire and fennel in the reserved oyster brine you kept when shucking the oysters, and add a little salt.

ASSEMBLE THE DISH

Arrange pigeon breast and leg pieces on each plate. Spoon some of the warm black fungus relish alongside and highlight with 2 oysters. Scatter the peas, sea banana, samphire and fennel about. Spoon some sauce onto the plates and serve.

Chinese-style blood sausage

This may be a rather cowardly way out for one with a slight fear or apprehension of eating offal: the blood in the sausage is disguised by interesting flavourings and textures so that it isn't the main focus. This is designed to be presented like a plate of charcuterie ... a sort of Chinese version.

Ingredients

SERVES 4

FOR THE SAUSAGES

- 300 G (10½ OZ) FAT-STREAKED PORK BELLY, FINELY DICED
- 100 G (3½ OZ) CASTER (SUPERFINE) SUGAR
- 700 G (1 LB 9 OZ) PORK SHOULDER MEAT
- 200 G (7 OZ) PIG'S BLOOD
- ½ TABLESPOON GINGER JUICE (SEE GLOSSARY)
- 1 TABLESPOON FIVE-SPICE
- 20 G (¾ OZ) SALT
- 1 TABLESPOON GROUND WHITE PEPPER
- 1 TABLESPOON BRANDY
- 1 TABLESPOON CHINESE ROSE WINE
- ½ TEASPOON DARK SOY SAUCE
- 250 G (9 OZ) SAUSAGE CASINGS OR PIG INTESTINES, WELL RINSED

FOR THE KIDNEYS

- 2 PIG'S KIDNEYS
- 50 G (1¾ OZ) SUGAR
- 75 ML (2½ FL OZ) SAKE
- 1 TEASPOON SALT
- 250 ML (8½ FL OZ) DARK CHICKEN STOCK
- 1 TABLESPOON GINGER JUICE (SEE GLOSSARY)
- 1½ TABLESPOONS VEGETABLE OIL

FOR THE VEGETABLES

- 2 CM (¾ IN) PIECE OF GINGER, BRUISED
- 200 ML (7 FL OZ) RICE VINEGAR
- 1 TEASPOON SUGAR
- ½ TEASPOON SESAME OIL
- 1 STEM CELTUCE (CHINESE LETTUCE/CELERY LETTUCE/STEM LETTUCE)
- 100 G (3½ OZ) KOHLRABI
- 1 TEASPOON SALT
- 2 TEASPOONS EXTRA VIRGIN OLIVE OIL

Method

MAKE THE SAUSAGES

Put the pork belly in a large bowl and toss with 1 tablespoon of the caster sugar. Set aside for 30 minutes. Use a meat mincer to finely grind the pork shoulder, then add to the bowl. Stir the pig's blood and ginger juice together and add to the bowl. Add the rest of the ingredients except the casings. Mix vigorously until the mixture comes together in a lump. Use a funnel or a sausage machine to stuff the filling into the sausage casings, tying each sausage off with string at 15 cm (6 in) lengths. Heat a pot of water to 75°C (165°F) and poach the sausages for 20 minutes. Drain, then set aside to cool. Preheat a gas oven to 50°C (120°F). String the sausages up on a rack in the oven and leave them overnight, or until they start to dry and wrinkle. Leave to age for 3 or 4 days in a cool dry spot before use.

PREPARE THE KIDNEYS

Peel off and discard any membrane from the kidneys and slice in half lengthways. Put them on a chopping board, cut side up, and trim the tubes at the core by shaving that side of the kidney with the blade of the knife at an oblique angle. Score the outer surface with perpendicular cuts. Blanch for 5–6 seconds in boiling salted water. Transfer to a rack to dry slightly while preparing the next step.

Put the sugar in a dry saucepan and melt over medium–low heat. When it colours and caramelises, add 2 teaspoons of water to dissolve the caramel. Add the sake and, when the alcohol has cooked off, add the salt, stock and ginger juice. Let the mixture reduce until quite syrupy. Quickly dip the drying kidneys in the liquid and then set aside again on a rack to dry for about 1 hour. Cut into 2 cm (¾ in) thick rectangles. Heat the oil in a frying pan and fry the kidneys until they curl and colour. Season with some salt and white pepper.

PREPARE THE VEGETABLES

Put the ginger, vinegar and sugar in a pan and bring to the boil. Cool, then stir in the sesame oil to make a marinade. Peel the tough outer skin off the celtuce. Cut into 5 cm (2 in) lengths and slice into thin cross-sections. Blanch in boiling salted water, refresh in cold water and dry thoroughly on paper towels. When cool, put in a clean bowl, add the marinade and leave for about 2 hours. Peel the kohlrabi and slice into very thin discs. Put in a bowl with the salt, toss well and leave for 10 minutes. Rinse, drain and squeeze gently to get rid of any excess moisture. Toss with the olive oil.

ASSEMBLE THE DISH

Pan-fry the sausages in oil and then cut into 2.5 cm (1 in) lengths. Arrange on a plate with the sautéed kidneys, celtuce and kohlrabi.

What would you do if you were politely offered the head of a fish to finish at a table in front of many people? It's a gesture of respect in most cultures, so in terms of courteous human behaviour you should finish the fish head with a great show of enthusiasm. However, what if you've become a little apprehensive about gouging out the eyes (part gluey gumminess and part inedible cartilage) or picking out the gelatinous flesh of the cheek or sucking out the soft brain tissue? And you're this way because you sometimes relate too much to the living creature the fish once was?

There was a time when it was great fun to race the other diners to get to the fish eyes (when, of course, there wasn't a guest of honour to whom we had to defer). I guess it wasn't part of my motivation at that time whether fish eyes were of any particular texture or something that might be a bit gruesome. I approached everything from the point of view of discovery and absorbed what other people did without judgement. A whole steamed fish — head, fins, tail, bones and all — was a bounty of delicious feasting. It was fascinating to hear of the customs associated with the whole fish: that we shouldn't turn it over when we'd finished one side because that's liable to bring a bad omen to the person who caught it and cause their boat to capsize.

With discovery came further questions. Do fears and apprehensions grow when questions are combined with imagined answers? I'd followed adults to the markets and had seen the fish either swimming or lying inert, in both instances with staring, unblinking eyes. They seemed strange and dangerous; they even had sharp teeth that could be seen through half-opened mouths. The markets were slippery places to wander through; the tiles constantly wet, which seeped uncomfortably into my sandals. The stall holders seemed to struggle to hold the fish, which were said to be cold and shiny with slime. I had already grown afraid of touching the fish. What then was the correlation between the whole fish lying on the table at the market stall and the steamed fish presented on the platter? Everything about the fish head was disgusting: it was slimy skinned, harboured the eyes and the sometimes big, fat lips, and those sharp, mean-looking teeth! What is that horror of a dish, fish-head curry, that the adults make such a great deal of fuss about? You don't mean to say that's all there is for dinner tonight?

Let's get back to the scene. I'm the guest being offered the fish head to savour. Let me get past the obligation to be polite that necessitates steeling myself to go through the motions of enjoying the head of the fish. I want to synthesise everything I like about eating fish, what I know I like about eating it, and work through the disgust of the untouchable fish head. I review my perennial favourite fish dishes: deep-fried whole fish with sweet and sour sauce; fish meat converted to a paste, formed into balls and served in curried sauces; little candied fishes (caramelised ikan bilis), which contain heads and all. I realise I'm no longer disgusted by the feel of raw fish. Their bodies are purpose formed for their environment. I've also learned to celebrate the texture of foods for their variety, including sliminess, sponginess, softness ...

All at once, the apprehension of touching this fish head is dispelled and I'm genuinely appreciating the experience of savouring it.

Fish Head Curry

Find the largest, fleshiest fish head you can (trevally or snapper will usually do). Remove any scales or gills from the fish. Rub the fish head with a couple of teaspoons of powdered spice comprising 5 g (¼ oz) each of coriander seed and black pepper, and 2 g (⅛ oz) each of fennel seed, powdered turmeric, chilli powder and fenugreek. Leave the fish head to marinate while preparing the spice paste (rempah). Pound together 4 dried chillies, 5 red Asian shallots, 4 garlic cloves, and turmeric, galangal and ginger all measuring the size of one-third of a little finger. Fry the combined spice paste and powdered spice with a generous amount of peanut oil in a wok until fragrant. Add a cupful of tamarind water extracted from 2 tablespoons of pulp mixed with a cupful of water. Add water so that the head isn't sitting out of the liquid, which would inhibit its cooking. Bring to the boil, add the fish head and gently simmer so the head doesn't fall apart. The head should almost be cooked through after 20 minutes, at which time add a couple of chopped Japanese eggplants (aubergines), a small handful of curry leaves and a cupful of fresh coconut milk. Cook until the eggplant is soft. Season with salt to taste. The curry can be served hot or warm.

Oyster omelette

This is inspired by the Penang and Taiwanese street stall versions I've seen. It's always been a quandary of mine whether to swallow an oyster whole or to chew on it. There's no choice here but to take things as they come when they are combined in an omelette, particularly if there are many components.

Oyster omelette

MAKES 1 OMELETTE

Ingredients

FOR THE SCALLOP CRISP

4 SCALLOPS
VEGETABLE OIL FOR BRUSHING

FOR THE RICE CRISP

50 G (1¾ OZ) JASMINE RICE
VEGETABLE OIL FOR BRUSHING

FOR THE OYSTERS

1 TEASPOON BLACHAN (SEE GLOSSARY), ROASTED
2 RED BIRD'S EYE CHILLIES, DESEEDED AND CHOPPED
2 LARGE RED CHILLIES, DESEEDED AND CHOPPED
1 SMALL GARLIC CLOVE, CHOPPED
JUICE OF 1 LIME
12 ROCK OYSTERS, FRESHLY SHUCKED

FOR THE OMELETTE

2 EGGS
1 TEASPOON VEGETABLE OIL
2 SPRING ONIONS (SCALLIONS), JULIENNED

60 G (2 OZ) LARDO, THINLY SLICED
4 STEMS OF CORIANDER (CILANTRO), DIVIDED INTO SMALLER SPRIGS

Method

MAKE THE SCALLOP CRISP

Preheat the oven to 180°C (350°F). Slice 4 scallops into the thinnest discs and brush lightly with vegetable oil. Spread on a silicone mat and put in the oven. Immediately reduce the temperature to 100°C (210°F) and dry-roast the scallops for 2 hours until crisp and orangey in colour.

MAKE THE RICE CRISP

Bring 350 ml (12 fl oz) water to the boil in a pot and drop in the rice. Cook for 5 minutes, when the rice should still be chalky in the middle. Drain, keeping the cooking water. Put the rice in a blender or food processor and break it up. Add the cooking water little by little until a runny batter is obtained. Heat a non-stick frying pan over medium heat and brush lightly with vegetable oil. Pour the rice batter into the hot pan. Cook until it dries out and turns from translucent to opaque white. Don't worry if there are cracks in it. Remove carefully and set aside.

DRESS THE OYSTERS

Make the dressing by pounding the blachan, chillies and garlic one after the other in a mortar and pestle to make a paste. Transfer to a bowl, add the lime juice, and season to taste with salt and pepper. Just before making the omelette, toss the oysters with 1–2 teaspoons of the dressing.

MAKE THE OMELETTE

Break the eggs into a bowl, season with a little salt and beat lightly. Heat a non-stick frying pan over high heat and, when hot, add the oil and swirl it around. Pour in the egg, tilting the pan so the egg covers the entire surface. The egg should sizzle when it hits the pan, then set quickly. Drop the oysters and spring onions onto the omelette and leave on the heat just long enough to heat through. Prepare to serve very quickly.

ASSEMBLE THE DISH

Put the omelette on a plate, arrange the lardo on top and arrange the coriander sprigs and scallop crisps around the plate. Position fragments of the rice crisp on top. Serve with the remaining dressing on the side if you'd like the additional chilli or sour hit.

Sweet and sour lamb

This is all about dispelling apprehension by using a favourite taste. It's also about the trickery of mixing the familiar with the not so well liked (sometimes not 'well liked' simply because it may not be so well understood).

Sweet and sour lamb

SERVES 4

Ingredients

FOR THE LAMB

- 250 G (9 OZ) LAMB BRAINS
- 600 G (1 LB 5 OZ) LAMB RIBS, SEPARATED AND FRENCH-TRIMMED (ASK YOUR BUTCHER TO DO THIS)
- TWO 3 CM (1¼ IN) PIECES OF GINGER
- 4 SPRING ONIONS (SCALLIONS), CRUSHED WITH THE SIDE OF A KNIFE
- 4 GARLIC CLOVES, CRUSHED WITH THE SIDE OF A KNIFE

FOR THE SWEET AND SOUR SAUCE

- 2 TABLESPOONS PEANUT OIL
- 3 CM (1¼ IN) PIECE OF GINGER, PEELED AND CRUSHED
- 4 SPRING ONIONS (SCALLIONS), CRUSHED
- 2 TABLESPOONS DRY SHERRY
- 2 TABLESPOONS CASTER (SUPERFINE) SUGAR
- 1 TABLESPOON RICE VINEGAR
- 1 TEASPOON DARK SOY SAUCE
- A FEW DROPS OF SESAME OIL

FOR FRYING THE LAMB

- ½ TEASPOON CORIANDER SEEDS
- ½ TEASPOON WHITE PEPPERCORNS
- 1 TABLESPOON SALT
- 185 G (6½ OZ) PLAIN (ALL-PURPOSE) FLOUR
- PEANUT OIL FOR DEEP-FRYING

FENNEL SHOOTS TO GARNISH

Method

PREPARE THE LAMB

Soak the brains in cold water for 2 hours. In the meantime, fill a saucepan with about 1 litre (34 fl oz) water and add the lamb ribs. Bring to the boil and add the ginger, spring onions and garlic. Simmer for 15 minutes until a skewer inserted into the lamb meets little resistance. Drain the poaching liquid into another saucepan, reserving the lamb ribs. Take out 250 ml (8½ fl oz) of the poaching liquid and keep for making the sauce. Drain the brains and remove the membranes. Gently poach the brains in the water for 10 minutes. Drain.

MAKE THE SWEET AND SOUR SAUCE

Heat a frying pan or wok over medium–high heat. Add the oil, ginger and spring onions and stir-fry until fragrant, reducing the heat if necessary to prevent scorching. Add the sherry, let the alcohol evaporate slightly and then add the sugar. Stir until the sugar dissolves. Add the reserved 250 ml (8½ fl oz) of poaching liquid and leave to reduce until the sauce is syrupy. Add the vinegar, cook briefly to let the rawness dissipate and then add the soy sauce. Taste that the sauce is as syrupy, sour, sweet and salty as you'd like it. Strain and discard the aromats. Finish with sesame oil.

FRY THE LAMB

Preheat the oven to 160°C (320°F). Put the coriander seeds and peppercorns on a tray and toast in the oven for 10–12 minutes. Grind with the salt to a fine powder. Stir into the flour and then pass through a sieve. Cut the brains into bite-sized pieces. Dredge them once in the seasoned flour, let the moisture come through, then dredge them again. Heat oil in a deep-fryer to 180°C (350°F) and fry the brains until golden. Drain on paper towels. Deep-fry the ribs (not dredged in flour), drain on paper towels and drop into the sauce.

ASSEMBLE THE DISH

I wanted to contrast the dark sauciness of lamb ribs with the crunch and softness of the brains, so place the sauced ribs on a plate and scatter the golden pieces of brains between them. Garnish with fennel shoots.

UNUSUALLY *foraged* FOODSTUFFS

I am, apparently, good at leading people on wild goose chases. There's not always a clearly discernible goal in what I want to do ... I may have articulated the general direction I'm heading, but the fun is in the experiences encountered on the way. And these, in turn, can lead to strange new directions previously unconsidered. The title 'Unusually foraged foodstuffs' is a reflection of this eccentric method of mine. 'Foraging' needn't necessarily mean hunting and seeking out edible items in the natural environment; I also take it to mean rummaging through my consciousness for events and memories that guide me to something edible.

From time to time, our family made excursions to plantations and estates. I'm not sure of the reason, for these weren't exactly family-friendly pleasure trips. We sometimes went by jeep and I remember perching precariously on side benches in the backs of these trucks, clutching to the seat as we bumped along uneven dirt tracks. For all the lack of comfort of our chosen transport, it was exhilarating to feel such excitement as to what discoveries the trip might bring.

On one of those days we ended up in what might have been the quietest, stillest spot that could ever be imagined. Long avenues of trees, strictly ordered in straight lines, stretched before us. On approaching, we could see there were parallel downward grooves cut into the trunks and leading to containers. The subtle grey colouring of the trunks gave the impression they should be smooth, but they were, in fact, rough with the multitude of these grooves. When I looked more closely, I could see a white resin trickling down into the container. We were, of course, among rubber trees being tapped for their milk. The milk was collected and put into a larger container by people who'd covered themselves up from the relentless rays of the sun with large hats. My memory is of how quietly they proceeded through the trees.

When I saw the milk being poured into the larger container, I wanted to put my hand in. And, when I saw the rubber coagulated and being cut into smaller blocks, I wondered if it were edible. Remembering this now, I feel something that most resembles the milk and the resilient rubber texture is the flesh of young coconuts charred over open fires. These are sometimes found in stalls by the roadside in places

like Kota Kinabalu. The heat that pours out when the coconut is opened, the extreme white and the sensation that I could bury myself in this pure whiteness fits my memory of the milk of rubber trees.

On other occasions, we would head uphill and come to a cocoa plantation. These seemed much more chaotic and action-filled places than the silent avenues of rubber trees. Perhaps because the workers weren't dwarfed by the size of the trees, or because it was more labour intensive to pick the oval fruits, the people here chatted to each other while they moved among the trees. Knowing what sweet satisfaction was to be found in eating bars of chocolate, I naively believed the same of the fruit from which chocolate began. When the nubbly skinned cocoa was split open, there was some promise there: the flesh was smooth and a pale caramel. In its raw state it tasted like melon, without much of the sweetness and with none of the creamy melting richness of real chocolate! What it did remind me of were the chocolate ice blocks at school, made of cocoa: slightly grainy in the mouth, insipidly sweet and a mere watery reminder of what chocolate might be like. It is not the most satisfying of food memories, I have to admit.

Industrial manufacturing also provides me with memories to be foraged. I won't be cowardly and not acknowledge how environmentally damaging and politically fraught the rise of the palm oil industry has been. But I can't help that one of my formative memories is of roving through a palm oil factory. It must have been a rather small factory because the manufacturing area was located close to where the palms were growing. The large bunches of red berries had clumps of rough, dried fronds attached, which people pulled off the trees with claw-like poles. These clumps looked fun to roll around but I was much too shy and too small to manage it.

The next scene I picture is in the factory: vats full of boiling, viscous, dark red oil separating out from dirty, orange-brown liquid. I find the sight of liquid separating from a mass into thick, coloured oil intriguing (and not because it might be a technical mistake of the cook's that has to be fixed). That process of extracting palm oil makes me think of thick curries such as rendang, where the fragrant oil that separates out is valued.

Blackened young coconut

Here I'm trying to make sense of a memory in a culinary context and convey a sense of texture and visual effect. You will need young, soft-fleshed coconuts of the kind we had in Malaysia when I was growing up.

Blackened young coconut

SERVES 4

Ingredients

2 YOUNG COCONUTS WITH SOFT FLESH (WITH GREEN HUSKS)
20 G (¾ OZ) RAW CASHEW NUTS
ABOUT 250 ML (8½ FL OZ) PEANUT OIL
50 FRESH CURRY LEAVES
2 TEASPOONS SALT
60 ML (2 FL OZ) BURNT GINGER AND GARLIC OIL (SEE BOX OPPOSITE)
A SELECTION OF YELLOW, GREEN, RED AND ORANGE TOMATOES
1 BUFFALO MOZZARELLA, TORN

Method

BLACKEN THE COCONUTS

Put the coconuts on the hot embers of a fire or barbecue, turning them over to thoroughly blacken the husks. Remove from the heat, cool enough to handle and then break away the blackened husk. Break open the top of each coconut, being careful not to spill any of the water. Pour out the water through a sieve and reserve. Scrape out the flesh in large chunks. If green husked coconuts can't be found, grill young coconuts on the highest heat to blacken the husks, but watch out for them catching fire.

MAKE THE CURRY LEAF SALT

Preheat the oven to 160°C (320°F). Spread the cashews on a tray and toast them in the oven for 15 minutes or until lightly golden and refreshed. When cool, finely grate them with a microplane. Heat the peanut oil to 180°C (350°F). Put the curry leaves in a sieve set over a bowl and pour the hot oil over them. Repeat until the leaves are dark green, translucent and crispy. Drain them thoroughly on paper towels and cool before proceeding. Rub the curry leaves through a fine sieve into a bowl and add the salt. Rub the grated cashew nuts through the sieve and into the bowl. Toss the contents to combine. Store in an airtight container away from sunlight (because exposure to sunlight will cause the green powder to turn a dull colour).

MAKE THE DRESSING

Combine the burnt ginger and garlic oil with 1 tablespoon of the reserved coconut water.

ASSEMBLE THE DISH

Cut the tomatoes into interesting pieces. Arrange the tomatoes, mozzarella and coconut meat on a serving plate, spoon some dressing over and sprinkle generous amounts of curry leaf salt over the arrangement.

TO MAKE BURNT GINGER AND GARLIC OIL

Deep-fry 5 thick slices of ginger and 2 smashed garlic cloves in 200 ml (7 fl oz) of olive oil over medium heat until the oil smells toasty and fragrant. Pass the oil through a sieve and discard the aromats.

A dessert inspired by cocoa fruit

This is how I think cocoa fruit should taste. The dish is a compilation of my idealised impressions of the cocoa fruit's appearance, feel (both of its exterior and interior), texture and scent.

A dessert inspired by cocoa fruit

SERVES 4

Ingredients

FOR THE CANDIED POMELO PEEL	1 POMELO 500 G (1 LB 2 OZ) SUGAR
FOR THE CHIFFON CAKE	25 G (1 OZ) PALM SUGAR (GULA MELAKA), CHOPPED 6 PANDAN LEAVES 8 EGGS, SEPARATED 200 G (7 OZ) CASTER (SUPERFINE) SUGAR 90 ML (3 FL OZ) GRAPESEED OIL 145 G (5 OZ) SELF-RAISING FLOUR, SIFTED
FOR THE COCOA WATER JELLY	100 G (3½ OZ) CASTER (SUPERFINE) SUGAR 2 TEASPOONS UNSWEETENED COCOA POWDER 1 TEASPOON POWDERED AGAR-AGAR 1 GELATINE LEAF
FOR THE CHOCOLATE SAUCE	2 TEASPOONS CASTER (SUPERFINE) SUGAR 2 TEASPOONS UNSWEETENED COCOA POWDER 30 G (1 OZ) CHOCOLATE WITH 75% COCOA FAT, CHOPPED
FOR THE MERINGUE	2 EGG WHITES 125 G (4½ OZ) CASTER (SUPERFINE) SUGAR

Method

CANDY THE POMELO PEEL

Cut the peel off the pomelo in large strips. Juice the rest of the fruit and reserve the juice. Blanch the peel in boiling water, then refresh under cold running water. Repeat this twice more to remove excessive bitterness and to soften the peel. Put the juice, sugar and 1 litre (34 fl oz) water in a pan and bring to the boil. Add the peel and simmer gently for 2–2½ hours, with the pan half-covered with a lid, until the peel is soft and translucent. When cool, transfer the peel and syrup to a jar and store for at least 24 hours before using.

MAKE THE CHIFFON CAKE

Make a syrup by heating the palm sugar and 60 ml (2 fl oz) water together until the sugar dissolves. Cool, then purée the pandan leaves with the syrup. Leave for 30 minutes and then wring through muslin to obtain 60 ml (2 fl oz) of syrup. Preheat the oven to 175°C (345°F). Oil and line two 30 cm (12 in) square cake tins with baking paper. In a large bowl beat the egg yolks and 60 g (2 oz) of the caster sugar until thick and light in colour. Combine the pandan syrup with the oil. Fold into the egg yolks, alternating with the flour, a third of each at a time. Beat the egg whites until just starting to soft peak, then gradually beat in the rest of the sugar with a pinch of salt until stiff peaks hold. Fold the whites into the egg yolk mixture. Divide between the tins and bake for 35–40 minutes until the cakes spring up when lightly pressed and have shrunk away slightly from the sides of the tins. Turn out onto wire racks to cool. Any excess cake can be eaten immediately or stored in the refrigerator for a few days.

MAKE THE COCOA WATER JELLY

Line a 20 x 7.5 cm (8 x 3 in) ice-cream tray with plastic wrap. Make a syrup by combining the sugar and 200 ml (7 fl oz) water in a saucepan and bringing to the boil, stirring only to dissolve. In a bowl mix the cocoa powder with a little of the sugar syrup, working it into a mixture without lumps. Stir in the rest of the syrup. Dissolve the agar-agar in the cocoa water using the same method. Transfer the mixture to a saucepan and bring to the boil. Remove from the heat. Have the gelatine leaf softening in cold water, drain it and wring dry. Stir into the cocoa water. Pour into the tray and put in the refrigerator for about 1 hour to set.

MAKE THE CHOCOLATE SAUCE

Bring the sugar and 100 ml (3½ fl oz) water to the boil, stirring to dissolve. Make a slurry with a little of the syrup and the cocoa. Put the chocolate in a saucepan and pour in the rest of the hot syrup. Once the chocolate starts to melt you can stir it. Stir in the cocoa slurry. Heat to 70°C (160°F) then remove from the heat. If you are worried about lumps in the sauce, whip it in a blender.

MAKE THE MERINGUE

Make this last and use immediately. I'd recommend using a copper bowl which has been rinsed out with salt, vinegar and hot water, then dried thoroughly. Otherwise use a very clean, dry mixing bowl. Beat the egg whites in the bowl until they start to hold soft peaks. Add the caster sugar gradually, while continuing to beat until stiff peaks form.

ASSEMBLE THE DESSERT

Spread one of the chiffon cakes with a thin layer of meringue and lightly brown with a blowtorch. Cut 4 small rectangles of cake. Cut the jelly into small circles with a ring cutter. Cut the candied pomelo peel into small squares. Serve the cakes with an arrangement of the cocoa jelly, pomelo chunks and the chocolate sauce. Additional garnishes could be toasted peanuts grated on a microplane, and deseeded custard apple.

The fat rendered from beef rendang

This dish explores the potential of the traditional beef rendang recipe for creating highly coloured, flavourful fat and unctuous shredded meat. I've tried to lighten the presentation of this dish and counter the comforting (but occasionally cloying) richness that can weigh down some Malaysian Nyonya cooking.

Ingredients

SERVES 4

FOR THE BEEF

- 1½ TABLESPOONS CORIANDER SEEDS
- ½ TEASPOON FENNEL SEEDS
- ½ TEASPOON DILL SEEDS
- ½ TEASPOON CUMIN SEEDS
- 2 CLOVES
- 500 G (1 LB 2 OZ) FATTY BEEF BRISKET

FOR THE PASTE

- 6 RED ASIAN SHALLOTS, CHOPPED
- 4 GARLIC CLOVES, CHOPPED
- 2 CM (¾ IN) PIECE OF GALANGAL, PEELED AND SLICED
- 2 CM (¾ IN) PIECE OF GINGER, PEELED AND SLICED
- 3.5 CM (1½ IN) PIECE OF TURMERIC, PEELED AND SLICED
- 1 LEMONGRASS STEM, PEELED OF TOUGH OUTER LAYER, SLICED
- 10 DRIED CHILLIES, SOAKED IN WATER FOR 30 MINUTES, DESEEDED AND CHOPPED

FOR BRAISING THE BEEF

- 20 G (¾ OZ) TAMARIND, SOFTENED IN 200 ML (7 FL OZ) WATER
- 2 TEASPOONS GULA MELAKA (MALAYSIAN PALM SUGAR), GRATED OR THINLY SLICED
- 2 TEASPOONS SALT
- 550 ML (18½ FL OZ) COCONUT MILK

- 1½ TABLESPOONS TOASTED COCONUT

Method

MARINATE THE BEEF

Grind the spices to a fine powder. Cut the beef into large cubes and toss with the spice mix, rubbing it in well. Leave overnight in the refrigerator, covered.

MAKE THE PASTE

If choosing to use a mortar and pestle, start with the first ingredient and pound it thoroughly before adding the next. Work your way like this until all the ingredients have been ground to a fine paste. If puréeing in a food processor, use a little water to help with getting the paste as smooth as possible.

BRAISE THE BEEF

Preheat the oven to 160°C (320°F). To extract the tamarind water, pass it through a fine sieve, firmly pressing the solids into the sieve. Discard the solids. Dissolve the palm sugar and salt in the tamarind water. Combine the paste, tamarind mixture and coconut milk in a large flameproof pot and add the beef. Bring to the boil. Cover and transfer to the oven. Cook for about 2 hours, stirring every 30 minutes or so. Remove the lid and cook further until it looks like a thick, oily but fragrant mass. At this stage it will probably stick to the bottom so make sure the mixture is stirred frequently. When the meat is spoon soft (about another 2 hours) take out of the oven.

ASSEMBLE THE DISH

Mix the toasted coconut into the beef. Taste and adjust the seasoning so that it's sour, salty, hot and slightly sweet. Serve as is or, alternatively, shred the beef after you have taken it out of the oven. Use a large spoon to scoop up any fragrant oil that remains and mix with the toasted coconut.

This now becomes like a condiment and, as a suggestion, it could be served with a meal of green papaya cooked in chicken stock, grilled okra, lime leaf, boiled peanuts, Vietnamese mint and thin slices of steamed eggplant (aubergine).

TE

AN OUTRAGE OF TASTES

As an adult I don't think twice about splicing chillies into any dish where there's a place for them. Observers comment that this is because of my Malaysian background, however, I do also remember a time when the sensation of chilli heat on my tongue was something quite unbearable.

I'm sure it was one of my mother's curries (probably her most mild chicken one, tempered with fresh coconut milk) that I remember. My mother, over the years, has developed the Malaysian-style chicken curry to a version that suits her sense of taste and the practicalities of her kitchen. Pungent with the smell of the ground spices that make up the paste, the knots of lemongrass and dark green curry leaves and the pools of coconut oil that have separated from the thick yellowish sauce, it now characterises 'balanced flavour' for me. I was probably quite curious about the taste of the visually arresting sight on the table, and was in likelihood warned off by my parents or other adults, aware that I was too young to endure the heat of chilli and pepper.

Of course it turned out to be an unpleasant experience. It was a 'nothing' sensation on my tongue, because something like numbing pain overpowered the other tastes of sweet and salty. It left me wondering why this was something people would choose to eat, and appear to enjoy eating. But I wasn't turned off by this initial encounter. Perhaps because I could see so many people around me enjoying chilli on a daily basis, I felt I had to be initiated into the group. So the introductory journey continued: discovering chillies in sauces (pickled green chillies or red chillies in dipping sauces) and gradually building up a forbearance and then an appreciation for their particular flavour and varying levels of heat.

Bitterness took me a lot longer to understand. 'Crestfallen' is the word that would have accurately described the look on my face, as well as the physical sensation I felt, when bitter melon featured at meal times. It might have been fragrantly fried with black beans and pork, stuffed with the tastiest of prawns, or accompanying the sweetest of fish, but the medicinal bitterness infected and dominated everything else. There was even a bitter quality to its smell which caught in my throat. How could anyone visibly smile when they tasted the dish? I don't recall my first encounter with bitter melon, but I do recall the many occasions I've tried to expel its bitter taste from my tongue, and the length of time it lingers (no one could criticise bitter melon for its lack of finish on the palate, I'm sure).

It certainly wasn't that I disliked all bitter things. A rich brew of pork soup with bitter and sweet dried Chinese herbs was, and will always remain, a favourite flavour. Tasting the meat from the pork bones dipped in dark soy sauce was a treat as a child. No other meat tasted more intense and sweet, for the very reason that it had been cooked for hours in essentially bitter herbs.

I'm not sure that I've reconciled myself to sitting down and enjoying a large dish of bitter melon; the memory of my distaste for it remains vivid. If I have any remaining apprehension, it would be against a lingering bitterness which has no rewarding taste — whether sweet, salty, sour or maybe hot — to balance it. Bitter tastes, then, have formed part of the spectrum of flavours with which I play around to create reactions from those tasting the dishes.

My Mother's Chicken Curry

Cut a 1.5 kg (3 lb 5 oz) chicken into pieces. Rub the pieces with 1 teaspoon of salt and 1 tablespoon of powdered curry spice. (You can buy curry spice or make your own: roast 1 tablespoon coriander seeds, 1 teaspoon fennel seeds, ½ teaspoon cumin seeds, a couple of cloves, a 3 cm/1½ in piece of cinnamon and a couple of cardamom seeds in a moderate oven for 10 minutes. Grind to a fine powder with 4 dried red chillies and 1 teaspoon white peppercorns and 1 teaspoon ground turmeric.) Leave to marinate for half an hour. Meanwhile, grind 1 chopped onion, 5 cloves of garlic and a 3 cm (1½ in) piece of peeled ginger to a fine paste with 1 teaspoon of roasted blachan. Fry the paste in 1 tablespoon of peanut oil over medium heat, sprinkle in another couple of tablespoons of the curry powder, add 1 smashed stem of lemongrass and 1 star anise and fry until fragrant. Add the chicken pieces and stir until coated with the aromatic ingredients. Add a cupful of water and simmer over medium heat for 30 minutes or so until the chicken is almost cooked. Add 3 peeled, quartered potatoes, a cupful of fresh coconut milk and 10 curry leaves and cook for a further 15 minutes until the potatoes are tender. Season with some salt and sugar to taste and serve hot.

Bitter melon with added rewards

It can be hard to like bitter ingredients. I think bitterness is tolerable when it is one of a number of elements in a dish, adding intriguing complexity, rather than the focal taste. Or, if there is an alternative source to quell the bitterness, such as the exaggerated aromatic and savoury elements in the recipe here. There's a touch of humour in the choice of the loofah here. Apparently loofahs can grow far longer than 30 cm (12 in), and when they reach full maturity these bland-tasting vegetables are actually quite bitter and can be used as a purgative.

Bitter melon with added rewards

SERVES 4

Ingredients

FOR THE LOOFAH

- 5 LARGE DRIED SCALLOPS (CONPOY, SEE GLOSSARY)
- 500 G (1 LB 2 OZ) FRESH LOOFAH (RIDGED GOURD/ANGLED LUFFA/SIGUA)
- 2 TABLESPOONS DRIED ANCHOVIES, SOAKED IN COLD WATER FOR 30 MINUTES
- 2 TEASPOONS DRIED GOJI BERRIES (WOLFBERRIES), SOAKED IN COLD WATER FOR 30 MINUTES
- 2 GARLIC CLOVES, THINLY SLICED
- 500 ML (17 FL OZ) LIGHT CHICKEN STOCK
- ½ TEASPOON SALT
- ¼ TEASPOON SUGAR
- 1½ TEASPOONS KUZU STARCH (SEE GLOSSARY)

FOR THE BITTER MELON DRESSING

- 100 G (3½ OZ) BITTER MELON (LOOK FOR THE GREENEST, WHICH IS THE MOST BITTER)
- 80 ML (2½ FL OZ) PEANUT OIL
- ¼ TEASPOON SALT, PLUS EXTRA FOR SEASONING
- 1 TABLESPOON SALTED/FERMENTED BLACK BEANS, FINELY CHOPPED
- 1 SPRING ONION (SCALLION), VERY FINELY DICED
- 1 TEASPOON FINELY CHOPPED GARLIC
- 1 TEASPOON FINELY CHOPPED GINGER
- 1 TEASPOON SUGAR, PLUS EXTRA FOR SEASONING
- 2 TEASPOONS LIGHT SOY SAUCE
- 1 TABLESPOON DRY SHERRY
- 3 GARLIC CLOVES, THINLY SLICED
- PEANUT OIL FOR DEEP-FRYING

Method

COOK THE LOOFAH

Soak the scallops in 100 ml (3½ fl oz) water for at least 2 hours to soften. Peel the loofah and slice into 4 cm (1½ in) rounds. Put the scallops and soaking water, anchovies, goji berries, garlic and chicken stock into a saucepan and bring to the boil. Turn down to a simmer and cook for about 30 minutes until the stock is tasty and smells rich. Season with the salt and sugar. Place the loofah in the hot liquid and simmer for about 5 minutes or until soft. Remove from the heat and leave to cool. Pass the poaching liquid through a fine sieve: you will need 200 ml (7 fl oz) of the strained liquid (any left over can be drunk as a broth or used as the stock for making any sauce or stir-fry). Pour the strained liquid into a saucepan. Blend the kuzu with a little water to make a slurry, stir into the liquid and cook until the sauce thickens. Fish out the scallops, tease into tresses and drain on paper towels.

MAKE THE BITTER MELON DRESSING

Cut the bitter melon in half and scrape out the pith (there's no need to pare down the nubbly bits of skin). Cut into 5 mm (¼ in) squares. Heat a frying pan over medium–high heat. Add 1 tablespoon of the oil and stir-fry the bitter melon for about 1 minute, moving it around constantly so it doesn't colour but turns deeper green and retains its crunch. Add 3–4 teaspoons of water and the salt and keep moving the melon around for another 1½–2 minutes. Take out of the pan and leave to cool. Heat a clean pan over medium–high heat and add the remaining oil. Add the black beans, spring onion, garlic and ginger and fry until fragrant, stirring constantly to prevent burning. Add the sugar, soy sauce and sherry. Taste that the oily mixture is highly salted but with some sweetness. Stir in the bitter melon and set aside in a bowl.

Bring a small saucepan of water to the boil. Blanch the garlic slices and then refresh them. Repeat the process of blanching and refreshing the garlic twice more, then drain and pat dry. Heat the oil in a deep-fryer to 180°C (350°F). Deep-fry the garlic and then the scallop tresses, draining them on paper towels. Season the garlic with sugar, and the scallop with salt.

ASSEMBLE THE DISH

Arrange pieces of loofah and some of the bitter melon dressing on each plate. Top with the deep-fried garlic and scallop tresses and spoon a little of the loofah sauce over the plate.

Mango chilli ice

This is an experiment in balancing tastes. I've combined something cold with raised spicy heat levels, and have tried to harmonise taste and temperature by introducing sweetness. The level of spicy heat, although heightened and placed out of context, is intended to be enjoyed.

Mango chilli ice

SERVES 8

Ingredients

FOR THE MANGO ICE CREAM

720 ML (25 FL OZ) MILK
2 EGGS
285 G (10 OZ) SUGAR
240 ML (8 FL OZ) THICKENED CREAM
900 G (2 LB) MANGO FLESH, PUREED
80 ML (2½ FL OZ) LIME JUICE
½ TEASPOON CAYENNE PEPPER

FOR THE PALM SUGAR CUSTARD

250 ML (8½ FL OZ) COCONUT MILK
50 ML (1¾ FL OZ) MILK
80 G (2¾ OZ) PALM SUGAR (GULA MELAKA), CHOPPED
1 EGG
3 EGG YOLKS
½ TEASPOON GROUND GINGER

FOR CARAMELISING WHITE CHOCOLATE

160 G (5½ OZ) WHITE CHOCOLATE (THE HIGHER THE FAT CONTENT THE BETTER), CHOPPED
½ TEASPOON SEA SALT FLAKES

2–3 TEASPOONS CHILLI OIL (SEE BOX BELOW) TO SERVE
NASTURTIUM FLOWERS TO GARNISH

TO MAKE CHILLI OIL

To make chilli oil, snip the stems off 50 g (1¾ oz) dried red chillies and halve them. Shake out and discard the seeds. Crush the chillies into smaller pieces in a food processor and put in a heatproof bowl. Heat 250 ml (8½ fl oz) of peanut oil to 140°C (285°F) and pour over the chillies: they will sizzle and toast. Set aside overnight before use.

Method

MAKE THE MANGO ICE CREAM

Heat the milk to near boiling point. Meanwhile, whisk the eggs and sugar together in a bowl. Pour the hot milk over the eggs and mix together well. Transfer to a clean saucepan and cook, stirring, over low heat until the mixture thickens slightly (it will be thinner than a normal crème anglaise). Sit a clean bowl over an ice bath and strain the custard into the bowl. When cool, whisk in the cream, mango, lime juice and cayenne pepper. Churn in an ice-cream machine according to the manufacturer's instructions.

MAKE THE PALM SUGAR CUSTARD

Lightly oil an ovenproof dish. Put the coconut milk, milk and palm sugar in a saucepan and bring to the boil. Simmer over medium heat, stirring to melt the palm sugar. Whisk the egg and yolks together in a bowl and stir the milk mixture into this. Strain to remove bits of egg which may not have been beaten into the mixture. Add the ground ginger and pour into the oiled dish. Leave for 30 minutes and then scoop off any foam that may have settled on the surface of the custard. Preheat the oven to 150°C (300°F). Put the custard dish in a larger roasting tin. Pour enough hot water into the tin to reach two-thirds of the way up the side of the custard dish. Bake for 30–40 minutes until there is a slight wobble in the centre of the custard. Check after 20 minutes or so, as everyone has different ovens and ovenproof dishes. Remove from the oven and leave to cool in the water bath. This is nice served warm.

CARAMELISE THE WHITE CHOCOLATE

Preheat the oven to 120°C (250°F). Put the chocolate and salt in a thick metal baking tin or metal ovenproof dish. Put in the oven until the chocolate softens, then take it out and spread it about to create a better surface area for caramelising. Return it to the oven for up to 1 hour, stirring it at intervals until it turns a uniform colour of peanut butter. The chocolate may become dry and chalky over time but stirring will smooth it out. Remove from the oven and leave to cool to room temperature and solidify before use.

ASSEMBLE THE DISH

The aim is to spread the elements around the plate so that the diner tastes some spicy heat alternating with comforting sweetness. Scoop a couple of small spoonfuls of custard onto each serving plate and crumble some of the caramelised white chocolate on top. Add a scoop of mango ice cream and a few droplets of chilli oil, not intermingling with each other. Decorate with petals of nasturtium flowers, if you like.

Look at the bounty on the table. There is a platter piled with Singapore fried noodles, festive in the yellowness of their turmeric. I know they will have some chilli heat because that's how all the family — aunts, uncles, cousins, grandparents — like them. Then there is the tureen of beef curry, offering comfort, creamy with coconut milk, yet finely tuned with the sharpness of curry leaf and woody spices. There is a multitude of condiments to go with it: pineapple sambal, cucumber salad, shrimp sambal, kalamansi lime and chilli. Large local prawns, shelled and deep-fried, sit at one corner of the table, the chilli sauce beside them to relieve their cloying sweetness.

But it's all getting cold because here's somebody bringing in a batch of satays from the charcoal brazier. We are urged to eat the satays while they're hot and at their best, so everyone grabs a skewer and makes for the peanut sauce, sweet from sugar, sour from tamarind and lime, and hot with more chilli. Someone points out that there are also chunks of cucumber and salty coconut rice in squares to use as an excuse for grabbing more of the mouth-watering peanut sauce.

What about the Hainanese chicken rice? That can't be neglected. And the casserole of Shanghainese lion's head meatballs? I'm not keen on the intensity of this rendition of Buddha jumps over the wall. The roast duck with plum sauce is beautifully plated; I'm craving the sour taste but am a little shy to disturb the orderly look of the dish, so will wait until someone else attacks it first. It becomes too easy to ignore the humble dish of amaranth leaf; its prickliness against the tongue is really off-putting. The scratchiness is as unpleasant as lashes of the whip, and it's not really softened by being cooked with fish and dried shrimp stock. I think, if I can keep far enough away from my mother, she won't notice I haven't eaten any greens.

I always loved the chaos and noise of large family gatherings. For one thing, the routines of the day were disrupted once again. There were always cousins to play with and we children weren't under the constant scrutiny of adult supervisors. How, I did wonder, was I meant to navigate this potluck arrangement on the banquet table? I would see people helping themselves to the sundry dishes, but how to know which dishes went with which? I didn't like the taste when the sauce from the lion's head meatballs mixed with the beef curry. So were the dishes supposed to be considered as if they were sitting on their own? What about the repetition of ingredients: could the cucumber in the pickle be dipped in the peanut sauce? No, it didn't taste quite right like that. Where is the logic of progression in this meal? Why are there such jarring and disparate tastes?

I've come to rethink what I then saw as a confusing proliferation of dishes. The pleasure lay in everyone bringing a dish they took pride in. The happiness came from sharing the table and enjoying each other's company. And, while I've been critiquing the choice of menu, I've forgotten the particular reason for the get-together.

There isn't always a rational order to things, but reason does lie somewhere. It's a matter of finding the level at which logical or rational order exists. It's futile to try to find it through examination of the dish combinations brought in a potluck context. The logic, if any, lies in the joy of the get-together. See how I like to trust there is a solution to everything; that I can find that last piece of the puzzle which will make everything fall into place? For example, there's no such thing as a bad combination of ingredients or flavours: adjustments can always be made in intensity and balance to reach a palatable result. (However, taste might dictate that, although interesting, the dish is not great and should be scrapped, even though the puzzle of the combination has been solved.)

Beef Satay with peanut sauce

The first thing requiring attention here is the necessity to marinate the meat overnight. Cut 500 g (1 lb 2 oz) of beef rump into small pieces. Prepare a fine paste by pounding together a 2 cm (¾ inch) piece of peeled fresh turmeric, a 2 cm (¾ inch) piece of peeled zedoary, 2 dried red chillies, 1 stalk of lemongrass and 2 thin slices of peeled galangal. Lightly roast 1 tablespoon of coriander seeds, 1 teaspoon of cumin seeds and 1 teaspoon of aniseed, blend to a fine powder and add to the mix. Finally, mix the marinade with 3 tablespoons sugar, 2 teaspoons salt, 1 teaspoon tamarind water and 2 tablespoons peanut oil. Thoroughly mix this paste with the beef and leave to marinate overnight. The next day, thread the meat onto skewers and grill over a charcoal fire. Baste with a mixture of 3 tablespoons of coconut milk mixed with 2 tablespoons of vegetable oil as the skewers are turned over the grill. Cook until browned.

The satays are traditionally accompanied by a peanut dipping sauce. Grind 1 tablespoon of coriander seeds, 1 teaspoon of cumin seeds and 1 teaspoon of aniseed to a fine powder. Combine with a smooth fragrant paste made of 10 deseeded dried red chillies, 3 garlic cloves, 8 red Asian shallots, 1 teaspoon of roasted blachan, 2 candlenuts and 1 stalk of lemongrass. Fry the paste over medium heat with a couple of tablespoons of peanut oil for about 15 minutes until well cooked and aromatic. Then stir in ½ cupful of roasted peanuts that have been roughly crushed, 4 tablespoons of sugar and 2 teaspoons of salt. Cook for a couple of minutes, then gradually add a cupful of fresh coconut milk and ½ cupful of tamarind water. Simmer for about 10 minutes until the sauce is quite thick. Serve warm or at room temperature.

A platter of duck with steamed buns and accompaniments

Presented at the table to be shared, this is an open invitation to celebrate the joy of eating together.

A platter of duck with steamed buns and accompaniments

SERVES 6

Ingredients

FOR BRAISING THE DUCK

PEANUT OIL FOR DEEP-FRYING, PLUS 1 TABLESPOON
2.5 KG (5½ LB) DUCK
12 RED ASIAN SHALLOTS, VERY FINELY DICED
6 GARLIC CLOVES, GRATED ON A MICROPLANE
5 CM (2 IN) PIECE OF GINGER, GRATED ON A MICROPLANE
2 TABLESPOONS SALTED SOY BEANS, PUREED
50 ML (1¾ FL OZ) DRY SHERRY
500 ML (17 FL OZ) LIGHT CHICKEN STOCK
10 G (¼ OZ) TAMARIND PULP MIXED WITH 200 ML (7 FL OZ) WATER AND THEN PRESSED THROUGH A SIEVE
½ TEASPOON DARK SOY SAUCE

FOR THE CUCUMBER AND CHRYSANTHEMUM LEAVES

2 LEBANESE (SHORT) CUCUMBERS, PEELED
1 TABLESPOON SALT
100 G (3½ OZ) CHRYSANTHEMUM LEAVES, WASHED, TOUGH LARGER LEAVES DISCARDED
100 ML (3½ FL OZ) PEANUT OIL

FOR THE SOURED JERUSALEM ARTICHOKES

125 ML (4 FL OZ) RICE WINE VINEGAR
60 G (2 OZ) SUGAR
2 TABLESPOONS SALT
1 TABLESPOON SALTED SOY BEANS, PUREED
1 TABLESPOON DARK SOY SAUCE
300 G (10½ OZ) JERUSALEM ARTICHOKES, PEELED, KEPT WHOLE

FOR THE GRILLED SPRING ONIONS

8 SPRING ONIONS (SCALLIONS), TRIMMED BUT KEPT WHOLE
PEANUT OIL FOR BRUSHING

FOR THE STEAMED BUNS

220 ML (7½ FL OZ) WARM WATER
14 G (½ OZ) DRIED YEAST
1½ TEASPOONS SUGAR
2 TABLESPOONS PEANUT OIL
430 G (15 OZ) STRONG FLOUR
1 TEASPOON SALT

Method

BRAISE THE DUCK

Heat oil in a deep-fryer to 180°C (350°F). Deep-fry the duck until lightly golden to tighten the skin and prevent it breaking apart during cooking. Preheat the oven to 180°C (350°F). Heat a large flameproof pot over medium heat and add 1 tablespoon of oil. Fry the shallots, garlic and ginger until fragrant and lightly coloured. Season with some salt during cooking. Add the soy beans and cook until fragrant. Pour the sherry into the mix, let the raw alcohol smell dissipate and then add the stock and tamarind. Bring to the boil. Add the soy sauce and taste for saltiness. Lower in the duck and bake uncovered for about 1½ hours until the duck is well-cooked. Baste constantly. Transfer the duck to a plate and keep it covered and warm. Check the consistency of the sauce: if too thin, reduce it by simmering for a few minutes, then strain. The final sauce should be salty, slightly sweet and rather sour. Pour over the duck when ready to serve.

DRESS THE CUCUMBER AND CHRYSANTHEMUM LEAVES

Slice the cucumber in half lengthways and cut into thin slices. Mix with the salt and leave for 30 minutes. Rinse and drain the cucumber, gently squeezing out excess moisture. Blanch the chrysanthemum leaves in boiling salted water and then refresh them in cold water. Drain and then squeeze out any excess water. In a blender or food processor purée the chrysanthemum leaves, adding the oil as you go. Season with freshly ground white pepper. When ready to serve, arrange the cucumber in a dish and spoon chrysanthemum leaf oil over the slices.

PREPARE THE SOURED JERUSALEM ARTICHOKES

Bring the vinegar, sugar, salt and 250 ml (8½ fl oz) water to the boil, stirring to dissolve the sugar. Add the salted soy beans and dark soy sauce. Put the jerusalem artichokes in a preserving jar and pour the liquid in. Seal tightly. Lower into a pan filled with enough cold water to cover the top of the jar. Bring to the boil and simmer for about 1 hour, when the artichokes should be soft. Take out the jar and leave to cool. Remove the artichokes and cut into cubes. Place on a serving dish, dressed with a little of the liquid in the jar.

GRILL THE SPRING ONIONS

Heat a grill plate to high heat. Brush the spring onions lightly with peanut oil and put on the grill until wilted, turning them once. Season with some salt and white pepper and slice thinly to serve.

MAKE THE STEAMED BUNS

These should be steamed just before serving. Combine the warm water and yeast in a large bowl and leave to activate. Mix in the sugar and oil. Add the flour and salt and mix to a rough dough which isn't sticky. This can be done in a mixer with a dough hook. If the dough feels too dry, add extra water. Knead until smooth and divide into balls, about 30 g (1 oz) each. Cover with a damp tea towel to avoid drying. Working a few at a time, flatten the balls into 7.5 cm (3 in) rounds. Brush half of each round with oil and fold it over to form a half moon shape. Spray lightly with water to prevent a crust forming and cover loosely with damp tea towels. Leave them all on the bench for 30 minutes or until doubled in size. Working in small batches, steam the buns in a bamboo steamer for about 12 minutes. Serve immediately.

ASSEMBLE THE DISH

Set the duck on the table with a serving fork, spoon and knife. Arrange the accompaniments and the buns on the table also. Invite guests to help themselves to whatever pieces of duck they wish. Let them know that they can sandwich the buns with one or more of the accompaniments and the duck meat.

Fish steeped in floral sweet vinegar

This was discovered through a chance encounter. I smelt brewing chrysanthemum tea at the same time as catching the waft of sweet black vinegar that was being used to cook pork. It made me decide that the marriage of these two could potentially bring out the best in each.

Fish steeped in floral sweet vinegar

SERVES 4

Ingredients

FOR THE SALTY FISH ROE RELISH

1 TABLESPOON OLIVE OIL
1 WHOLE FRESH FISH ROE, MULLET PREFERRED
LIGHT SOY SAUCE TO TASTE
LEMON JUICE TO TASTE

FOR POACHING THE FISH

250 ML (8½ FL OZ) LIGHT CHICKEN STOCK
4 CM (1½ IN) PIECE OF GINGER, SMASHED
2 SPRING ONIONS (SCALLIONS), BRUISED
1 TABLESPOON DRIED CHRYSANTHEMUM
60 ML (2 FL OZ) CHINESE SWEET BLACK VINEGAR
4 FINGERS (ABOUT 90 G /3 OZ EACH) CUT FROM A STRONG-FLAVOURED WHITE FISH (EG MULLOWAY, MACKEREL, KING GEORGE WHITING)

FOR THE WILTED MUSHROOMS

100 G (3½ OZ) ENOKI MUSHROOMS
1 TABLESPOON EXTRA VIRGIN OLIVE OIL
25 ML (¾ FL OZ) CHINESE RICE WINE

4 SEA URCHIN ROE

Method

MAKE THE SALTY FISH ROE RELISH

Heat the oil and fry the whole roe over medium heat for about 10 minutes or until cooked through. When cool enough to handle, open the sac and use a fork to tease out the roe into a bowl. Season with salt, some light soy sauce and some lemon juice so the relish is salty and slightly acid.

POACH THE FISH

Pour the chicken stock into a saucepan and add the ginger and spring onions. Bring to the boil and add the chrysanthemum and vinegar. Leave off the heat to steep for 10 minutes. Now heat to 75°C (150°F) and lower in the pieces of fish. Poach for about 10 minutes (the fish should be just cooked).

WILT THE MUSHROOMS

Trim the mushrooms at the base so they separate into individual stems. Heat the oil in a saucepan over medium heat, add the mushrooms and pour in the rice wine. Cook long enough for the mushrooms to wilt and begin to soften. Season with salt and white pepper and remove from the heat.

ASSEMBLE THE DISH

Put a piece of fish on each plate, sliced into smallers pieces if you like, and allow some of the poaching liquid to drain onto the plate. Arrange some of the mushrooms, the sea urchin roe and a spoonful of the salty fish roe relish around the fish and serve immediately.

Peanut and tannic greens

I was remembering the potluck nature of some of our family banquets. I felt a salad of greens with the addition of a number of interesting textures would be a good foil for the richly flavoured dishes competing against each other for attention at those family feasts... in particular, when satays were served.

Ingredients

SERVES 4

FOR THE SPICED SALT

- 1 TEASPOON CORIANDER SEEDS
- ½ TEASPOON CUMIN SEEDS
- ½ TEASPOON ANISEED
- 1 DRIED CHILLI, SEEDS REMOVED, COARSELY CHOPPED
- 1 TEASPOON SALT

FOR THE PEANUT TOFU

- 80 G (2¾ OZ) RAW PEANUTS
- 250 ML (8½ FL OZ) FILTERED WATER
- 50 G (1¾ OZ) POTATO OR KUZU STARCH

FOR SERVING

- 1 TABLESPOON PEANUT OIL
- 1 BUNCH LEAF AMARANTH (SEE GLOSSARY), WASHED, STEM AND LEAF KEPT IN ONE PIECE, PLUS A FEW BABY LEAVES TO GARNISH
- 3 TABLESPOONS WILD RICE
- 50 G (1¾ OZ) ROASTED PEANUTS, ROUGHLY GROUND
- 1 HANDFUL CORIANDER (CILANTRO) SPRIGS
- 1 LARGE HANDFUL BEAN SPROUTS, ROOTS TRIMMED, BLANCHED AND REFRESHED
- 1 HANDFUL THAI BASIL LEAVES
- 1 LIME

Method

MAKE THE SPICED SALT

Preheat the oven to 160°C (320°F). Toast the coriander seeds, cumin and aniseed on a tray in the oven for 10 minutes until fragrant. Grind to a fine powder with the chilli and salt.

MAKE THE PEANUT TOFU

In a blender or food processor, finely process the peanuts with the water until a fairly smooth milk forms. Strain through muslin into a jug. You will need 420 ml (14 fl oz) of milk. In a small bowl mix some of the milk with the starch. Beat until totally smooth, then stir it back into the milk. Pour into a saucepan and cook over medium–high heat, stirring often, for 10 minutes. It will thicken and have large, stretchy bubbles. Keep scraping the bottom of the pan to prevent sticking. Taste to check that the uncooked starchiness has gone and then remove from the heat and stir for 2 minutes. Line a shallow baking tray with plastic wrap and spray with water. Pour in the tofu and leave at room temperature to set.

ASSEMBLE THE DISH

Heat a frying pan over high heat and swirl with the oil. Fry the amaranth in small batches for a couple of seconds each batch, just long enough for it to wilt (any more, and it will become really soft and tannic). Season with a little of the spiced salt. Deep-fry the wild rice in 180°C (350°F) oil for a few seconds until puffed up. Drain on paper towels. Take teaspoonfuls of the peanut tofu and toss in the ground peanuts. Place the ingredients for the salad together in a serving bowl: the amaranth, wild rice, peanut tofu, coriander sprigs, beans sprouts and basil leaves. Squeeze the juice of the lime over this and sprinkle with more spiced salt. Conceived to accompany satay and satay sauce.

CHICKENS AND PIGS

At home we ate in a manner typical of most Chinese families: very simply, with lots of shared vegetable dishes, fewer meat dishes, rice and sometimes a soup. Given that the emphasis was on variety to balance out what defined a meal, the meat element represented just one part of the array. In this way, the quality of the meat and fish was just as important as how deliciously they were rendered by the cooking process.

From a child's point of view, our meals were structured around a reward and punishment system. Certain dishes that I didn't like included spinach poached to an incredible softness in dried shrimp stock (this had a weird tannic taste that stung my tongue) and strong-tasting batons of spring onion and thin slices of ginger stir-fried with strips of beef, which was too rich for my childlike sense of taste.

Dishes I did enjoy included soy sauce chicken: intensely salty and highly flavoured with spring onion and garlic, but balanced by the sweetness of meat and sauce. Also, salted chicken steamed with ginger and shallot; this was cut with the bones in, red at their centres, chewy but with an appealing meatiness, and, again, with the sweetness of light soy, fried onion, ginger and scallion oil dressing and with mustard mixed from powder. (I think it's also important to mention how much of a thrill and sometimes annoyance were the shards of bone found in the dish.) And dried lily buds steamed with chopped pieces of chicken on the bone: oniony and garlicky, the taste spiced up by ginger. Also, chicken braised with chestnuts (which we bought dried) for sweetness and savouriness.

I recall the sense of pride expressed by family members, male and female, when they found what they asserted was the best purveyor of pork or chicken in the markets. I always felt like a voyeur during these adult exchanges, but they might explain my early fascination with the facts and fictions associated with food: the logistics of choosing the right live chickens; how to determine the age of a bird by looking at the state of the claws; feel out the thickness of breast meat for tenderness; the state of the feathers; the history of the farm or grower; the correct colour of pork meat;

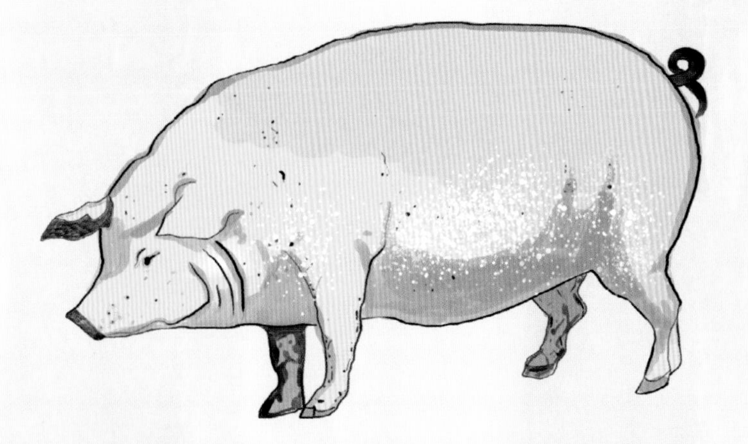

the smell and sex of the pig; the ideal age of a pig ... I also vividly recall accounts from cousins, and even my younger sister, of the killing of live chickens in our home after their purchase from the market; the disproportionate spray of blood and the poor chicken running around the yard headless. I've heard them all before. (I can still only tolerate watching horror or violent films with one eye closed or my ears covered so that at least one of the senses is blocked out to filter what might be too much to bear.)

When my family arrived in Australia, we maintained our eating traditions, but were without our extended family with whom to share meals. What was more startling for us innocents abroad was how different the produce was from the ingredients we were used to sourcing at the wet markets and small market gardens.

My mother kept mentioning that the texture of the chickens she bought in Australia was much softer. She made it one of her missions to find the scrawny, chewy, yellow-skinned little chickens that she missed, but to no avail. In recent years, one of my highly individualistic pig-farming friends has offered the chickens from the brood that runs wild around his property. And there are also now chickens bred for Chinese tastes available through specialist providores. But these options have never been wholly satisfactory to her and, by extension, to me. I suspect we have a static concept based on imperfect recall. Times do change through economic and social necessity and I believe the chickens we would find in our old home town now are probably better fed and less likely to have run around in yards developing muscle. Moreover, since we live in a vacuum outside the progressive change happening in Malaysia, our tastes are probably no longer aligned; what for us is an 'ideal' might no longer be found, or indeed considered 'ideal' any more.

Steamed Chicken with lily buds

Cut a 1.5 kg (3 lb 5 oz) chicken into pieces. Make a marinade of 1 tablespoon of dry sherry, 1 tablespoon of light soy sauce, 1 teaspoon of cornflour (cornstarch), a 3 cm (1 in) piece of thinly sliced ginger, 1 teaspoon of salt and 1 teaspoon of sugar. Leave the chicken in the marinade. Meanwhile, soak 30 dried lily buds (from golden day lilies) for 30 minutes, changing the water as the lily buds colour it yellow until the water remains clear. Remove the hard part of the buds at the base of the flowers and tie each into a knot. Fry a chopped onion in a pan with a couple of tablespoons of vegetable oil until translucent and soft, add the soaked lily buds and heat through. Season with salt and some sugar. Place the vegetables on the bottom of a heatproof platter and place the chicken pieces on top. Put the platter in a steamer and steam over high heat for 30 minutes until the chicken is cooked through. When cooked, garnish with sliced spring onion (scallion) and fresh coriander (cilantro) and serve in the same platter.

Salted and steamed chicken

This dish is a celebration for me of the chewy leanness of chicken that I thought was the ideal. The presentation as described here is meant to emphasise what has now become the elusive tastiness and chewiness of chicken, so is designed as a titbit.

Salted and steamed chicken

SERVES 4

Ingredients

FOR THE SALTED CHICKEN

1 SMALL CHICKEN
1 TABLESPOON SAND GINGER POWDER (SHAJIANG) (SEE GLOSSARY)
1½ TABLESPOONS SALT

FOR THE CLAMS

1 TABLESPOON PEANUT OIL
8 LARGE MEATY CLAMS (I USE DIAMOND CLAMS)

FOR THE DRESSING

500 ML (17 FL OZ) GRAPESEED OIL
3 RED ASIAN SHALLOTS, PEELED AND FINELY SLICED
2 TABLESPOONS LIGHT SOY SAUCE
4 SPRING ONIONS (SCALLIONS), COARSELY SLICED
3.5 CM (1¼ IN) PIECE OF GINGER, PEELED AND CHOPPED
1 TEASPOON SALT

Method

STEAM THE CHICKEN

Take the legs off the chicken and use elsewhere. Trim away the wing tips and then dry the cavity and the outside of the chicken. Mix the sand ginger and salt together and rub into the chicken, both inside and out. Leave the chicken to marinate for 1½–2 hours in a cool spot, or in the refrigerator if the kitchen is hot. Place the chicken on a metal tray with a lip and steam over high heat for about 25 minutes until just cooked. Remove from the steamer and leave to cool, covered with foil so it doesn't dry out.

COOK THE CLAMS

Heat a frying pan over high heat. Add the oil and clams and any juices collected in the tray when steaming the chicken. Put a lid on the pan and cook until the clams open, then immediately take them out of the pan, reserving the juices. When cool enough to handle, extract clam meat and put into the reserved juices.

MAKE THE DRESSING

Heat the oil in a deep-fryer to 160°C (320°F). Add the shallots and fry until golden and crisp. Remove, drain on paper towels and then put in a bowl. Add the soy sauce so they soften. Set the oil aside to cool. Put the spring onions, ginger, salt and 250 ml (8½ fl oz) of the cooled oil in a blender and purée until the oil is green and the spring onions are broken up. The aim is to incorporate the spring onions and ginger with the oil, rather than making an emulsion. Strain through muslin by letting the oil drip through slowly. It's not appropriate here to press the solids through the sieve.

ASSEMBLE THE DISH

Take the breast fillet off the chicken and cut into slices. Arrange on plates with a couple of clams per person. Moisten the chicken with drops of the heated clam juices. Drizzle 2 teaspoons of dressing on each plate and scatter with some of the softened deep-fried shallots.

The transformed taste of chicken

Instead of being wistful about the remembered taste of chicken, I've decided to create something that I might now latch onto as a new favourite taste. This is intended to be texturally interesting so the chicken wings are not falling-apart soft. Serve as a large shared dish so that everyone gets their hands dirty while they're eating.

The transformed taste of chicken

SERVES 4

Ingredients

FOR THE BRINE AND CONFIT

- 250 G (9 OZ) SALT
- 250 G (9 OZ) SUGAR
- 24 CHICKEN WINGS, SPLIT INTO 3 PARTS OF WING TIP, MIDDLE PART AND LITTLE DRUMSTICK
- 1.5 LITRES (51 FL OZ) OLIVE OIL, DUCK OR PORK FAT
- 1 TABLESPOON CORIANDER SEEDS
- 1 TABLESPOON WHITE PEPPERCORNS

FOR THE SAUCE

- PEANUT OIL FOR FRYING
- 500 G (1 LB 2 OZ) PRAWN SHELLS AND HEADS, RINSED AND DRIED
- 4 CM (1½ IN) PIECE OF GINGER, CRUSHED AND ROUGHLY CHOPPED
- 3 GARLIC CLOVES, CRUSHED
- 3 SCALLIONS (SPRING ONIONS), BRUISED AND CUT INTO LONG LENGTHS
- 100 ML (3½ FL OZ) SAKE
- 100 ML (3½ FL OZ) MIRIN

- JUICE OF ½ LEMON
- 1 SMALL HANDFUL CORIANDER (CILANTRO) LEAVES
- 1 SCALLION (SPRING ONION), WHITE PART ONLY, THINLY SLICED
- ¼ TEASPOON EACH OF BLACK AND WHITE SESAME SEEDS, TOASTED

Method

BRINE AND CONFIT THE CHICKEN WINGS

Put the salt and sugar into a pot with 1.5 litres (51 fl oz) cold water and bring to the boil. Turn the heat off and completely cool the brine. Add the middle parts and drumsticks of the chicken wings, keeping the wing tips for later. Refrigerate for 2–3 hours, then lift out the chicken wing pieces, discarding the brine. Pat them dry with paper towels. Preheat the oven to 160°C (320°F). Put the oil, coriander and peppercorns in a flameproof dish large enough to also hold the chicken wings in a snug fit. Heat the oil to 80°C (175°F), then add the wings, cover the pot and transfer to the oven. Bake for 30 minutes or until the chicken is cooked through. Remove from the oven and leave to cool in the oil. If you wish to store the chicken overnight or longer, remove from the oil, strain out the spices and decant any chicken juices that may have collected at the bottom of the pot. (The juices don't help to prolong the storage life of the chicken but they are flavoursome and can be combined in some sort of sauce if you like.) Pour the oil over the chicken pieces and refrigerate.

MAKE THE SAUCE FOR THE CHICKEN

Heat a very small amount of oil in a frying pan over medium heat. Brown the wing tips until dark golden. Remove from the pan and put in a flameproof pot. Scrape off whatever has stuck to the bottom of the frying pan (adding some water helps) and add a little more oil. Stir-fry the prawn shells over medium–high heat. Once they start to smell fragrant, add the ginger, garlic and spring onions and fry until these wilt. Add the sake and cook until the alcohol dissipates. Transfer the prawns and aromats to the pot containing the chicken wing tips and cover with about 1 litre (34 fl oz) water. Bring to the boil and simmer for 45 minutes. The broth should be fragrant with prawns and ginger, and taste sweet from the prawn shells. Strain the liquid into a clean saucepan and put over high heat to reduce. Once it becomes syrupy, pour in the mirin and add salt and pepper to taste. The syrup should be highly seasoned with the primary tastes being salty and sweet.

ASSEMBLE THE DISH

Heat a non-stick frying pan over medium heat and add 1½–2 tablespoons of oil. Brown the confited chicken wings in batches for about 2 minutes each side until golden brown and crisp. Bring the sauce to simmering point and toss in the wings. Turn them over to coat well and then transfer them to a large serving dish. Squeeze the lemon juice over and garnish with coriander leaves, spring onion slices and a sprinkling of sesame seeds.

Chestnuts and chicken liver, mixed together

This is inspired by my remembered fondness for chicken braised with dried chestnuts. The flavour of those fragrant chestnuts braised with chicken is blended with the sweet richness of chicken liver and served as an appetiser.

Ingredients

SERVES 4

FOR THE SAUTEED CHICKEN LIVERS

- 50 ML (1¾ FL OZ) COGNAC
- 1 TEASPOON GINGER JUICE (SEE GLOSSARY)
- 1 TABLESPOON THICK SOY SAUCE
- 1½ TEASPOONS BROWN SUGAR
- ½ TEASPOON SALT
- 100 G (3½ OZ) CHICKEN LIVERS, TRIMMED
- 1 TABLESPOON VEGETABLE OIL

FOR THE BRAISED CHESTNUTS

- 1 TABLESPOON VEGETABLE OIL
- 4 GARLIC CLOVES, PEELED
- 2.5 CM (1 IN) PIECE OF GINGER, PEELED AND SLICED
- 4 CHICKEN WINGS, CHOPPED
- 50 ML (1¾ FL OZ) DRY SHERRY
- 1 TABLESPOON LIGHT SOY SAUCE
- 1 TABLESPOON DARK SOY SAUCE
- 250 G (9 OZ) CHESTNUTS, PEELED

FOR SERVING

- CRUSTY BREAD OR WAFERS
- CORIANDER (CILANTRO), VIETNAMESE MINT AND SPRING ONIONS (SCALLIONS)

Method

SAUTE THE CHICKEN LIVERS

Make a marinade by mixing together half the cognac, the ginger juice, soy sauce, brown sugar and salt in a bowl. Toss in the livers and leave for 1½–2 hours. When ready to eat, take the livers out of the marinade and drain over a sieve. Heat the oil in a non-stick frying pan over medium heat. Add the livers and brown them on each side for 3–4 minutes until they are crisp on the outside but pink and just cooked through on the inside. Remove from the pan and sprinkle with the rest of the cognac.

BRAISE THE CHESTNUTS

While the chicken livers are marinating, braise the chestnuts. Heat the oil in a saucepan over high heat. Drop in the garlic and ginger and fry until they become fragrant. Reduce the heat if they begin to scorch. Add the chicken wings and fry until the skin is golden. Reduce the heat and add the sherry. When the raw alcohol smell has cooked off, stir in 125 ml (4 fl oz) water and both the soy sauces. Add the chestnuts and cook at a low simmer, covered, for 20–25 minutes or until they become very soft and sweet. Scoop out of the liquid.

Pound the livers and the chestnuts with a mortar and pestle to make a rough paste, adding a little strained liquid if the paste is too dry.

ASSEMBLE THE DISH

The resulting paste of ground chestnut and liver can be served from a central bowl with crusty bread or crispy wafers of some sort. Garnish with fresh herbs such as a mixture of coriander and Vietnamese mint and shredded spring onions.

I suppose this could just as easily have been about sour, salty or bitter memories, but those words don't quite conjure up such warm evocations, do they? There are some early encounters with sweet tastes that have stayed with me. I still use these memories as my reference point for what tastes good sweet-wise, because of the strong early affinity I developed for the taste. (I hope this emphasises that likes and dislikes are based on personal preference and there is almost always no objective standard.)

Let me gather my thoughts on what I consider to be the good sweet tastes. I don't remember my first taste of cereal porridge, but it seems to have been a part of my life since the days I was first taught to eat solid food. It came in a big, very bright yellow, blue and red tin that gave an impression of largesse for some time ahead, and offered comfort in its own way. The small dried flakes are the makings of this porridge: once combined with some liquid, a transformation occurs and they become a porridge mixture. We simply poured water over the flakes and sugared the mix slightly. If we were ill or just feeling pathetic, warm water was added as an alternative and the mixture thinned out to become a drinkable thing. The taste of it was malty and never overly sweet or rich.

This elusive 'maltiness' seems very finely tuned to a particular memory that represents an ideal of taste for me. For a long while I held red bean pancakes, the sweet snack presented to us as an occasional treat, as fulfilment of my subjective view of malt-like goodness, from the filling to the intriguing flavour of the pancake.

Flakes of corn are also a cereal I've known almost all my life. These too have a maltiness, but I'm distracted first by the crunch, and then by the cardboard-like texture that they decline into if left for a bit too long in the milk. Oatmeal porridge was also distracting: it looked like the other cereal porridge but had nothing of the taste. It had to be cooked for a long time, milk was added and it had a harder texture, which required some chewing. It was a little too grown-up for me at that time.

Reminiscing about the taste and smell, I feel a physical need to have this cereal porridge right now. These days, when a dessert hints at malt, whether through its use or another similar flavour profile, or by a fortuitous combination of ingredients, I'm transported to an early happy time.

Avocados belong in the sweet foods category for me; I still find it difficult to comprehend how they can be considered a savoury ingredient. Split in half, the pale green flesh sprinkled with sugar, an avocado snack was a cooling salve against the humid heat. It tasted rich but wasn't sickly; the sugar accentuated its subtly pleasant sweetness. The combination of texture and taste is what arrests me. Baked creams, sweet tofu dishes, Cantonese custard tarts, Macanese and Portuguese custard tarts — all have that same combination in my view.

Coconut is not such an unconventional sweet ingredient. It can be shredded and desiccated, its milk and cream extracted, and oil refined from it. The multiple ways in which the coconut can be processed results, obviously, in a multitude of coconut dishes both sweet and savoury. My paternal grandmother made a Nyonya paste called kaya. This steamed coconut custard, with the addition of a generous amount of butter, was usually spread over bread (soft white loaf bread preferred; toasted bread also an acceptable alternative). Kaya is not very appetising in appearance; it can be olive brown, perhaps with a green tinge if pandan juice has been added, and its appearance slightly reminiscent of mucus if I'm to be honest. I struggled to make myself even approach it, let alone taste it, because of its repulsive appearance. However, the flavour of it is absolutely satisfying. I think in this instance the richness of the combined eggs, sugar and coconut creates a feeling of contented fulfilment.

My other favourite coconut titbits are the New Year biscuits called kuih bangkit. They are rather ornate things, the dough shaped by being pressed into wooden moulds and transformed into floral shapes. I would describe these biscuits as crunchy: they are composed of toasted tapioca brought together with egg and coconut cream. Some might describe their taste as unpleasantly chalky without any saving grace, but I recall how they radiated warmth when I popped them into my mouth and started chewing and that I liked how the flour crumbled all at once and sucked all the moisture out of my mouth. Perhaps, for me, the interest lay there and the coconut sweetness merely played the foil.

Red bean pancake

Soak 150 g (5½ oz) of dried red beans in water overnight. The next day, boil the drained red beans in plenty of water for about 30 minutes until completely soft. Drain and rub through a bamboo sieve placed over a bowl of water. Pour off the water in the bowl and place the red bean purée in a saucepan with 140 g (5 oz) of sugar. Stir over low heat until completely dry. Gradually stir in 3 tablespoons of corn oil over the low heat until a thick shiny paste is formed. Set aside to cool.

The pancake batter is made by beating together 150 g (5½ oz) of plain (all-purpose) flour, 2 tablespoons of custard powder, 1 tablespoon cornflour (cornstarch) and 2 eggs. Add ⅔ to 1 cupful of water to the mixture to make a smooth thin batter. Pour a small ladle of batter into a frying pan over medium heat to make as thin a pancake as possible and cook until set only on one side. Take the pancake out of the pan, spread a spoonful of red bean paste on one half of the pancake and fold over, sealing the edge of the pancake with a cornflour slurry. Fry both sides of the filled pancake in a hot pan until golden and cut into fingers to serve.

Coconut jam ice cream

The richness of the traditional kaya has been translated into a densely textured ice cream confection. It's a compilation of favourite coconut-based taste sensations. The proportions will leave you with leftover kaya and kuih bangkit. I'd suggest eating them in the traditional manner: spread on bread for the kaya and as a sweet snack for the kuih bangkit. Store the kaya in sterilised jars in the refrigerator.

Coconut jam ice cream

SERVES 4

Ingredients

FOR THE KAYA (COCONUT JAM)	6 EGGS 2 EGG YOLKS 150 ML (5 FL OZ) THICK COCONUT CREAM 220 G (8 OZ) CASTER (SUPERFINE) SUGAR ⅛ TEASPOON SALT 10 PANDAN LEAVES, TIED IN A KNOT
FOR THE KAYA ICE CREAM	235 G (8½ OZ) KAYA 60 ML (2 FL OZ) SUGAR SYRUP (MADE WITH 1½ TABLESPOONS SUGAR AND 1½ TABLESPOONS WATER) 235 ML (8 FL OZ) WHIPPING CREAM
FOR THE KUIH BANGKIT (TAPIOCA AND COCONUT BISCUITS)	75 G (2¾ OZ) CORNFLOUR (CORNSTARCH) 300 G (10½ OZ) TAPIOCA FLOUR 1 PANDAN LEAF, SLICED INTO PIECES 2 CM (¾ IN) THICK 1 LARGE EGG 75 G (2¾ OZ) CASTER (SUPERFINE) SUGAR 200 ML (7 FL OZ) THICK COCONUT MILK
FOR THE AVOCADO PASTE	50 G (1¾ OZ) AVOCADO FLESH 1 TABLESPOON POURING (SINGLE/LIGHT) CREAM 30 G (1 OZ) WHITE CHOCOLATE, CHOPPED 1 TEASPOON GRAPESEED OIL

Method

MAKE THE KAYA

Place all the ingredients in a large bowl. Using your hands mix everything together, crushing the pandan leaves to extract the juices. Keep going until all the sugar has dissolved. Strain through a sieve into a stainless steel bowl, squeezing the pandan dry so that all the mixture is extracted. Put the bowl over a saucepan of near boiling water. Cook as for custard, stirring regularly for 35–40 minutes until it thickens. It may appear grainy because of the relatively high amount of egg to liquid, but beat out the lumps. When cooked, place over an ice bath to cool.

MAKE THE KAYA ICE CREAM

Combine all the ingredients. Churn in an ice-cream machine until the consistency of whipped cream. Transfer to an ice-cream tray and freeze until set to your liking.

MAKE THE KUIH BANGKIT

Place the cornflour, tapioca flour and pandan leaf in a wide stainless steel saucepan. Dry-fry over low heat until the flour is completely dried out (it will collapse from the side of the pan). Set aside to cool completely. Preheat the oven to 150°C (300°F) and dust a baking tray with cornflour. Sift the pandan out of the flour. Whisk the egg and sugar in a bowl until thick and frothy. Mix in the flour; it will resemble breadcrumbs. Add the coconut milk gradually to form a pliable dough (you might not need to use all the coconut milk). Knead to form a smooth dough (but it won't be like any Western dough, given the different flour). Form into 2 cm (¾ in) balls. Put on the tray and flatten slightly. Or, if you're lucky enough to have a kuih bangkit mould, press dough into that to form the traditional shape. Bake for no more than 20 minutes. There shouldn't be any colour on the biscuits and their centres will be slightly soft but will crisp up when cooled.

MAKE THE AVOCADO PASTE

Purée the avocado flesh with the cream, then pass it through a sieve. Melt the chocolate in a stainless steel bowl over a saucepan of very hot water. Stir the avocado, chocolate and grapeseed oil together just until combined (over-agitating white chocolate will make it seize). Keep unrefrigerated until required.

ASSEMBLE THE DISH

Spread a spoonful of the avocado paste on the plate. Add a scoop of the ice cream with the kuih bangkit, roughly crumbled.

A dessert celebrating malty flavours

Some classic French elements feature in this recipe, chosen for their malt flavours: sugar caramelising on pastry; vanilla bean in combination with egg and milk; and, of course, malt itself as an ingredient. The kouign-aman (caramelised leavened pastry) is a highly involved piece of work. I am fond of this pastry because of the way the sugar caramelises during the baking and how it all comes together from such a messy sticky process.

A dessert celebrating malty flavours

SERVES MANY

Ingredients

FOR THE KOUIGN-AMAN

275 G (9½ OZ) STRONG FLOUR
1½ TEASPOONS SALT
5 G (¼ OZ) DRIED YEAST
2 TEASPOONS UNSALTED BUTTER, MELTED BUT NOT SEPARATED
225 G (8 OZ) UNSALTED BUTTER, AT THE SAME TEXTURE AS THE DOUGH (PLIABLE BUT NOT SOFT)
225 G (8 OZ) CASTER (SUPERFINE) SUGAR, PLUS EXTRA FOR DUSTING

FOR POACHING THE PEARS

600 G (1 LB 5 OZ) SUGAR
200 ML (7 FL OZ) FILTERED WATER
500 ML (17 FL OZ) CHARDONNAY
6 SMALL CORELLA PEARS, PEELED

FOR THE MALT MERINGUE POWDER

60 G (2 OZ) ICING (CONFECTIONERS') SUGAR
20 G (¾ OZ) MALT POWDER
160 G (5½ OZ) EGG WHITES (ABOUT 4 EGG WHITES)
100 G (3½ OZ) CASTER (SUPERFINE) SUGAR

FOR THE PRALINE PASTRY CREAM

275 ML (9½ FL OZ) MILK
½ VANILLA BEAN, SPLIT WITH SEEDS SCRAPED
4 EGG YOLKS
75 G (2¾ OZ) CASTER (SUPERFINE) SUGAR
20 G (¾ OZ) CORNFLOUR (CORNSTARCH)
1 TEASPOON UNSALTED BUTTER
POWDERED PRALINE (SEE BOX BELOW)
2 TEASPOONS WHITE RUM

TO MAKE POWDERED PRALINE

To make the powdered praline, scatter 80 g (2¾ oz) of toasted almonds over a sheet of lightly oiled foil. Melt 125 g (4½ oz) of sugar in a pan and cook without stirring until it caramelises and turns golden brown. Pour over the almonds and leave to cool and harden. Break up into smallish pieces and then process to a fine powder.

Method

MAKE THE KOUIGN-AMAN

Put the flour, salt and yeast in an electric mixer with a dough hook attached. Start to mix slowly and gradually add the melted butter and then 170 ml (5½ fl oz) water. Keep mixing until the dough comes together and is elastic (it springs up when a finger is pressed into it). Put in a lightly oiled bowl, cover with plastic wrap, then a tea towel and leave for 1 hour.

On a lightly floured surface, roll the dough into a rectangle that is 1.5 cm (½ in) thick. If the dough is sticking to the rolling pin or work surface, avoid using a lot of extra flour, and, if you must, brush off the excess. Place the block of butter between two sheets of plastic wrap and roll into a shape that will cover two-thirds of the length of the block of dough, leaving a margin of 2.5 cm (1 in) on the three outside edges. Remove the plastic wrap and sit the butter in place on the dough. Sprinkle a tablespoon of sugar over the butter. Fold the outside margins over the butter and then fold the butter-free end of dough over the butter. Again sprinkle a tablespoon of sugar over the surface of the dough. Now fold again to cover the exposed third of butter and dough (so, fold it up as you would a business letter). Roll out into a rectangle that is 1.5 cm (½ in) thick again and fold in three, repeating the sprinkling of sugar over the surface of the dough. Cover with plastic wrap and leave in the refrigerator for about an hour.

Roll out once again into a rectangle that is 1.5 cm (½ in) thick. Sprinkle another couple of tablespoons of the sugar over the dough. Press the sugar into the dough and fold a third of the pastry over. Sprinkle a couple more tablespoons of the remaining sugar over the unsugared surface, then fold the last third of dough over this. Wrap once again in plastic wrap and refrigerate for about 30 minutes. Preheat the oven to 220°C (430°F). Butter a 23 cm (9 in) square tart or cake tin and dust it with sugar. Roll the dough out to 40 x 30 cm (16 x 12 in) and roll into a cylinder. Cut along the length of the cylinder, gather the pastry, cut side up, and place into the tin. Scatter the remaining sugar on the pastry. Put in the oven and reduce the temperature to 180°C (350°F). Bake for 40–45 minutes until the top is deep golden brown from the caramelisation of the sugar and the bottom is well cooked and golden. Remove from the tin while hot and cool on a rack.

POACH THE PEARS

Combine the sugar, water and wine in a saucepan and bring to the boil. Add the pears and simmer for 30 minutes. Leave to cool in the syrup.

MAKE THE MALT MERINGUE POWDER

Preheat the oven to 120°C (250°F) and line two baking trays with paper. Sift the icing sugar and malt powder together, then put to one side. Beat the egg whites until soft peaks form. Gradually beat in the caster sugar and continue beating until glossy stiff peaks form. Fold in the icing sugar and malt mixture. Pipe meringues of 4 cm (1½ in) diameter onto the trays. Bake for about 1 hour until dry but not coloured. When cool, grate on a microplane to yield 4 tablespoons.

MAKE THE PRALINE PASTRY CREAM

Heat the milk with the vanilla pod and seeds to just below boiling point. Meanwhile, beat the egg yolks and sugar together until thick and pale. Stir in the cornflour. Whisk the heated milk into the yolk mixture and discard the vanilla bean. Pour the custard into a clean saucepan and bring to the boil, stirring constantly. Simmer for 1½–2 minutes. Remove from the heat and stir in the butter. Cover the surface with plastic wrap to prevent a skin forming and leave to cool. Measure the volume of the powdered praline in a cup and mix with an equal amount of pastry cream. Stir in the rum and then cover and keep refrigerated. Beat just before using, so that it is pliable.

ASSEMBLE THE DISH

Cut everyone a slice of kouign-aman and place, cut side down, on each plate. Add a few small spoonfuls of the praline pastry cream, a poached pear and a sprinkling of malt meringue powder.

Salt-baked chicken and salty avocado accompanying

I still have a lingering disbelief of avocado as a savoury flavour. I'm taking the cooling and creamy aspect of the avocado, which is what I associate with fruit, and translating it into a savoury presentation.

Ingredients

SERVES 4

FOR SALT-BAKED CHICKEN

- 2 TEASPOONS PEANUT OIL
- 3 GARLIC CLOVES, SMASHED
- 4 SPRING ONIONS (SCALLIONS), BRUISED
- 4 CM (1½ IN) PIECE OF GINGER, BRUISED
- 2 TABLESPOONS DRY SHERRY
- 2 TABLESPOONS LIGHT SOY SAUCE
- 100 ML (3½ FL OZ) LIGHT CHICKEN STOCK
- 4 CORIANDER (CILANTRO) STALKS
- 2 KG (4 LB 6 OZ) CHICKEN
- 3 KG (6 LB 10 OZ) ROCK SALT
- 1 TEASPOON FENNEL SEEDS
- 2 STAR ANISE, ROUGHLY CRUSHED
- 3 CLOVES, ROUGHLY CRUSHED
- 1 TEASPOON SICHUAN PEPPERCORNS
- 2 TEASPOONS CORIANDER SEEDS
- 4 CM (1½ IN) PIECE OF CASSIA BARK, ROUGHLY CRUSHED
- 1 LARGE PIECE OF CAUL FAT, ABOUT 200 G (7 OZ)

FOR THE AVOCADO PUREE

- 2 TEASPOONS VEGETABLE OIL
- 4 RED ASIAN SHALLOTS, THINLY SLICED
- 2 GARLIC CLOVES, THINLY SLICED
- 5 CM (2 IN) PIECE OF GINGER, PEELED AND JULIENNED
- 500 ML (17 FL OZ) LIGHT CHICKEN STOCK
- 100 ML (3½ FL OZ) GLUTINOUS RICE WINE
- 1 AVOCADO
- A FEW DROPS OF SESAME OIL

Method

SALT-BAKE THE CHICKEN

Make the marinade first. Heat the oil in a frying pan over high heat and add the garlic, spring onions and ginger. Stir-fry until fragrant and wilted. Add the sherry, fry for a few seconds, then add the soy sauce, chicken stock and coriander. Cool before proceeding. Carefully fill the cavity of the chicken with the marinade. Sew or skewer shut any openings, then sit the chicken, covered with a cloth, in a cool place for about 2 hours. Preheat the oven to 180°C (350°F). Put the rock salt in a dutch oven or similar ovenproof dish that is big enough to take the salt plus chicken. Put in the oven uncovered for 1 hour, stirring occasionally. Add the spices to the pot and return it to the oven for 10 minutes for the salt to become fragrant with the spices.

Take out one-third of the salt to use as a covering and make a nest of the salt left in the pot. Wrap up the chicken with the caul fat and sit in the nest of salt. Pour the one-third of salt back in to totally cover the sides and top of the chicken. Cover the pot and return to the oven for 1½ hours. Remove the chicken and brush off all the salt stuck to it. Remove the caul fat. Drain the marinade out of the chicken's cavity before cutting the chicken into serving pieces.

MAKE THE AVOCADO PUREE

Heat the oil in a saucepan over medium heat. Throw in the shallots, garlic and ginger and sweat them until cooked but not coloured. Pour the chicken stock into the pan. Bring the mixture to the boil and simmer for about 30 minutes until syrupy. The amount should be 100 ml (3½ fl oz). Add the rice wine and bring up to simmering point again. Strain, then leave the liquid to cool. Purée the flesh of the avocado in a blender or food processor. Quickly add the strained liquid. Season with salt and white pepper to emphasise the sweetness of the avocado mixture. Mix in a couple of drops of sesame oil.

ASSEMBLE THE DISH

I like to serve the chicken hot as a contrast to the coldness of the avocado. For each serve take some breast fillet and boned thigh or leg meat and serve with a dollop of avocado purée. You could also serve with an accompaniment of lightly fried, shredded ginger, garlic, spring onions and sliced fresh shiitake and shimeji mushrooms, seasoned with salt, white pepper and a little rice vinegar.

WHAT ARE COLOURS MEANT TO TASTE LIKE?

At this late stage in the book I have to confess to a failure of memory. The central inspiration for this memory is an instance of imagination taking over reality, but it remains one of my most vivid, nevertheless. We were attending a wedding in the kampong area where some Malay friends lived. We arrived in our car late in the day and parked it by the roadside. Our parents guided us down stone steps that led to a house set on stilts.

I recall how shy my sister and I were about being in that environment, for we knew no one yet there were so many laughing happy faces milling around. We were guided to the verandah and settled on rattan chairs with some kindly faced older women. On a low table there were a number of large jars containing snacks. I recall my mother taking the lead in tasting everything. The thing that astounded me was a cookie that looked like a lump of coal. My mother pointed it out and said, 'Try it: it's delicious'. I was thrown into a whirlwind of hesitancy yet wanting to satisfy my curiosity — this black thing surely was not edible? But my mother had already tasted it and pronounced it delicious. I overcame my negative feelings about the coal-black cookie and took a tentative bite. It was the crunchiest, hardest, lightest, sweetest, most fragrant, complex-flavoured coconut cookie I have ever tasted.

And my problem is, how much of this is fabrication created in my mind over the years, and how much actual reality? Neither my sister nor my mother has any recollection of the cookie, and I haven't found reference to it in any literature. So it has come to occupy a mythical place in my world and pushes me to explore what it might represent.

The incident reinforces a question that keeps appearing in my head: what are colours meant to taste like? One of my favourite sweet snacks, kuih cha guo, is a patty made of glutinous rice flour dough, wrapped around crunchy crushed peanut and steamed over rounds of banana leaves. My grandmother was an expert at making these; she didn't have the wooden moulds that you could press the dough into, so hers were simply flattish patties, dull white but translucent, showing a hint of the golden peanut filling. On occasion she coloured them red, but they didn't really taste any different. I had an inkling that this was symbolic of something but it was only later confirmed that these snacks were eaten to celebrate the Lunar New Year.

What was even more perplexing, once I had absorbed the tenuous state of certainty that cha guo could be white or red and still contain my favourite sweet peanut filling, was that, when we went to visit other households or when my mother brought them back from the market, the familiar shape and format of the cha guo could encase a multitude of fillings: red bean paste, green bean paste, savoury or sweet dried shrimp, salty peanut, salted turnip and pork. The colour meant nothing — it could be white, red or even a green version — but any one of them could contain the filling that I most looked forward to. How was a child to process that?

The seven-layered kuihs presented me with a similar problem. Home cooks prided themselves on being able to achieve seven or more perfectly thin and even layers by pouring a flour-thickened coconut cream mixture onto a tray and steaming it to set, pouring layer after thin layer until the required number was achieved. However, the way to differentiate the thin stripes was to colour the mixture. So, a kuih could have alternating layers of white and green, or white and pink, or even white, green and pink. I liked to peel off each layer individually to taste it. And I was continually disappointed to realise that the different colours bore no correlation to any difference in taste. You see how this playing around with colouring confused me?

I didn't have the same difficulty in comprehending taste and colour when different foods were of similar colours. Take, for example, orange-coloured foods. The flesh of the pumpkin, when cooked, usually becomes a deeper translucent orange: sweet, pasty, and easily crushed up into mush. Ripe papaya flesh is also orange: its sweetness tempered by a musty smell and a more resilient texture than cooked pumpkin. I understood that I could eat papaya raw, but not pumpkin; it was simply the way these things were. Was it, then, adults playing tricks of manipulation that I found so hard to accept and comprehend?

I also didn't have a problem accepting that the same object could appear different when presented in a different context. Whole eggs in their shells are hard-boiled, then dyed red. These are presented to guests at the month-long celebration of a newborn child: and the eggs taste simply like hard-boiled eggs. They do taste noticeably different if presented in the form of tea eggs. The marbled look of the whole egg results from staining with a fragrant mixture of tea and spices. An egg tastes leathery and sweet, sour and also savoury when steeped in a mixture of black vinegar, ginger and pork hock and trotter. (I mean to describe this as a delicious mixture, although it may appear rather odd when itemised.) However, there is no pretence about the egg being anything other than egg in that particular mixture. Perhaps my acceptance of the differing appearance and taste of egg showed an early favouring of function over form?

Steamed rice dumplings filled with peanuts

The filling is made by roughly grinding 50 g (1¾ oz) roasted peanuts and mixing with 25 g (1 oz) sugar. To make the dough, put 1½ cupfuls of glutinous rice flour in a bowl and gradually add about ¾ cup of water until the dough is soft and not completely holding together. To make it malleable, break off a quarter of the dough, roll into a flat disc and drop into a pan of boiling water to poach. The dough will rise to the top in a couple of minutes. Reduce the heat at that stage and let it poach for a further 20 seconds before lifting out. Combine the cooked dough with the raw dough and the result now should be more supple and malleable. Use vegetable oil to prevent the dough sticking to fingers and the work bench. Divide the dough into 15 balls, flatten each one in the palm of your hand and make a disc measuring 7 cm (2¾ in) in diameter that is thicker at the centre than at the edge. Place a teaspoon of the peanut mixture in the middle of the disc and bring the edges together to make a dumpling. Turn the dumpling over and press it down flat onto a 7 cm (2¾ in) circle of banana leaf that has been lightly brushed with vegetable oil. Repeat with the remaining dough and filling. Steam the dumplings over medium heat for 15 minutes until soft and cooked.

There are a number of variations on this sweet snack. What they have in common is a skin made, in its basic form, of a glutinous rice flour and water dough. Balls of the dough are rolled out and filled, then sealed, flattened and perhaps pressed into purpose-made wooden moulds, then steamed. I recall there was always a gloss on these dumplings, for they are brushed with oil after steaming. Fillings can be a mixture of ground peanuts, sesame and sugar, sweetened mung bean or sweetened red bean paste. Alternatively, the savoury ones (which were contrary to what I expected, since my grandmother never made such things) were a sautéed mixture.

A multi-coloured dessert

This recipe tries to answer the question of how different colours might taste. I also wanted to involve the diner in the excitement of colour changing in front of them.

A multi-coloured dessert

SERVES 4

Ingredients

FOR THE AVOCADO BLANCMANGE

125 G (4½ OZ) SKINLESS WHOLE ALMONDS
250 ML (8½ FL OZ) FILTERED WATER
1 TEASPOON VANILLA EXTRACT
60 G (2 OZ) (CASTER (SUPERFINE) SUGAR
3 GELATINE LEAVES
240 G (8½ OZ) AVOCADO FLESH (ABOUT 1½ AVOCADOS)
60 ML (2 FL OZ) MILK
55 ML (1¾ FL OZ) THICK (DOUBLE/HEAVY) CREAM

FOR THE GOLDEN EGG THREADS

5 EGG YOLKS
500 G (1 LB 2 OZ) SUGAR
4 PANDAN LEAVES, CRUSHED AND KNOTTED

FOR THE BUTTERFLY PEA FLOWER SYRUP

15 DRIED BUTTERFLY PEA FLOWERS (BUNGA TELANG)
70 G (2½ OZ) SUGAR
50 G (1¾ OZ) HONEY
4 PANDAN LEAVES, CRUSHED AND KNOTTED

FOR THE SWEET POTATO DUMPLINGS

350 G (12½ OZ) ORANGE SWEET POTATO, PEELED AND CUT INTO LARGE CHUNKS
50 G (1¾ OZ) GLUTINOUS RICE FLOUR
1 TABLESPOON CASTER (SUPERFINE) SUGAR
¼ TEASPOON SALT
GLUTINOUS RICE FLOUR OR CORNFLOUR (CORNSTARCH) FOR DUSTING
VEGETABLE OIL FOR DEEP-FRYING

LIME WEDGES

Method

MAKE THE AVOCADO BLANCMANGE

Grind the almonds and mix with the water. Leave overnight in the fridge to infuse, then strain through muslin to make almond milk. Combine 150 ml (5 fl oz) of almond milk, the vanilla and sugar in a saucepan. Put over low heat until just warmer than blood temperature (test with a finger). Meanwhile, soak the gelatine in cold water until soft. Drain, squeeze out any excess water and stir into the almond milk, then set aside. Purée the avocado and pass it through a sieve so that there are no lumps. Mix in the milk. Whip the cream to soft peaks and then fold in the avocado mixture. Once the almond milk mixture is cool but not set, fold the avocado cream through. Pour the mixture into a container and refrigerate for 2 hours or until set.

MAKE THE GOLDEN EGG THREADS

Beat the egg yolks in a bowl, cover with plastic wrap and rest for at least 2 hours in the refrigerator. Make a syrup by combining the sugar, pandan leaves and 950 ml (32 fl oz) water over medium heat until the sugar has dissolved. Leave to infuse for 30 minutes and then discard the pandan. Pour three-quarters of the syrup into a narrow saucepan and keep at a constant 75°C (150°F). Fit the very smallest round piping nozzle into a piping bag. Hold over the syrup and pass the egg yolks through, making long thin threads. Poach them for a couple of minutes until cooked. You might need to adjust the temperature of the syrup to get the desired result. Once cooked, scoop out the threads and drop into the remaining one-quarter of the syrup to steep and keep.

MAKE THE BUTTERFLY PEA FLOWER SYRUP

Using a mortar and pestle, crush the butterfly pea flowers with a teaspoon of the sugar to a fine powder. Set aside. In a saucepan combine the rest of the sugar with the honey and 250 ml (8½ fl oz) water and bring to the boil. Drop in the pandan leaves, remove from the heat and leave to infuse while the syrup cools. Remove the pandan then mix the butterfly pea flower powder into the syrup. Strain to remove any debris.

MAKE THE SWEET POTATO DUMPLINGS

Steam the sweet potato until soft and mushy, then leave to cool. Mash the sweet potato, rice flour, sugar and salt together. Shape into 2.5 cm (1 in) balls and dust with rice flour. Heat the oil in a deep-fryer to 170°C (340°F) and fry the dumplings in batches until golden. Drain on paper towels and serve immediately.

ASSEMBLE THE DESSERT

For each serving, place a spoonful of avocado blancmange in a wide bowl. Arrange 3 hot sweet potato dumplings and some golden threads of egg yolk in the bowl. Spoon over some of the butterfly pea flower syrup. Invite eaters to try the dessert as is, then offer the lime wedges to add a few drops of juice onto the syrup. Observe what happens and taste what is different.

Reminiscences on the black Malay cookie

It was a figment of my imagination, perhaps, but the mysterious black cookie still occupies a space in my thoughts. This is a meditation on what that particular memory means to me.

Reminiscences on the black Malay cookie

SERVES 4

Ingredients

FOR THE ORANGE BLOSSOM ICE CREAM

4 EGG YOLKS
2 TABLESPOONS CASTER (SUPERFINE) SUGAR
100 ML (3½ FL OZ) POURING (SINGLE/LIGHT) CREAM
250 ML (8½ FL OZ) ORANGE BLOSSOM SYRUP (SEE BOX BELOW)
250 ML (8½ FL OZ) THICK (DOUBLE/HEAVY) CREAM

FOR THE SESAME SEED SWEET

175 G (6 OZ) SESAME OR SUNFLOWER SEED PASTE
140 G (5 OZ) SUGAR

FOR THE COCONUT ASH PASTRY

115 G (4 OZ) ALMOND MEAL (GROUND ALMONDS)
2 TABLESPOONS UNSWEETENED COCOA POWDER
40 G (1½ OZ) TAPIOCA FLOUR, TOASTED IN A PAN UNTIL BONE DRY BUT UNCOLOURED
55 G (2 OZ) HONEY
½ LARGE EGG, LIGHTLY BEATEN
½ TEASPOON VANILLA EXTRACT
35 G (1¼ OZ) UNSALTED BUTTER, SOFTENED
COCONUT ASH (SEE BOX BELOW)

FOR THE COCONUT SAUCE

50 G (1¾ OZ) PALM SUGAR (GULA MELAKA)
2 PANDAN LEAVES, CRUSHED AND KNOTTED
10 G (¼ OZ) GLUTINOUS RICE FLOUR
70 ML (2¼ FL OZ) THICK COCONUT MILK
¼ TEASPOON SALT

TO MAKE ORANGE BLOSSOM SYRUP

To make orange blossom syrup, bring 500 ml (17 fl oz) of water and 350 g (12½ oz) of sugar to the boil, stirring to dissolve. Remove from the heat and, when the temperature drops to 80°C (175°F), add 55 g (2 oz) of fresh orange blossoms. Store in sterilised preserving jars for at least 12 hours before use.

TO MAKE COCONUT ASH

Dry the husk of a coconut in the sun for a few days. Set it alight and let it burn until black. Break up into smaller pieces and pass through a sieve to obtain a fine powder.

Method

MAKE THE ORANGE BLOSSOM ICE CREAM

In a bowl beat the egg yolks and sugar until the sugar dissolves. Combine the pouring cream with the orange blossom syrup in a pan and bring to simmering point. Beat into the egg yolk mixture and pour into a clean saucepan. Cook over low heat until the custard thickens enough to coat the back of a metal spoon. Strain into a bowl set over iced water and cool quickly. When cold, mix in the thick cream. Transfer to an ice-cream machine and churn following the manufacturer's instructions.

MAKE THE SESAME SEED SWEET

Place the sesame seed paste in a bowl and beat until the oil and the paste comes together again. Place the sugar and 50 ml (1¾ fl oz) water in a small saucepan and bring to the boil. Continue boiling until the syrup reaches 125°C (255°F). Beat into the sesame seed paste bit by bit. This mixture should be crumbly and melt-in-your-mouth. Set aside until required.

MAKE THE COCONUT ASH PASTRY

In a food processor blend the almond meal and cocoa together as finely as possible. Add the tapioca flour. Combine the honey, egg, vanilla and butter and quickly process into the dry ingredients. With your hands, press the dough into a block 1 cm (½ in) high. Cover with plastic wrap and leave for 30 minutes in the refrigerator. Preheat the oven to 170°C (340°F) and line a baking tray with baking paper. Cut the block of dough into 1.5 cm (½ in) squares. Spread evenly on the baking tray and bake for 10 minutes. Reduce the temperature to 150°C (300°F) and leave the biscuits in the oven to dry out thoroughly for up to 30 minutes. If they start to blacken, reduce the temperature by 10°C (20°F). Cool on cake racks, then dust with coconut ash.

MAKE THE COCONUT SAUCE

Put the palm sugar and 125 ml (4 fl oz) water in a saucepan and bring to the boil, stirring to dissolve the sugar. Drop in the pandan leaves and remove from the heat. Leave to infuse for 30 minutes then strain out the leaves. Mix the glutinous rice flour, coconut milk and salt together in a saucepan. Stir in the palm sugar syrup. Cook over low heat, stirring, until thickened. Serve warm.

ASSEMBLE THE DESSERT

Scatter some of the sesame seed sweet onto each plate and arrange a few coconut ash pastries around. Drizzle with a spoonful of the coconut sauce and then place a scoop of the ice cream amongst the arrangement.

A monochromatic dish

This recipe aims to express the idea that, within the self-enforced limitations of a monochromatic white scheme, the contrasting tastes, textures and temperatures of the dish now become its primary distinguishing factors. If you can't help yourself and have the urge for some colour relief, then, after putting the cream on the plate, dust it with a mixture of crushed crystallised violets and finely grated toasted almonds.

Ingredients

SERVES 4

FOR THE WHITE SPONGE

- 70 G (2½ OZ) PLAIN (ALL-PURPOSE) FLOUR
- ½ TEASPOON DRIED YEAST
- 100 G (3½ OZ) CASTER (SUPERFINE) SUGAR
- 80 G (2¾ OZ) PLAIN FLOUR, ADDITIONAL
- 50 G (1¾ OZ) GLUTINOUS RICE FLOUR
- 2 TEASPOONS VEGETABLE OIL

FOR THE WHITE BEAN AND ALMOND CREAM

- 50 G (1¾ OZ) WHITE NAVY BEANS, SOAKED IN COLD WATER OVERNIGHT
- 80 G (2¾ OZ) ROASTED ALMONDS
- 2 TABLESPOONS CASTER (SUPERFINE) SUGAR
- 200 ML (7 FL OZ) THICKENED (DOUBLE/HEAVY) CREAM
- 40 G (1½ OZ) UNSALTED BUTTER, SOFTENED

FOR THE MERINGUES

- 180 G (6½ OZ) EGG WHITES (ABOUT 5 EGGS)
- 350 G (12½ OZ) CASTER (SUPERFINE) SUGAR
- 100 G (3½ OZ) ALMOND MEAL (GROUND ALMONDS)
- ZEST OF 1 LEMON

Method

MAKE THE WHITE SPONGE

Combine the plain flour with the yeast and 100 ml (3½ fl oz) water to make a smooth paste and leave to ferment in a warm place for a couple of hours. Combine the caster sugar with 125 ml (4 fl oz) water in a pot over heat to dissolve and form a syrup. Set aside.

When the yeast mixture is sufficiently fermented, sift together the additional 80 g (2¾ oz) plain flour with the glutinous rice flour and mix with the yeast mixture. Stir in the vegetable oil and then the sugar syrup. Cover and leave again to ferment for 4 hours in a warm spot. Grease and line a 20 cm (8 in) round cake tin. Pour in the fermented mixture and prove for a further 30 minutes. Steam over medium heat for 15 minutes until the sponge springs up when pressed. Turn out when ready to use and serve hot or warm.

MAKE THE WHITE BEAN AND ALMOND CREAM

Drain the beans. Put in a saucepan, cover generously with cold water and bring to the boil. Cook until tender. Purée with a blender or food processor, then pass through a sieve into a bowl. Measure out 80 g (2¾ oz) and set aside. Pulverise the almonds with the caster sugar using a mortar and pestle. Bring half the cream to the boil and add the almond and sugar mixture. Leave off the heat for 1 hour to infuse. Strain through muslin, reserving the cream only. Add to the beans along with the butter and mix well. Whip the remaining half of the cream to soft peaks and fold into the bean and almond mixture. Keep chilled until needed.

MAKE THE MERINGUES

Preheat the oven to 110°C (230°F) and line two baking trays with baking paper. Beat the egg whites until they form soft peaks. Gradually beat in the sugar and continue beating until stiff peaks form. Fold in the ground almonds and lemon zest. Use a piping bag to pipe meringues of varying sizes ranging from 2 to 3 cm (¾ to 1¼ in) in diameter. Bake for 30 minutes, then reduce the temperature to 100°C (210°F) and bake for 1 hour. Do not allow to colour.

ASSEMBLE THE DESSERT

For each serving spread a tablespoon of cream on the plate. Break off a few small pieces of white sponge for each person and arrange around the cream. Add meringues of various sizes to the plate and serve. (You will have leftover meringues, which can be stored in an airtight container and eaten another time.)

Glossary

AMARANTH LEAVES

AVAILABLE FROM ASIAN GREENGROCER STORES, AMARANTH LEAVES GROW IN A VARIETY OF COLOURS FROM RED, PURPLE AND GOLD, TO GREEN (SOMETIMES ALL ON THE SAME PLANT). THEY HAVE A MILDLY SWEET FLAVOUR, A LITTLE LIKE ENGLISH SPINACH, AND BECOME TANNIC WHEN COOKED UNTIL SOFT, ALSO LIKE ENGLISH SPINACH.

BETEL LEAVES

THESE GLOSSY, HEART-SHAPED LEAVES WITH THEIR SWEET, RESINOUS, SMOKY AROMA COME FROM A CREEPING PLANT. THEY ARE USED IN SOUTH-EAST ASIA AS A HERB OR A LEAF WRAPPING.

BLACHAN (BLACAN)

THIS DRIED SHRIMP PASTE IS BOUGHT IN A FIRM BLOCK. IT KEEPS WITHOUT REFRIGERATION AND IS ALWAYS TOASTED OR ROASTED BEFORE USE. TO ROAST BLACHAN, COVER WITH FOIL AND PUT IN A PREHEATED 160°C (320°F) OVEN FOR 15 MINUTES UNTIL DRIED OUT AND 'TOASTY'.

BUTTERFLY PEA FLOWERS (BUNGA TELANG)

PICKED FROM A CREEPING PLANT, THESE VIVIDLY BLUE FLOWERS ARE USED AS A NATURAL FOOD COLOURING IN SOUTH-EAST ASIAN CUISINE IN SUCH DISHES AS GLUTINOUS RICE SWEETS. USE EITHER DRIED OR FRESH.

CHILLI BEAN PASTE (DOU BAN JIANG)

THIS HIGHLY SALTED AND SPICY FERMENTED PASTE IS MADE FROM BROAD BEANS AND SOY BEANS AND MOST COMMONLY ASSOCIATED WITH SICHUAN CUISINE. THE VARIETY I PREFER IS THE PIXIAN DOUBANJIANG.

CHINKIANG VINEGAR

ALSO KNOWN AS ZHENJIANG VINEGAR, THIS ORIGINATES FROM JIANGSU PROVINCE, CHINA. MADE FROM BLACK GLUTINOUS RICE, IT IS A VERY SHARP, DARK-COLOURED VINEGAR WITH SMOKY OVERTONES.

COCONUT CREAM AND MILK

WHERE A RECIPE CALLS FOR EITHER OF THESE, IT IS BEST TO USE CREAM OR MILK THAT HAS BEEN FRESHLY EXTRACTED. THIS IS DONE BY PROCESSING THE WHITE COCONUT FLESH WITH AN EQUAL AMOUNT OF HOT WATER. SQUEEZE THE MASS THROUGH MUSLIN CLOTH INTO A NON-METALLIC BOWL OR CONTAINER. LEAVE FOR ABOUT HALF AN HOUR TO ALLOW THE CREAM TO RISE TO THE TOP. THE APPROXIMATE YIELD PER COCONUT IS 250 ML (8½ FL OZ) OF CREAM. THE RESIDUE CAN BE STEEPED IN HOT WATER AND SQUEEZED OUT AGAIN TO YIELD A LARGER AMOUNT OF COCONUT MILK. IF USING TINNED COCONUT CREAM, USE THE SOLID MASS AT THE TOP OF THE TIN AS YOU WOULD FRESH COCONUT CREAM.

CURRY LEAVES

THESE ARE ALSO KNOWN AS SWEET NEEM LEAVES. THEY ARE VERY AROMATIC AND ARE USED FOR FLAVOURING DISHES SUCH AS CURRIES AND RELISHES.

DRIED SCALLOPS

THESE ARE ALSO KNOWN AS COLPOY. THEY MUST BE RECONSTITUTED IN WATER BEFORE USE. BUY FROM CHINESE FOOD STORES AND CHOOSE LARGE ONES AS THEY HAVE A BETTER FLAVOUR.

FERMENTED RED BEAN CURD

BEAN CURD THAT HAS BEEN FERMENTED IN RICE WINE AND RED RICE YEAST, THIS COMES IN LITTLE BRICKS SUSPENDED IN RED LIQUID IN GLASS JARS. IT IS USED IN SMALL QUANTITIES AS A SEASONING OR FLAVOURING IN CHINESE CUISINE, MOST OFTEN IN PORRIDGE, STIR-FRIES AND BRAISES.

FISH MAW

THE SWIM BLADDER OF THE FISH IS USED TO CONTROL BUOYANCY AND STABILITY. THIS IS DRIED AND USED AS A LUXURY DELICACY IN CHINESE CUISINE, AS A TEXTURAL FOOD THAT TAKES ON THE FLAVOUR OF THE SAUCES OR BROTHS IN WHICH IT IS COOKED. IT'S BEST PURCHASED IN LARGE THICK PIECES.

GINGER JUICE

FOR 1 TEASPOON OF GINGER JUICE, PUREE A 3 CM (1¼ IN) PIECE OF FRESH YOUNG GINGER, THEN PRESS THROUGH A FINE SIEVE. FOR 10 TEASPOONS OF GINGER JUICE, PUREE 60 G (2 OZ) PEELED GINGER, THEN PRESS THROUGH A FINE SIEVE.

GULA MELAKA

THIS MALAYSIAN PALM SUGAR IS MADE FROM SAP EXTRACTED FROM THE PALM TREE AND IS USUALLY SOLD IN SMALL CYLINDRICAL BLOCKS.

IKAN BILIS

THIS IS DRIED ANCHOVY, USED IN SOUTH-EAST ASIAN COOKING TO FLAVOUR SOUPS AND STIR-FRIES, OR AS A SNACK IN ITSELF. IT CAN BE BOUGHT IN ASIAN SUPERMARKETS (I BUY MALAYSIAN OR THAI BRANDS).

JASMINE FLOWERS

THESE SMALL, IVORY WHITE FLOWERS ARE FROM THE ARABIAN OR BIBLICAL JASMINE (JASMINUM SAMBAC). THE FLOWERS ARE STEEPED IN WATER TO EXTRACT THEIR SCENT TO PERFUME SWEETS AND DESSERTS.

KALAMANSI LIME

THIS SMALL, VERY SOUR LIME, ALSO KNOWN AS CALAMANSI OR MUSK LIME, IS VERY POPULAR IN THE PHILIPPINES AND IN MALAYSIA, WHERE IT IS CALLED LIMAU KESTURI.

KUZU STARCH

THIS IS OBTAINED FROM THE ROOTS OF THE KUZU (ALSO KNOWN AS KUDZU) PLANT. IT CAN BE PURCHASED IN ASIAN GROCERS, OR IN JAPANESE GROCERS UNDER THE NAME OF KUZUKO.

PANDAN LEAVES

THESE LONG GREEN LEAVES ARE USED IN SOUTH-EAST ASIAN CUISINE AS A WRAPPING OR FLAVOURING, MOST OFTEN IN SWEETS. THE LEAF HAS A SWEET, GRASSY, GREEN AROMA THAT COMPLEMENTS COCONUT IN PARTICULAR.

PRESERVED MUSTARD GREENS (XIAN CAI)

THE PUNGENT MUSTARD GREEN VEGETABLE IS PRESERVED IN BRINE, LOSING ITS VIVID GREEN TO BECOME OLIVE COLOURED. IT IS USED IN CHINESE AND SOUTH-EAST ASIAN CUISINES.

PURSLANE LEAVES

THE LEAVES OF THIS SUCCULENT HAVE A SLIGHTLY SOUR AND SALTY TASTE. ALSO KNOWN AS PURSLEY, PIGWEED AND LITTLE HOGWEED, THEY ARE AVAILABLE FROM SPECIALIST GREENGROCERS.

QUARK

QUARK IS A SOFT, WHITE, UNSALTED, UN-AGED CHEESE, MADE BY WARMING SOURED MILK. IT IS NOT MADE WITH RENNET LIKE COMMERCIAL CURD OR COTTAGE CHEESE, SO ITS CLOSEST SUBSTITUTE WOULD BE THE FRENCH FROMAGE FRAIS OR INDIAN PANEER.

RED SEDIMENT (HONG ZAO)

THIS RICE WINE IS MADE BY GRINDING TOGETHER YEAST BALLS AND RED RICE YEAST AND THEN LAYERED WITH STEAMED GLUTINOUS RICE. LEFT TO FERMENT FOR 4 DAYS, IT DEVELOPS VERY INTERESTING FRUIT FLAVOURS WITH LOTS OF FLORAL TOP NOTES. LEFT FOR A WEEK OR MORE, IT BECOMES QUITE POTENT.

ROSE WINE

THIS CHINESE COOKING WINE IS MADE OF SORGHUM AND DISTILLED ROSE PETALS. IT'S HIGH IN ALCOHOL CONTENT, SO SLIGHTLY SWEET. OFTEN USED FOR SEASONING MEAT.

SAMPHIRE

ROCK SAMPHIRE OR CRITHMUM IS AN EDIBLE WILD SUCCULENT THAT GROWS IN ROCKY OUTCROPS. IT HAS A HOT, SPICY TASTE. MARSH SAMPHIRE, ALSO KNOWN AS PICKLEWEED, GLASSWORT AND SEA BEANS, GROWS IN SALTY MARSHES AND HAS A HIGH SALT CONTENT. BOTH TYPES CAN BE EATEN RAW OR COOKED.

SAND GINGER (KAEMPFERIA GALANGAL)

SAND GINGER IS USED IN CHINESE AND SOUTH-EAST ASIAN CUISINES AND TRADITIONAL MEDICINE. SAND GINGER POWDER IS OFTEN USED AS A FLAVOURING IN CHICKEN DISHES, SUCH AS SALT-BAKED OR STEAMED CHICKEN.

SEA (BEACH) BANANA

THIS IS A TYPE OF SUCCULENT. GENERALLY THERE IS NO NEED TO CHOP, AND IT IS USED WHOLE LIKE SAMPHIRE.

SHISO (PERILLA)

ALSO KNOWN AS BEEFSTEAK PLANT, SHISO IS A RELATIVE OF BASIL AND MINT AND HAS A DISTINCTIVE ANISEED FLAVOUR.

SPRING ONION (SCALLION) JUICE

TO MAKE 2 TEASPOONS OF JUICE, PUREE THE WHITES OF 2-4 SPRING ONIONS AND THEN PRESS THROUGH A FINE SIEVE TO EXTRACT THE JUICE.

SWEETENED BLACK VINEGAR

THIS RICE VINEGAR IS MADE BY A PROCESS OF COMBINING RICE WINE, YEAST, GLUTINOUS RICE AND BACTERIA TOGETHER OVER A NUMBER OF STAGES. IT IS THE KEY INGREDIENT IN THE TRADITIONAL CHINESE DISH OF PORK KNUCKLE, GINGER AND EGG, WHICH IS SERVED TO WOMEN AS A RESTORATIVE AFTER CHILDBIRTH.

TAMARIND

THIS SOURING AGENT IS POPULAR IN SOUTH-EAST ASIAN CUISINE. I PREFER TO USE THE PULP, WHICH IS SOLD IN BLOCKS IN ASIAN PRODUCE STORES. THE PODS OF THE TAMARIND FRUIT ARE STRIPPED OF THEIR HUSKS AND COMPRESSED. TO USE, MIX WITH WATER TO FORM A PASTE AND THEN PASS THROUGH A SIEVE TO GET RID OF ANY UNWANTED FIBRES OR SEEDS.

TOMALLEY

THIS IS THE LIVER OR PANCREAS OF SHELLFISH. THE SHELLFISH USED MUST BE VERY FRESH, NEVER FROZEN.

WINE YEAST

IN ASIAN COOKING, WINE BALLS OR WINE CUBES ARE BALLS OF BREWER'S YEAST USED TO CONVERT SUGAR INTO ALCOHOL AND CARBON DIOXIDE. THEY HAVE A HIGH ALCOHOL AND SUGAR TOLERANCE AND ARE AVAILABLE FROM ASIAN PRODUCE STORES. BAKER'S YEAST IS NOT A SUCCESSFUL SUBSTITUTE.

Index

A
A dessert celebrating malty flavours 318
A dessert inspired by cocoa fruit 264
A different type of tuile 194
A gritty, fibrous shrimp paste 214
A jumble of shapes and colours masked by yellow 126
A monochromatic dish 336
A multi-coloured dessert 328
A platter of duck with steamed buns and accompaniments 286
A savoury tropical fruit salad 92
A searingly hot braise of goat 156
A surprising fruit flavour appears in the rabbit pie 100
A traditional recipe for fallen mangoes 90
Abalone 146, 148
almond
  Almond milk 66
  White bean and almond cream 337
An alcoholic dumpling 180
An unassuming dish of scallops 202
Ants' nest cake 198
artichoke
  The ritual of preparing globe artichokes 96
  Soured Jerusalem artichokes 288
asparagus: Oyster mushrooms with asparagus and botarga 84
Assam paste 25
aubergine *see* eggplant
avocado
  Avocado blancmange 330
  Avocado dressing 22
  Avocado paste 316
  Avocado purée 323

B
Bamboo shoot, glazed 84
Bamboo, young
  preparing 166
  roasting 167
banana
  A savoury tropical fruit salad 92
  Banana fritters 27
bean sprouts: Laksa lemak 209
beans
  Grilled squid and white beans 110
  Red bean pancake 313
  White bean and almond cream 337
beef
  Beef satay with peanut sauce 284
  The fat rendered from beef rendang 268
  Numbing ox tongue 226
  Ox tongue with five tastes 228
  Sirloin and accompaniments 166
Betel leaves, spiced lentils and grilled okra 16
Birthday tomato and chilli crab 144
biscuits
  A different type of tuile 194
  Deep-fried coconut crescent puffs 63
  Love letters 51
  Reminiscences on the black Malay cookie 332
  Tapioca and coconut biscuits 316
  Wafers 58
Bitter melon with added rewards 274
Bitter melon with celery 230
Bitter melon dressing 276
blachan
  Blachan paste 185
  Stir-fried kang kong with blachan 185
Black fungus relish 242
the black Malay cookie, Reminiscences on 332
black moss, Braised dried oysters with 235
Black sesame croquant 174
Black sesame dust 58
Black sesame pudding 58
Blackened mashed chillies 165
Blackened young coconut 260
blood sausage, Chinese-style 244
borage
  Borage and other cucumber-like flavours 44
  Walnut and borage salad 46
Borlotti beans 112
Bouillon, spiced 218
Braised chestnuts 309
Braised dried oysters with black moss 235
bread: Hollow bread chicken 72
Brine 46
Briny concoction 204
broth
  Laksa broth 209
  Spiced mushroom broth 139
  Tomato broth 192
brussels sprouts: Roasted fish: Chinese herbal concoction 40
Burnt ginger and garlic oil 263
Burnt orange sauce 66
Butterfly pea flower syrup 330

C
cakes
  A different type of tuile 194
  Ants' nest cake 198
  Chiffon cake 266
  White sponge 337
Candied ikan bilis 108
Candied pomelo peel 266
Candied walnuts 226
capsicum: Red capsicum salt 30
Caramelised white chocolate 280
Caraway seasoning 18
Cashew salt 230
Cassia bark oil 266
celery, Green bitter melon with 230
chestnuts
  Chestnuts and chicken liver, mixed together 308
  Mushrooms with walnuts and chestnuts 130
  Roasted fish: Chinese herbal concoction 40
  shelling chestnuts 132
  Walnut and chestnut garnish 132
chicken
  Chestnuts and chicken liver, mixed together 308
  Chicken braised with dried shiitake mushrooms 129
  Chicken liver parfait 127
  Chicken and other bits 236
  Chicken sauce 306
  Chicken steamed with lily buds 299
  Chicken stock 185
  Chicken threads and green tomato 30
  Chicken wing confit 306
  Green tomato, hazelnut and shiitake 28
  Hollow bread chicken 72
  My mother's chicken curry 273
  Salt-baked chicken and salty avocado accompanying 322
  Salted and steamed chicken 300
  The transformed taste of chicken 304
  Vadouvan sauce 160
Chiffon cake 266
chilli
  Birthday tomato and chilli crab 144
  Blackened mashed chillies 165
  Chilli oil 280
  Green chilli, coriander and chilli relish 73
  Green peppercorn and chilli paste 230
  Mango chilli ice 278
  Rose petal and chilli paste 34
Chinese herbal concoction 42
Chinese-style blood sausage 244
chocolate
  Caramelised white chocolate 280
  Chocolate and coffee cream 58
  Chocolate sauce 266
Chrysanthemum and cucumber leaves 288
Citrus oil 179
Clams with salted and steamed chicken 300
cocoa fruit, A dessert inspired by 264
Cocoa water jelly 266
coconut
  Blackened young coconut 260
  Coconut ash pastry 334
  Coconut cream and blachan sauce 188
  Coconut, gula melaka and sweet potato 64
  Coconut jam ice cream 314
  Coconut sauce 334
  Deep-fried coconut crescent puffs 63
  Love letters 51
  Palm sugar custard 280

Sago pudding 171
Tapioca and coconut biscuits 316
coffee
Chocolate and coffee cream 58
Plums, curry leaf syrup and baked coffee cream 36
The concept of celebration 86
cookies *see* biscuits
Coral trout, steamed 148
Corn and egg flower soup 185
crab
Birthday tomato and chilli crab 144
Corn and egg flower soup 185
Stuffed crab claws 197
crackers, Hand-made prawn 144
Crayfish, poached 136
cream
Chocolate and coffee cream 58
Cumin cream 200
Vanilla cream 80
White bean and almond cream 337
Crescent puffs, deep-fried coconut 63
Croustades 49
cucumber
Cucumber, dressed 167
Cucumber and chrysanthemum leaves 288
Cucumber juice 112
Marinated cucumber 46
Turmeric pickle 127
Cumin cream 200
cumquat, Mullet steamed with salted 15
curry
Curry leaf salt 263
Fish head curry 249
Frosted curry leaves 37
My mother's chicken curry 273
Plums, curry leaf syrup and baked coffee cream 36

D

Deep-fried coconut crescent puffs 63
desserts
A dessert celebrating malty flavours 318
A dessert inspired by cocoa fruit 264
A multi-coloured dessert 328
A savoury tropical fruit salad 92
Banana fritters 27
Coconut jam ice cream 314
Luminous things 78
Mango chilli ice 278
Plums, curry leaf syrup and baked coffee cream 36
Reminiscences on the black Malay cookie 332
Sago with ginger milk pudding 172
Sago pudding 171
Shards, things hidden, shattered and revealed 56
Steamed rice dumplings filled with peanuts 327
dressings *see* sauces/dressings
duck
A platter of duck with steamed buns and accompaniments 286
A savoury tropical fruit salad 92
Duck tongues 239
dumplings
An alcoholic dumpling 180
Steamed rice dumplings filled with peanuts 327
Sweet potato dumplings 330

E

eggplant
Eggplant relish 164
Oysters, eggplant custard and rose petals 32
eggs
A different type of tuile 194
Corn and egg flower soup 185
Golden egg threads 330
Lobster siam 186
Oyster omelette 250
Enoki mushrooms
fried in butter 167
wilted 292

F

The fat rendered from beef rendang 268
Fermented shiso and pickled mussels 52
figs, Honey-spiced 200
Fingers of purple potato 122
fish
Borage and other cucumber-like flavours 44
Fish fragrant watermelon 20
Fish head curry 249
Fish presented in its natural shape 158
Fish steeped in floral sweet vinegar 290
Green mango pickles with other things that make me shiver 224
Mullet steamed with salted cumquat 15
Oyster mushrooms with asparagus and botarga 84
Painted and smoked kingfish 68
Pickled fish 120
Roasted fish: Chinese herbal concoction 40
Salty fish roe relish 292
Sand whiting with spinach 224
Smoked rainbow trout 46
Steamed coral trout 148
Three kinds of fish 146
see also seafood
floral sweet vinegar, Fish steeped in 292
Fragrant black noodles from outdoor stalls 105
Frosted curry leaves 37
fruit salad, A savoury tropical 92

G

garlic
A searingly hot braise of goat 156
Burnt ginger and garlic oil 263
Garlic juice 152
Garlic and scallion oil 105
garnish, Walnut and chestnut 132
The gills of shiitake mushrooms 134
ginger
Burnt ginger and garlic oil 263
Ginger juice 152
Sago with ginger milk pudding 172
globe artichokes, The ritual of preparing 96
Glutinous rice wine 174
goat
A searingly hot braise of goat 156
Goat sausage and a spiced tomato sauce 162
Green bitter melon with celery 230
Green chilli, coriander and chilli relish 73
green mango
A traditional recipe for fallen mangoes 90
Green mango pickles 222
Green mango pickles with other things that make me shiver 224
Green papaya pickle 108
Green peppercorn and chilli paste 230
Green tea dressing, shoots and fungi 82
Green tomato, hazelnut and shiitake 28
greens, Peanut and tannic 294
Grilled squid and candied ikan bilis 106
Grilled squid and white beans 110

H

Hand-made prawn crackers 144
hazelnuts
Green tomato, hazelnut and shiitake 28
Hazelnut meringue 80
Hazelnut and shiitake paste 30
herbal concoction, Chinese 40
Hollow bread chicken 72
Honey-spiced figs 200
Honeyed prawn sauce 152
Hot oil 230
Hot and sour pork hock 222

I

ice cream
Coconut jam ice cream 314
Mango chilli ice 280
Orange blossom ice cream 334
Ikan bilis, candied 108
The intense colour of pickled radishes 118

J

Jam, coconut (kaya) 316
Jasmine syrup 49
jelly
Cocoa water jelly 266
Sweet potato jelly 66
Jerusalem artichokes, soured 288
John dory, presented in its natural shape 158

K

kang kong, Stir-fried, with blachan 185
Kaya 316
Kidneys, pig's, in sake 245
kingfish, Painted and smoked 68
Kouign-aman 320

L

Laksa lemak 209
reworking into a spiced bouillon 216
lamb, Sweet and sour 254
leaves
Cucumber and chrysanthemum leaves 288
Leaves and stems treated meticulously 190
Lemon curd 58
Lemon salt 124, 230
Lemon syrup 192
lentils: Betel leaves, spiced lentils and grilled okra 16
lily buds, Chicken steamed with 299
liver
Chestnuts and chicken liver, mixed together 308

Chicken liver parfait 127
'liver' of shellfish (tomalley) 150
Lobster siam 186
Loofahs 274, 276
Love letters 51
Luminous things 78

M
Malt meringue powder 320
malty flavours, A dessert celebrating 318
mango
A traditional recipe for fallen mangoes 90
Green mango pickles 222
Green mango pickles with other things that make me shiver 224
Mango chilli ice 278
Marron tails, roasted 148
Marshmallow buttons 80
melon
Bitter melon with added rewards 274
Green bitter melon with celery 230
meringues 231, 266, 337
Hazelnut meringue 80
Malt meringue powder 320
milk
Almond milk 66
Ginger milk pudding 174
Soy milk sheets 136
Mullet steamed with salted cumquat 15
Mung bean noodles 84
mushrooms
Chicken braised with dried shiitake mushrooms 129
Enoki mushrooms, fried in butter 167
The gills of shiitake mushrooms 134
Green tea dressing, shoots and fungi 82
Green tomato, hazelnut and shiitake 28
Mushrooms with walnuts and chestnuts 130
Oyster mushrooms with asparagus and botarga 84
Pickled pine mushrooms 178
Spiced mushroom broth 139
Squid cooked in its own ink 176
Wilted enoki mushrooms 292
Mussels, pickled, with fermented shiso 52
My mother's chicken curry 273

N
noodles
Fragrant black noodles from outdoor stalls 105
Mung bean noodles 84
Numbing ox tongue 226

O
offal: Chicken and other bits 236
oils
Burnt ginger and garlic oil 263
Cassia bark oil 266
Chilli oil 280
Citrus oil 179
Garlic and scallion oil 105
Hot oil 230
Prawn oil 153
okra: Betel leaves, spiced lentils and grilled okra 16
omelette, Oyster 250
onions
Marinated onions 94
Spiced onion mixture 160
orange
Burnt orange sauce 66
Orange blossom ice cream 334
Orange blossom syrup 334
ox tongue, Numbing 226
Ox tongue with five tastes 228
oyster mushrooms
Green tea dressing, shoots and fungi 82
Oyster mushrooms with asparagus and botarga 84
oysters
Braised dried oysters with black moss 235
Deep-fried oysters 34
Oyster omelette 250
Oyster sauce 242
Oysters and black fungus with pigeon 240
Oysters, eggplant custard and rose petals 32

P
Painted and smoked kingfish 68
Palm sugar custard 280
pancake, Red bean 313
pancetta: Green mango pickles with other things that make me shiver 224
papaya: Green papaya pickle 108
pastes
A gritty, fibrous shrimp paste 214
Assam paste 25
Avocado paste 316
Blachan paste 185
Green peppercorn and chilli paste 230
Hazelnut and shiitake paste 30
Peanut paste 212
Pistachio paste 70
Rempah 249
Rose petal and chilli paste 34
The softest, smoothest spice paste 210
Spiced mushroom paste 139
Walnut paste 132
pastry
Coconut ash pastry 334
Peanut pastry 66
Sour cream pastry 37, 101
Strudel pastry 48
Pastry cream, praline 320
peaches
Pickled peaches 117
White peach in pastry, drenched with jasmine syrup 48
peanuts
Beef satay with peanut sauce 284
Peanut paste 212
Peanut pastry 66
Peanut and tannic greens 294
Peanut tofu 295
Puréed peanuts 212
Steamed rice dumplings filled with peanuts 327
Pears, poached 320
Peppercorn and chilli paste 230
pickles
Green mango pickles 222
Green papaya pickle 108
The intense colour of pickled radishes 118
Pickled fish 120
Pickled mussels 54
Pickled peaches 117
Pickled pine mushrooms 178
Pickled rose petals 34
Turmeric pickle 127
pigeon, Oysters and black fungus with 240
Pine mushrooms, pickled 178
pineapple
A savoury tropical fruit salad 92
Hot and sour pork hock 222
Piquant shrimp dressing 98
Pistachio paste 70
Plums, curry leaf syrup and baked coffee cream 36
Poaching liquid 239
Pods and roots treated meticulously 190
pomelo peel, Candied 266
pork
An alcoholic dumpling 180
Braised dried oysters with black moss 235
Chinese-style blood sausage 244
Hot and sour pork hock 222
Kidneys in sake 245
Steamed pork belly 124
potato
The concept of celebration 86
Fingers of purple potato 122
Potato crisps 86
praline
Powdered praline 320
Praline pastry cream 320
prawns
An alcoholic dumpling 180
Hand-made prawn crackers 144
Honeyed prawn sauce 152
Laksa lemak 209
Prawn oil 153
Prawn relish 218
Prawns out of their shells 150
Stuffed crab claws 197
Purple potato dough 124

R
rabbit pie, A surprising fruit flavour appears in the 100
Rabbit sauce 101
Radicchio, marinated 46
radishes, The intense colour of pickled 118
Rainbow trout, smoked 46
Red bean pancake 313
Red capsicum salt 30
relish
Black fungus relish 242
Eggplant relish 164
Green chilli, coriander and chilli relish 73
Prawn relish 218
Salty fish roe relish 292
Reminiscences on the black Malay cookie 332
Rempah (spice paste) 249
Reworking laksa lemak into a spiced bouillon 216
rice
Glutinous rice wine 174
Rice crisps 252
Sago with ginger milk pudding 172
Steamed rice dumplings filled with peanuts 327
rice wine
Sago with ginger milk pudding 172

Sago and rice wine sauce 174
The ritual of preparing globe artichokes 96
Roasted fish: Chinese herbal concoction 40
Roots and pods treated meticulously 190
Rose petal and chilli paste 34
Rose petal syrup 35
Rose petals, pickled 34
Rose petals in syrup 80

S

Sago with ginger milk pudding 172
Sago pudding 171
Sago and rice wine sauce 174
salads
A savoury tropical fruit salad 92
Walnut and borage salad 46
salt
Cashew salt 230
Curry leaf salt 263
Lemon salt 124, 230
Red capsicum salt 30
Spiced salt 295
Salt-baked chicken and salty avocado accompanying 322
Salted and steamed chicken 300
Salty fish roe relish 292
Sand whiting with spinach 224
Sardines, pickled 120
sauces/dressings
Avocado dressing 22
Bitter melon dressing 276
Burnt orange sauce 66
Chicken sauce 306
Chocolate sauce 266
Coconut sauce 334
Green tea dressing 84
Honeyed prawn sauce 152
Oyster sauce 242
Peanut dipping sauce 284
Piquant shrimp dressing 98
Rabbit sauce 101
Sago and rice wine sauce 174
Shiitake sauce 136
Shrimp dressing 98
Soy dipping sauce 181
Soy dressing 105
Spiced tomato sauce 164
Sweet and sour sauce 256
Vadouvan sauce 160
sausage
Chinese-style blood sausage 244
Goat sausage and a spiced tomato sauce 162
Scallion and garlic oil 105
Scallion juice 152
Scallions, grilled 288
scallops
An unassuming dish of scallops 202
Loofah in scallop broth 276
Scallop crisp 252
seafood
A gritty, fibrous shrimp paste 214
Abalone 146, 148
An alcoholic dumpling 180
An unassuming dish of scallops 202
Birthday tomato and chilli crab 144
Blachan paste 185
Braised dried oysters with black moss 235
Corn and egg flower soup 185
Fermented shiso and pickled mussels 52
Grilled squid and candied ikan bilis 106
Grilled squid and white beans 110
Hand-made prawn crackers 144
Laksa lemak 209
Lobster siam 186
Loofah in scallop broth 276
Marron tails, roasted 148
Oyster omelette 250
Oysters and black fungus with pigeon 240
Oysters, eggplant custard and rose petals 32
Piquant shrimp dressing 98
Poached crayfish 136
Prawns out of their shells 150
Reworking laksa lemak into a spiced bouillon 216
Salted and steamed chicken 300
Scallop crisp 252
Squid cooked in its own ink 176
Stir-fried kang kong with blachan 185
Stuffed crab claws 197
seasoning, Caraway 18
sesame seeds
Black sesame croquant 174
Black sesame dust 58
Black sesame pudding 58
Sesame seed sweet 334
Shards, things hidden, shattered and revealed 56
shiitake mushrooms
Chicken braised with dried shiitake mushrooms 129
The gills of shiitake mushrooms 134
Green tomato, hazelnut and shiitake 28
Shiitake sauce 136
Shiso leaves, fermented 52
shrimp paste, A gritty, fibrous 214
Sirloin and accompaniments 166
Smoked rainbow trout 46
The softest, smoothest spice paste 210
soup
Corn and egg flower soup 185
see also broth
Sour cream pastry 37, 101
Soy dipping sauce 181
Soy dressing 105
Soy milk sheets 136
spice paste, The softest, smoothest 210
Spiced bouillon 218
Spiced mushroom broth 139
Spiced onion mixture 160
Spiced salt 295
Spiced tomato sauce 164
spinach, Sand whiting with 224
squid
Grilled squid and candied ikan bilis 106
Grilled squid and white beans 110
Squid cooked in its own ink 176
Steamed buns 288
Steamed coral trout 148
Steamed rice dumplings filled with peanuts 327
Stems and leaves treated meticulously 190
Stir-fried kang kong with blachan 185
stock
Chicken stock 185
Squid stock 178
Strudel pastry 48
Stuffed crab claws 197
sweet potato
Coconut, gula melaka and sweet potato 64
Sweet potato dumplings 330
Sweet potato jelly 66
Sweet and sour lamb 254
sweetbreads, Veal, soured and grilled 24
syrup
Butterfly pea flower syrup 330
Jasmine syrup 49
Lemon syrup 192
Orange blossom syrup 334
Rose petal syrup 35

T

Tapioca and coconut biscuits 316
Three kinds of fish 146
Tofu, peanut 295
tomalley 150
tomato
Birthday tomato and chilli crab 144
Green tomato, hazelnut and shiitake 28
Spiced tomato sauce 164
Tomato broth 192
tongue
Numbing ox tongue 226
Ox tongue with five tastes 228
The transformed taste of chicken 304
tropical fruit salad, A savoury 92
trout
Borage and other cucumber-like flavours 44
Steamed coral trout 148
tuile, A different type of 194
Turmeric pickle 127

V

Vadouvan sauce 160
Vadouvan spice mix 161
Vanilla cream 80
Veal sweetbreads, soured and grilled 24
Vegetables with ginger and rice vinegar 245

W

Wafers 58
walnuts
Candied walnuts 226
Mushrooms with walnuts and chestnuts 130
Walnut and borage chopped salad 46
Walnut and chestnut garnish 132
Walnut paste 132
Watercress, wilted 204
watermelon, Fish fragrant 20
White bean and almond cream 337
White chocolate, caramelised 280
White peach in pastry, drenched with jasmine syrup 48
White sponge 337

Y

Young bamboo
preparing 166
roasting 167
young coconut, Blackened 260

For my family and those who shared the experience along the way.

An SBS book

Published in 2013 by Hardie Grant Books

Hardie Grant Books (Australia)
Ground Floor, Building 1
658 Church Street
Richmond, Victoria 3121
www.hardiegrant.com.au

Hardie Grant Books (UK)
Dudley House, North Suite
34–35 Southampton Street
London WC2E 7HF
www.hardiegrant.co.uk

A Cataloguing-in-Publication entry is available from the catalogue of the National Library of Australia at www.nla.gov.au

Green Pickled Peaches
ISBN 9781742702407

Publishing Director: Paul McNally
Editor: Jane Price
Design Manager: Heather Menzies
Design and illustrations: Studio Racket
Photographer: Chris Chen
Stylist: Deborah Kaloper
Food preparation: Amira Georgy
Production Manager: Todd Rechner

Colour reproduction by Splitting Image Colour Studio
Printed in China by 1010 Printing International Limited